Riding the

My Story

Jane McDonald

Riding the Waves

My Story

PENGUIN BOOKS

3 5 7 9 10 8 6 4

Virgin Books, an imprint of Ebury Publishing
20 Vauxhall Bridge Road
London SW1V 2SA

Virgin Books is part of the Penguin Random House group of companies
whose addresses can be found at global.penguinrandomhouse.com

Copyright © Jane McDonald Limited 2019

First published by Virgin Books in 2019
This paperback edition published in 2020

www.penguin.co.uk

A CIP catalogue record for this book is available from the British Library

ISBN 9780753554340

Typeset in 9.89/13.82 pt ITC Galliard Pro by Jouve (UK), Milton Keynes
Printed and bound in Great Britain by Clays Ltd, Elcograf S.p.A.

Penguin Random House is committed to a sustainable future for our
business, our readers and our planet. This book is made from Forest
Stewardship Council® certified paper.

For my amazing mum . . . words will never be enough.
I miss you so much.

Also, to everyone who has been a part of my life,
good and not so good, I thank you all. I've loved and
learned from everyone.

Contents

Contents

Introduction

May 2019

I'm lying in my cabin on the high seas when the ship's horn sounds. I wasn't expecting that. Hopefully, it doesn't mean anything sinister, like a collision ahead. I'm being silly now. I'm tucked up in my cosy bed, tired but happy. The ship's motion is soothing. Through my porthole I can see the moon shining in the darkness, casting a silvery light across the waves. It's been a long day of filming and now I'm ready to drift off. But I can't sleep, I'm too excited. My mind is miles away in Wakefield.

Sometimes I can't believe how lucky I am. Even though I've been in show business for 20 years now, I still have to pinch myself. I mean, who'd have thought I'd have two primetime TV shows and a sold-out tour at my time of life? It's an incredible position to be in and I never stop counting my blessings.

We've had a lot of fun filming, these past few weeks. Everyone knows I love a cruise and the latest programmes in my Channel 5 *Cruising with Jane McDonald* series have taken me to some beautiful places. But now that we're about to wrap in October 2019 and I'm shifting my focus on to the tour, I'm starting to feel giddy with excitement. I've been getting emails from my band and crew, saying, 'Can't wait to get on that bus!'

'And me,' I keep replying. 'Brass knobs an' all!'

There's nothing like that first moment we get on board our huge, gleaming tour bus. Fourteen people yelling, 'Whee, here we go!' as we step through the door, one by one. It's like we're going on holiday together.

It's such a special group of people, too, from the crew up. We're an eclectic bunch, but we're all really good mates, all family people, all having a blast, which makes our tour bus the most uplifting place in the world. There's always something going on – the laughter never stops – and the banter and the good times flow with us onto the stage. We'll be up there during the show, smiling at each other and remembering the laughs we had the night before, and all the fun we're having comes across to the audience and flows back to us again. It's addictive, for us and for them; it's a joy. We're a little tour family and everyone wants to be a part of it.

I can't wait, because everything about this tour is going to be stratospheric. It's going to be the best thing I've ever, ever done. We've got every aspect covered: the venues are booked, the stage set designed, the tickets sold, the posters up and, best of all, I've got the most wonderful fans in the world coming to see me perform, from all over the country.

My musicians are the best in the business, the band is tighter than ever and my backing singers are fantastic. We've rehearsed a new medley to get everybody up and dancing and I'll be singing some big, big numbers: I'm doing *The Greatest Showman*, I'm doing Queen; I'm doing songs that I would never have challenged myself to sing before. It's going to look incredible, too: we've got our own dedicated lighting guy and he's an artist in his own right; and Kay Heeley, who makes my gowns, has surpassed herself for this tour. (Also, no one has seen it yet, but I've bought something special to wear during the last section of the show. It was unbelievably expensive, but it's just going to look *amazing* – all crystals, sparkle and shine.)

Touring used to be quite tough, but it's so much easier now we've got the tour bus. It was my tour manager, Martin Hudson, who suggested it. He's brilliant, is Martin – he fixes everything. I said, 'I need a fridge and a microwave, I need a bed I can sleep in,' and he came up with the perfect solution.

Long ago, my dad and I used to rattle across the Pennines in an old van, battling through all weathers to get to my next working men's club gig, so I can't help smiling when I think of how he'd react if he looked inside our spanking new home on wheels. It would knock his socks off to see that it has beds for everyone upstairs and its own little kitchen and sitting area downstairs. It's got air conditioning and smooth suspension; it doesn't rattle, it hums.

I think he'd be most impressed by the inbuilt satnav, though. He was always screeching to a halt in the middle of some out-of-the-way village high street so I could wind down my window and frantically ask for directions to a club – before we pulled off in a flurry of beeping horns, none the wiser, exhaust pipe clanging at the rear. There's none of that anymore, no fuss and bother leading up to a turn, and the cherry on top is that I can have tea and toast when I want and hot meals when I'm hungry.

We've always got a fridge full of stuff: I stack it up with all sorts of things before we set out; I go to my local farm store and get sausage rolls, cheese-and-onion rolls, fabulous bread, vegetarian pâté, avocados and wine. I make a big bowl of salad and veg every day and everybody's welcome to it. We've got a couple of vegetarians on the bus, so there's lots of cheese and salad; there's always some food going on somewhere.

The bus is my safe haven in every way; it's my home from home. I have my own private area and my own little door; I have my cases with me and I always take my own pillow. So, instead of waiting up with my eyes on stalks until we get to our next scheduled hotel stop in the dead of night, I can go to bed when I'm tired and stay there all day long if I need to. What a revelation! It has completely transformed my life on tour.

I'm very cosy on the bus and wear tactile fabrics, because onstage I'm dressed to the nines in sequins and lashes. I've usually got a nice velour tracksuit on, or my pyjamas, dressing gown and slippers. I do love my slippers! We each have our own customised ear plugs that we put in of a night, so if there's someone who snores, we can sleep in peace. You've got to think of these things, haven't you? That was Martin, again: when we had individual moulds done for the in-ear monitors we wear onstage, he said, 'Why don't we have ear plugs made at the same time?'

It's great: you put your eye shades on and your ear plugs in and you're out for the count. It's the best sleep we ever have.

There's a party atmosphere on the bus on the first weekend back. After the first show, everybody is high-fiving each other and the alcohol comes out. You can't go straight to bed when you've given a show and brought the crowd to their feet – there's so much adrenaline pumping that you need to take time to wind down. So, the first night or so we'll probably stay up and celebrate with a bevvy or two. We'll catch up with each other's news and talk shop. Then, as the tour goes along, the partying tends to tail off and people start going to bed earlier and earlier. They'll get on the bus, have one beer, say, 'Right, I'm off to bed now.' And I'll just have a cuppa, because I hardly drink these days, especially when I'm touring. Now and again I do like to have a drink. Not very often, but I like to have a glass of wine.

Martin and the crew get up really early – they're always the first into the theatre of a morning to set up the stage while the rest of us are still in bed. Martin runs around, making sure everybody has everything they need to do their job, from the onstage sound monitor to the lighting guy. He puts our signs on the dressing-room doors: 'Singer/dancers', 'Band', 'Jane', 'PA' and 'Tour manager'; he checks the showers are working and lays out enough towels for everyone. The wardrobe with all my gowns in is wheeled into my dressing room, along with my shoes and make-up. He makes sure we're all set for the soundcheck. Everything runs like clockwork: that's Martin.

Before the show, I warm up my voice with singing exercises. In the old days, I just used to have a Drambuie and walk on – I had a brilliant time! – but I don't do that anymore. Brandy is good for the voice because it is said to warm and relax your vocal cords, but I don't need it now, because when I've done my vocal warm-up and I've hit that top C, I know I'll be fine.

My nerves still kick in a bit as I'm getting ready, but luckily my PA, Sue Ravey, is there to diffuse the tension. Sue is a singer in her own right, so she understands, and she's my very dear friend, so she's the perfect PA for me. She is also a force of nature, so when she decided it would be a good idea for my PA to be able to do make-up and hair, she made sure she learned how to do it professionally. Sue once had her own hair salon, which she co-owned with a friend before giving it up to become a professional singer. Years later, she gained a City & Guilds Advanced Diploma in hair and make-up. Now, she does my hair and make-up on tour and for TV.

Sue also helps with my quick costume changes backstage, when I only have four or five bars of music to get out of one outfit and into another. Wearing a torch on her head to light the way, she unzips me, holds my dress while I step out of it and takes it off to hang up. My backing singers get me into my next outfit. Those girls move like lightning – they've worked on cruise ships, so they know that it's all about getting the zips up and down. I just stand there and it's like the tyre changes at a Formula 1 pitstop, it's that quick.

It will be especially nice to have Sue and the girls with me on this tour, because for the first time ever, my mother won't be coming to see me. That is my only sadness, that Mum won't be out there in the audience, or slipping quietly into the dressing room after the show, asking, 'Where's my star? Where's Jane?'

I know Mum's absence is going to make me very sad along the way. It's only six months since she passed and there will definitely be tears. I miss her so, so much and not for a moment do I ever forget that I wouldn't be here without all the support she's given me. But I'll get through.

Mum is always in my heart.

Leading up to a performance, I always give myself a little pep talk. 'These people need cheering up,' I tell myself. 'They've come for a really good night out. They've paid to see you, make it a good 'un.'

After that, a little prayer: 'Please may these people have a brilliant time tonight.'

Then come the finishing touches to my appearance, completing my transformation. Once the hair doubles in size, with all the backcombing that goes into it, and when the lashes go on, that's it: she's arriving, Jane McDonald, the performer. The gown goes on and then the shoes. As soon as I've got my high heels on, I think, 'Right, I'm ready to rock and roll.'

Out in the auditorium, the lights go down and a continuous bass drone starts up. There's tension in the room, anticipation, a bit of a rumble. The band build the music up and then I make my entrance at the back. As I walk onstage, the rhythm section kicks in to add to the drama of the moment.

Oh heck, my throat's gone dry. Will I be all right?

I'm so tired that I'm wired. So why can't I get to sleep? The moon's glow is beginning to dim.

I know why it is: it's because I can't wait to get on that tour bus. I can't wait! Every tour is better than the last, every show more spectacular, and I'm just about to set out on the most amazing adventure. Here I am, in a luxury cabin on a cruise ship, making my own TV series. Here I am, enjoying the best time of my life as a singer. And back home in Wakefield I've got the loveliest man in the world, waiting patiently for me.

I just feel so lucky.

Of course, it hasn't all been plain sailing, I've had some very stormy times. I know what it's like to sink down to the lowest ebb and more than once I've had to bail myself out of deep trouble. But I'm still here, which is why I originally wanted to call this book *Unsinkable*. Only, some of my friends weren't at all sure about it when I mentioned it to them.

'You're not the flipping *Titanic*, Jane!' they said.

So, I chose a title that hopefully reflects where I am, riding the waves (lifejacket at the ready, just in case).

I've always loved reading books, because there's something special about losing yourself in someone else's world. I hope you enjoy reading this book, but I'm warning you: there are choppy waters ahead, maybe even a tidal wave or two, so sea legs at the ready, hold on to your hats . . .

1

The Hand That Leads Me

People find it hard to believe that I used to be painfully shy. A shy, maungy (peevish) child who grew up hiding behind her mother's skirts, that was me. I was a nightmare – even my mother said so – because I never wanted to go anywhere. For years, I was fearful of the world beyond our front door, and even when I was older, and a little bolder, my stomach would start to dissolve at the thought of venturing out of my safe haven.

My idea of happiness was being at home in the parlour with my piano, singing away on my own. That was heaven to me. But I didn't want an audience: I hated drawing attention to myself and the idea of appearing on a stage filled me with terror. Just the thought of it gave me clammy hands, sweats and nausea.

Despite this, every summer without fail, at the holiday park in Bridlington where we rented a caravan for a week in June, my mother would find a way to coax a public performance out of me. If there was a beauty pageant, she would suggest I join the parade. If there was a talent contest, she would cajole me into the line-up. She always managed to gently rope me into something or other.

When they had an open mic in the bar at lunchtime – and if they didn't, she would refuse to book our annual holiday there, in later years – we'd find ourselves sitting up front around midday, at a table close to the stage. I'll never forget the first year I was old enough to be allowed into the bar. It was called the Harbour Lights and I must have been 13 or 14.

As we sat at our table, my skin started to prickle with a horrible sense of what was coming next. Up onstage, an organist and a drummer were waiting expectantly for someone to take the mic.

'Get up and do a song, Jane,' my mother said, giving me a nudge in the ribs.

Clammy hands. Sweats. It was my worst nightmare. 'Oh no, please don't make me,' I pleaded.

'Go on, love,' she wheedled. 'I've worked hard all year for the chance to listen to you sing.'

In a torment of agony, I sat rooted to the spot. I desperately wanted to please my mother, but every nerve in my body was resisting.

'I can't, Mum!' I whimpered.

'Yes, you can,' she soothed. 'Come on, you know you can. You're going to get up there and sing.'

'Don't make her do it, Jean,' my father weighed in.

'She'll be fine, trust me,' Mum said crossly.

'Please don't make me,' I begged.

'Just leave her alone,' Dad growled.

'All right, then,' Mum huffed, pointedly turning her attention back to the stage and whoever had taken the mic in my absence.

Then, just as soon as the spot was free again, she said sweetly, 'I was so looking forward to hearing you sing, Jane. It'll spoil my holiday if you don't . . .'

That was my mother. Mick McManus might have been Britain's all-star wrestler at the time, but Mum didn't need muscles (or black pants) to floor her opponents. I'm not saying she wasn't strong, because she was every bit as solid and sturdy as my father was lean and athletic, but she was also very clever, was Mum, and very persuasive with it too. She never pushed, she just coaxed, and this strategy always won the day, especially with Dad in a supporting role.

My mother's words having hit my tenderest spot, I shook physically at the prospect of the challenge looming ahead. 'Just get it over and done with,' I thought, my ears whooshing as I rose to my feet. 'Mum works so hard, I can't ruin her holiday.'

Gritting my teeth, I climbed what felt like a mountain to reach the stage, where I stood behind the microphone awkwardly, beset by stage fright and the worry that I might be sick on my shoes.

With an indulgent smile, the organist asked, 'What'll it be, love?'

' "Who's Sorry Now?" ' I whispered, my throat dry.

'Why am I doing this?' I thought miserably, drawing in a deep breath as the music started up. But then everything changed the moment I started singing. My nerves melted away and I was in my element, belting out Mum's favourite Connie Francis number onstage. I enjoyed it even more when I reached the end of the song. That was always the pattern: I never enjoyed performing until it was over, but afterwards, wow, I felt fantastic!

When I'd finished, I rejoined my parents at their table in a happy daze, thrilled by the sudden roar of applause around me. Leaning over to give me a hug, Dad said, 'That was good, Jane.'

Mum gave me a look as if to say, 'See?'

They didn't agree on a lot of things, but in one respect my mother and father were in perfect accord: there was something a little bit different about their youngest daughter.

'I'm not different!' I used to insist whenever they mentioned it. Along with most other children, I just wanted to be like everybody else.

'You are, love,' Mum would say. 'I can't put my finger on it, but you are definitely different.'

Clearly, she had decided that it was her job to bring it out of me, whatever it was.

I think it would be fair to say that my pretty, vivacious mother, Jean Ferguson, and my gruff, handsome father, Peter McDonald, were not ideally suited. I can only imagine that love's young dream shone so brightly when they met in 1953, at the Palais de Danse in Coatbridge, near Glasgow, they were blinded to what a mismatched pair they made.

'What attracted you to Dad in the first place?' I used to ask Mum, whenever she was having a bit of a moan – as you do from time to time when you've been married to someone for what feels like eternity.

'Oh, Jane, he was such a good dancer,' she'd say fervently, 'and very charming with it, and I assumed he must have money, because he always had a new shirt on when we were courting. Only, it wasn't new at all,' she'd add, starting to giggle. 'Instead, he had a whole collection of new collars and cuffs that he used to clip to his only shirt. I was conned!'

My father was always something of a mystery. He rarely mentioned his upbringing in Kirkaldy in Fife, or his time in the army during World War Two. He was Scottish, but of Lithuanian descent, which explains his dark looks: his mother and father met on the boat coming over from Lithuania during the First World War and we haven't been able to trace his family beyond that meeting. I do know that Dad's mother died when he was very young and he was brought up by his father, which had a huge effect on him, being a boy. His childhood was all rough edges, without any softness, and I think that's why he went on to develop such an abrupt manner. He was so different from my open, bubbly mum.

Funnily enough, it's also difficult to trace the family back on Mum's side, because my grandmother and her mother were both illegitimate. Everything stops at my great-grandmother, Jane Ann Fenton, whose father was a French nobleman. I'm Jane Ann McDonald because my mother named me after her and it was always said that my colouring came from the French side of my mother's family, rather than my father's.

After Jane Ann Fenton had a baby out of wedlock by a local lad – that baby being my grandmother, Janet Ferguson – her life might easily have gone to rack and ruin. Instead, as soon as Janet was old enough, she left the child with someone called 'Grandpa', who lived in Sidlaw Cottage, overlooking the sea in Monifieth near Dundee. Grandpa wasn't a blood relative, but he was a kind, gentle man whom my grandmother loved very much.

Passing Janet off as her little sister, Jane Ann Fenton went to work for a rich, entitled employer called Lady Pilditch, whose name changed to Yenkin when she remarried, and whose daughter later married into the Darling family, who were diplomats. Jane Ann Fenton was nanny to two generations of the family's children, the Yenkins and the Darlings, and her work with the Darlings took her all round the world, providing fantastic opportunities for travel and sightseeing. Yet the price was high and I imagine there were many moments along the way when her heart was in Monifieth with her daughter.

Gran found it very hard to understand, or forgive, her mother for the choices she made. 'How could she have left me like that?' she used to fret. Her thoughts were often with her mother, but I never heard her speculate about her father or who he might have been. My Auntie Nancy, who is now in her nineties, says that he was either the butcher or the baker in Monifieth, but my Auntie Barbara, now in her eighties, says it was the chemist. It's all a bit unknown. If I had to hazard a guess, I'd go for the baker, because Gran could bake absolutely anything and make it taste good and perhaps this was a talent she inherited from her dad. Gran was renowned for her baking – so much so, during the war, her neighbours in the tenement building where she lived all clubbed together and brought their rations to her, saying, 'Can you make your delicious bread and scones for us?'

With my granddad James (Jim) Ferguson working in a steel factory making bullets by day, and on patrol as a warden by night, and with four kids to feed, wash and iron for, my amazing grandmother somehow managed to do her bit to bolster morale on the home front by baking treats for everyone in her building. Sadly, my grandfather died only a few years later, at the age of 45, in 1950, leaving Gran widowed with four children. Even then, she managed to keep the family going, taking in extra washing and baking from home. Mum took after her in many ways, as she was a great organiser and an excellent cook. But while Gran was always a bit of a loner and enjoyed her own company, Mum was very outgoing and loved being around people.

I wonder how long it took for Mum and Dad to realise they were like chalk and cheese. They should probably never have married, but marry they did – within three months of their first foxtrot – and before too long my older sister, Janet, was on the way. There's a proverb, isn't there, *Marry in haste, repent at leisure*? Only there wasn't much leisure to be had in Scotland during the postwar years, especially in places like Kirkaldy and Mum's home town, Coatbridge, where unemployment was rising as fast as the iron and steelworks were declining.

Mum was so friendly and sociable that it can't have been long before Dad showed his jealous streak, but there wasn't time to dwell on any doubts she might have had about marrying her sweetheart from Fife. It was sink or swim for many working families in Scotland and, since few fancied going down with the shipbuilding industry, most of my family, like many others, moved south in search of work.

The first to go was my Auntie Nancy, with her bus-driver

husband, Bill. Once settled in Wakefield, Nancy wrote to Mum to say, 'If you hurry, I can get you a house in the same street as me.'

It only took that one sentence to set off a chain reaction. Mum read the letter out to Dad and he said, 'Get packing, lassie.' Jimmy, Mum's younger brother, popped in, heard the news and said, 'I'm coming too.' He dashed back to Gran's to tell her they were leaving and, to everybody's surprise, Gran agreed to come as well, bringing her youngest, Barbara, along with a pot of paint she'd bought to spruce up her living room. So, they all moved from Scotland to a run-down area of Wakefield, West Yorkshire, known as Piccadilly, where Gran and Barbara moved into Auntie Nancy's tiny back-to-back terraced house and, just a few doors down the same street, Uncle Jimmy lived with Mum, Dad and baby Janet, who was now six months old.

Since my earliest memories of Janet are of a sulky teenager whose last wish on earth was to share a bedroom with her irritating little sister, it's funny to think of her as a fat-cheeked, smiling baby. Even then I bet she used to lie in her pram scanning the horizon for signs of unwelcome siblings. Luckily, she was safe for the time being, as our brother Tony didn't come along for another four years and I arrived five years after him.

I gave Janet a run for her money on the night I was born, though. As Mum laboured with me in the bedroom and Gran ran round, making sure she was supplied with plenty of hot water and towels, Janet sat at the top of the stairs, wringing her hands and in muttered undertones willing Mum to get on with it.

When Gran found her up there, long after her bedtime, she assumed Janet must have heard Mum moaning and was worried about her. After all, Janet knew that Mum was having me at home because she'd had a bad experience in the hospital, having Tony five years previously, when the nurses left her all alone on a trolley.

'Don't leave,' Mum said. 'I'm going to have it now.'

'No, you're not. It's not coming for hours yet, love,' they laughed, before going off to deal with another labour.

Fifteen minutes later, Tony was on his way and Mum was left to give birth to him all on her own. That didn't impress her one bit, which is why, with me, she decided, 'No, I'm going to have this one at home,' and there was a midwife with her throughout.

It turned out Janet wasn't at all anxious about Mum, as Gran soon realised. She was far more concerned her new sibling might arrive after midnight, on 5 April.

'I'm going to be nine tomorrow and I don't want the baby to share my birthday,' she told Gran crossly.

It was lucky for me I was born at 11.30pm on 4 April 1963 or I might not have lived long enough to tell the tale!

Once Mum was all cleaned up and Dad was allowed upstairs to see the new baby – Janet having finally gone to sleep after mistaking the shriek of the kettle for the sound of my first cry – Mum had recovered enough to declare herself hungry. Everyone felt very sorry that she hadn't been able to finish the fish and chips she'd been eating ravenously when her waters broke.

'I'll go and find you something to eat, love,' Gran said.

When she'd gone, Dad asked Mum how she was feeling.

'Och, fine,' she said, her cheeks glowing pink. She smiled down at the baby in her arms. 'This one was the easiest of the three.'

My father grinned. 'Good, then you'll have nae trouble getting up to do the breakfasts in the morning.'

Mum's eyebrows shot up. Surely he didn't expect her to be up and bustling around in the kitchen, cooking bacon and eggs, the morning after she had given birth?

Mum opened her mouth to respond just as Gran hurried into the room with one of her delicious plain scones on a plate.

'Don't be daft, I'll sort out the breakfasts,' she said. 'Now, get this down you, love. You must be starving.'

By then, we were living in a large, roomy Victorian house in Eastmoor Road, on the posh side of Wakefield. After a spell as a coach builder, Dad had gone down the mines and was working at the coalface, the most highly paid and treacherous of all the pit jobs. Mum didn't like him doing such dangerous work, but they were keen to move away from the grimy, overcrowded streets of Piccadilly and their cramped back-to-back with its tin bath, earth closet and dirty heap of coal in the back yard. Gran had spent the years since their move from Scotland as a 'live-in domestic' worker and was able to lend them enough for a deposit, and with Dad earning a steady wage and Mum doing part-time shop work to bring in the extra they needed, they were able to move to their dream house in a better area.

There was a catch, though. Isn't there always? With next to nothing left over for furnishings after they had bought their lovely big house, they had to trawl second-hand shops for cheap bargains, making do with the sort of heavy, Edwardian furniture that nobody else wanted. So, they had none of the mod cons, shiny formica surfaces and geometric patterns that were starting to come into fashion. What's more, in order to afford the mortgage on the house, they had to take in boarders – who were expecting their breakfast as usual the day after I was born.

As it happened, having lodgers suited my mother at the time, for several reasons. First and foremost, it meant she could stay at home and be around for Janet and Tony – and me, when I came along. Secondly, she wanted Gran to be able to leave her job as a domestic, move in with us and work a little less hard. Thirdly, Mum was very independent and, working from home, she could be in control of the household finances while earning her own money. My dad would give her a weekly sum to look after the house, with a gruff, 'You'll have to manage on that.' Often as not, it wasn't enough. Last, but not least, my mother liked to be needed and since the boarders we attracted were often trainee officers from around the world, who were attending courses at the nearby West Yorkshire Police College, she was always very much needed, if only for a snippet of friendly conversation when they were missing home. Being from Scotland, she knew exactly how it felt to be homesick.

There were sometimes as many as six boarders in the house at any one time and Mum and Gran went beyond the call of duty to make them feel comfortable. A full English every morning. Fresh sheets and tidy rooms every day. A three-course meal every evening, cooked using the best cuts of meat. They were constantly on the go and it's a wonder they made any money, if indeed they did – and I have my doubts.

It used to exasperate my father. 'You do too much for them,' he'd complain as he watched my mother lining up a row of juicy lamb chops, ready for the grill. For him, the lodgers were a constant niggling reminder that he wasn't bringing in enough money to support his family.

'You know my rule: "Don't ever skimp on shoes and meat",' Mum replied cheerfully.

Dad also got annoyed at the way she fussed over the lodgers at mealtimes. Mum had a lovely, open nature and couldn't help but serve up a little good-natured banter as she was seeing to their tea. Equally, the lodgers couldn't help but be charmed by her pretty, vivacious presence as they ate their tasty chops and steamed pudding. It made Dad jealous and he would accuse Mum of being over-familiar. He resented the way people naturally gravitated towards her. Eventually, Gran took over seeing to the boarders directly and, to keep the peace, Mum would stay downstairs in the big basement kitchen during their meals.

With Mum being so busy, often I found myself alone, but not

lonely. Mum told me that I never fussed about staying in the parlour in the mornings. 'Now, I'm going to be busy for two to three hours,' she'd say. 'I'll keep popping in and seeing you're all right, but you have to be quiet.'

After putting the radio on to keep me company, she and Gran went off to do the sheets, change the beds, make all the dinners and get everything sorted. I was perfectly happy on my own and they never got a peep out of me. Whenever Mum popped in to say, 'Are you okay?' I used to nod and carry on listening to the radio.

There was a bus stop right outside the house and, when I was about 18 months old, I discovered the fun to be had from sitting in the window and waving to the people in the queue below. That was my first audience. Whole crowds used to stare up at me, saying, 'Look at that baby in the window.'

'See what she's doing,' Mum exclaimed to Gran one morning when they found me waving at a crowd of people down below. 'She's such an intelligent bairn.'

The swell of pride in her voice made Gran chuckle. 'Aye, there's something a wee bit special about that one,' she agreed, 'and it could well be she's preparing for her destiny.'

Those mornings in the parlour definitely made an impact. After many hours, days and weeks of listening to the radio on my own, the first word I ever said was 'Downtown', which I must have picked up from the Petula Clark record that was at the top of the charts then. Before too long, I knew all the words to 'Downtown' and several other pop songs, and by the time I was three, I was singing and dancing in the kaleidoscope spotlight in the hall that appeared whenever the sun shone through the coloured glass at the top of our front door. Razzle dazzle! There was something very magical about that rainbow spotlight.

My mother loved music and was a lovely singer herself. She

was a happy person to be around and used to sing to me all the time: nursery rhymes, hymns and songs from the radio. She knew every word of every song and I revelled in her renditions, saying, 'Again, again, again.' I just remember her being so loving, always looking after me.

I may have had an inkling of the career in store for me – who knows? I certainly knew what I didn't want to do. One day, when I was about four, Mum pulled out a little fold-up green table and said, 'I'll make you a little shop like the one I used to work in. There's your till, let's arrange a display of the things you're going to sell.'

I shook my head. 'I won't be working in a shop,' I said.

'Really?' Mum looked at me in surprise.

I was adamant: 'No, I'm not going to work in a shop.'

Gran nodded sagely, convinced as I was that my destiny lay elsewhere.

By now Gran was president of the Wakefield Spiritualist Church and a highly respected psychic counsellor and demonstrator there. My Uncle Harold was one of the top ministers and my mother, who had no gift herself, had become the church treasurer. This had all come about just after the move from Scotland, when a neighbour invited Gran along for a social evening at the church: she went along out of curiosity and was told by an elderly medium that she had important work to do there. It was news to Gran, yet it wasn't long before she discovered that she had a rare gift for clairvoyance.

The Wakefield branch of Spiritualists believed in God, the brotherhood of Man and the continual existence of the human soul. Their golden rule was 'Do unto others as you would have done unto yourself' and the ministers practised prophecy and healing through mediumship, which is a way of communicating with spirit guides, angels and spirits who have passed over.

Dad used to call it the 'spook church' because the idea of spirits and clairvoyance frightened him to death. One day, Mum came home to find him nailing a crucifix to the wall above their bed.

'No, no,' he said, 'I'm putting this cross up here, just in case.'

He never tried to prevent Mum and Gran going, though. They played a huge part in the running of the church and went there almost every evening, often taking me with them if Dad was on a late shift and there was no one at home to babysit. The church had a really friendly atmosphere and I used to enjoy going there: I loved the people, the sense of community, the music and the hymns. What was funny was that Gran would present herself as someone far posher than she actually was when she was on the stage. The first time I saw her up there, I thought, 'That's my grandmother. What's she talking like that for?'

The church Easter rally was one of the highlights of our year. It conjures up memories of cake, bunting and the smooth, crisp fabric of my brand-new Whitsuntide dress. Although I was too shy to leave my mother's side and run off to play with the other kids, it was always a joyful occasion: you could sense everybody was happy that spring was here. It was a wonderful time of year because, added to the rest of the fun, the painted Easter eggs and chocolate, there was my birthday on 4 April, Janet's birthday on the 5th and Tony's on the 15th. The only problem was that Tony used to cry when his sisters' birthdays arrived, because we were getting all the attention and he still had ten long, agonising days to wait until his special day. To spare his tears, Mum took to buying him a little present and giving it to him early so that he didn't feel left out – that was my mother.

When Mum and Dad threw parties, you knew about it. Mum was very much a family person, so my aunties, uncles and cousins would come over at times like Easter and Christmas and there would be music and singing into the night. Hogmanay at the end of the year was always massive for us, because everyone was Scottish and homesick for the motherland. Being shy, I wasn't keen on these get-togethers, with so many relatives in the house making a hubbub and commotion with their hearty auld lang synes and bonailie toasts to absent friends. What did 'Lang may yer lum reek' mean, anyway? I used to hide under the heavy oak dining table so that I didn't have to talk to any of them.

The confidence I'd had as a baby had left me now. I was fast developing into a nervous, sickly child who was scared of her own shadow. Loud noises made me jump: I couldn't stand the telephone ringing and, whenever we had to pass under a railway bridge near the house, I couldn't do it if there was a train speeding across because of the racket it made. Even worse, we lived next door to the Stanley Royd Lunatic Asylum, known locally as 'the Loony Bin', and its spectre began to cast a looming shadow in my mind as I grew older and more aware. Stanley Royd was a large purpose-built Victorian hospital set in leafy grounds that sloped down to the road, where tall green railings enclosed the land. It was quite a disturbing place and, being next door, we heard all sorts of goings-on, at all times of the day and night. There was howling, moaning and screaming. I used to clamp my hands over my ears to block it out and I never ventured into the yard behind our house.

When the inpatients walked around the asylum grounds for their exercise, some of them would wander down towards the road and reach eerily through the railings when we were passing. Even at my young age I quickly picked up on their despair. I sensed there was a great deal of chaos and suffering within those grounds, a lot of depression and sadness. It frightened me to death, especially as my father would constantly warn: 'Don't go near the railings.'

Janet and Tony were of an age when they weren't scared of anything, or so they pretended. 'Let's go through the railings,' they suggested one day when we were on our way back from the local shop.

'I don't want to,' I wailed, pulling my hand out of Tony's.

'Come on,' Janet urged, squeezing herself through a gap. Tony went next and I followed reluctantly, feeling I had no choice.

We ran around for a while and then Janet asked, 'Do you want to play hide and seek?'

'No, I want to stay with you,' I said.

'Go on! I bet I'll find you in no time.'

I ambled off dutifully to hide behind a tree, but soon panicked and jumped out to see my brother and sister pelting back to the gap in the railings. Some of the patients had come outside to go for a walk and they were heading straight towards us.

'Wait for me,' I screamed, running helter-skelter after Janet and Tony.

Once I'd scrabbled back through the railings, I burst into floods of angry tears.

'Hush, you're fine, aren't you?' Janet said, breathing hard, her eyes shining with excitement.

To her, it was just a funny teenage escapade, but it scared the living daylights out of me. It even infiltrated my dreams. For years afterwards, I had a recurring nightmare of being chased out of the asylum and not being able to run fast enough, however hard Janet and Tony tried to drag me along with them. I would wake up terrified, my heart beating like thunder, electrified by the fear of being caught.

'Mum!' I'd scream in the dead of night. 'Mu-um!'

It must have been around this time that I developed a nervous stomach. I was sick a lot and stopped wanting to leave the house altogether. I didn't even like going to school – I had to be coaxed and cajoled out of the house and past the asylum railings every single day. Once there, I found the kids too boisterous and the dinners indescribably revolting. I had a poor appetite at the best of times and the food they served up at school didn't tempt me in the least. I remember spending the mornings feeling sick at the thought of the disgusting dinner ahead and the afternoons dreading the walk home.

At around the age of six, I became so thin that my mother began to worry. I was a beanpole. She couldn't even fatten me up with sugary things – I wasn't one for sweets and preferred water to pop. What made matters worse was my father was very partial to fatty meat like pork belly, which I just couldn't eat, and while Mum gave the best cuts of meat to the boarders, often we had to make do with leftover strips of fat and scraggy scraps. In those days parents didn't say, 'What would you like for your tea?' A meal was served up and you ate it or you went hungry. If it wasn't to your taste, there wasn't enough money for your mum to say, 'Well, what do you want to eat instead?'

Sitting down for meals could be an ordeal because Dad was a disciplinarian and Mum was also strict: we had to sit at the table, eat properly and use manners. We always sat at the dinner table, the table was set just so and we had to eat with the correct knives and forks, as our grandmother had taught us, just as she had been taught by her own mother, the Darlings' nanny. If we wanted to blow our noses, we had to say, 'Please may I leave the table . . . ?' There wasn't much fun or laughter and, despite Mum's cooking skills, pig's trotters, brawn and brisket all made my stomach turn. I'd eat just enough to survive: a little gravy and maybe some chips.

Mum used to take me to the doctor all the time: 'I can't get anything down her,' she'd say anxiously. 'What can I do?'

The doctor was brilliant. 'She will eat when she's hungry, don't force-feed her,' he said, recognising I was a nervous child.

It was the best advice he could have given, because by then the teachers at school had decided forcibly feeding me was the only answer. One lunchtime, when it was noticed that I hadn't touched my food again, a teacher was called (one of those teachers from a bygone age who believed in good old-fashioned discipline).

Visibly annoyed, she sat down next to me, her lips pursed. 'You have to eat your dinner, Jane,' she told me briskly. 'No ifs or buts.'

I shook my head resolutely. 'I will not eat this,' I said.

There was just no way on earth.

Sensing trouble, the other kids on my table bolted their food and rushed off to stack their plates. Dinnertime was nearing an end and gradually the dining room emptied out. The standoff between me and the teacher lasted for what felt like hours.

'What a waste of time,' I thought as she kept urging me to eat the now congealed food in front of me.

Clearly not used to being bested by a pupil in the dinner hall, the teacher had a sharp word with my mother: 'She outright refuses to eat the school food.'

'Well, I can give her some sandwiches that I know she will eat?' Mum suggested.

The teacher frowned. 'None of the other children are allowed to bring in their dinner from home,' she said.

'Oh dear, then, what can we do? I'm so worried,' Mum said.

Which is how I became the first person at the Parish School to be allowed to take in my own ham sandwiches.

I felt I had won an important battle, but it turned out to be a hollow victory. Taking my own sandwiches into school meant that I stood out from everybody else and being different attracted the attention of the very people I least wanted to notice me.

There was a group of girls in my class who liked to pick on timid kids like me. Being nervous, weak and sickly, as well as shy, I was their perfect victim. They used to gather round me in the playground and say nasty things, pushing and prodding me, sometimes giving me a slap or two. One morning, as I carried my little dinner package into school, I suddenly found myself surrounded by four or five of them.

Sarah, their ringleader, snatched the package out of my hands. 'What you got in here?' she asked.

'Ham sandwiches and a scone,' I whispered.

She ripped it open to see for herself. 'Oh, plain and boring, just like you,' she sneered, throwing the entire contents into the hedge at the back of the playground.

'She's just a plain Jane,' one of the other girls piped up with a snigger.

'Plain Jane, plain Jane!' they started to chant, closing in on me.

'Stop it!' I shouted. I burst through a gap in the circle and ran away as fast as my legs would carry me.

That afternoon, I trudged home, wondering if I would just have to accept that life got worse with every passing day, the older you grew – little knowing salvation lay just around the corner.

2

The Way We Were

I don't remember the day the ambulance arrived at our door, bringing Dad back from hospital. I was very protected as a child, so maybe I was kept out of view. Or perhaps I've just forgotten, as I have a very clever mind that won't acknowledge anything really bad. Yet, although I can't remember it, that day had huge significance for our family – and for me, in particular, because of what came afterwards.

Dad didn't talk about what had happened, he kept a lot inside. I once had a letter from a man named Roy Brooke, saying, 'Your dad saved my life when he dragged me out of the pit after an accident. I wouldn't be here without him.'

What a powerful story, but it was news to me because Dad was so tight-lipped about his life. He buried everything. We had a photograph of him in his paratrooper uniform, looking horribly thin, somewhere really hot, but that was the only evidence we had in the house that he'd fought in the war, and he never spoke about it. We worked out that he must have lied about his age to get into the army, as the dates don't tally unless he joined up when he was 15. It was confusing: we were always saying, 'How old is our father again?'

It was years before I learned how close Dad came to being killed the day the ambulance brought him home. He was making his way to the face of the mine when a trolley broke loose and hurtled straight towards him. As the trolley clipped him, he had a fraction of a second to jump onto it or be crushed to death. He jumped. Clinging on for dear life as it careered along, he kept his nerve until he was thrown free.

The accident left Dad with a shattered ankle and broken ribs, but he wasn't one to make a fuss. He brushed Mum aside when she tried to help him out of the ambulance into the house and never once complained about the pain. He was off work for weeks and did a lot of sitting around, that much I do remember. Poor Dad, he hated not being able to get up to his allotment, where he could escape life's stresses and strains and have a bit of man time. He really missed being out in nature.

'My veg'll go to seed if someone doesn't go an' pick them,' he groaned.

It was hopeless sending Tony and Janet up there to do it for him. They didn't have a clue and used to come home with nothing but a bunch of carrot tops or sweet peas. To add to Dad's misery, it was summer and the television was all repeats. He probably wouldn't have minded being stuck in an armchair, watching his favourite programme – a Western series called *The High Chaparral* – but the good stuff never seemed to be on more than once.

As the school holidays approached and the lodgers began leaving for the summer break, Mum started fretting. 'Where are we going to take Jane and Tony this year?' she said to Gran. 'We can't go to Brid without Peter, it would break his heart.'

Of all the places in this wide world, my father loved Bridlington on the Yorkshire coast best and Mum felt it wouldn't be fair to go there without him. Luckily, this had also occurred to Gran, who was one step ahead as usual.

'These past few weeks I've been thinking about going home,' she told Mum. 'Let's take them to the Scottish seaside.'

*

I have such happy memories of that holiday in Monifieth, where Gran grew up. Yet whenever Tony and I think back to it, all we do is laugh about what happened on the journey there. Being nine years older than me, Janet was more interested in being with her friends, so she stayed at home in Wakefield with Dad, while Mum, Gran, Tony and I took the train to Dundee, an adventure in itself to us kids. From there, we were set to catch a local bus that would take us along the coastal road to our caravan site.

When the bus arrived, the kindly driver stacked our cases in the luggage space under the stairs, including a round case of Gran's that was slotted in on its side. Why she had a round case, I don't know – it didn't have a hat in, it wasn't a vanity case and it didn't stack neatly. As the bus pulled away, it rolled out of the luggage space and onto the road. Then it went on rolling all the way down the street.

A few minutes later, Tony noticed a car flashing and beeping behind us, its driver frantically waving.

'I wonder what's happened?' he said.

The car wouldn't give up. Every now and then it would try to come alongside the bus, but our driver had an obstinate streak and held to his speed, so it kept dropping back again.

'It's a man!' Tony exclaimed, his face glued to the rear window.

By now, everybody was thinking, 'What the flipping heck is up with him? He's going mad with all that flashing, there must be something really wrong.'

When our bus finally pulled into a stop, the car screeched to a halt behind us and we were amazed to see the driver holding up Gran's beautiful cream case triumphantly as if it were a Grand Prix trophy.

'Miles, that car followed us for miles,' Tony always says, laughing his head off.

*

Monifieth was our best holiday ever. There was nothing there: it was just running around sand dunes all day, probably in the freezing cold, but you didn't care about that when you were a kid, did you? We relished the freedom of not having to do anything. No school, nothing. It was heaven.

On a morning, we woke up in our caravan to the smell of bacon frying and Mum making us each a big, fresh bacon bap. She was a great cook, my mother. Then Tony and I would go off for the whole day, flying his kite on the beach, making up games and having fun from morning till night. We were at just the right ages when the five-year gap between us didn't seem to matter and Tony was good to me. He was a lovely soul and still is – takes after our mother.

On the fourth day of our holiday, we caught the bus to Edinburgh Zoo, but I don't remember any of the animals we saw because they've been completely overshadowed in my mind by the hordes of pigeons flocking outside the zoo gates: there were hundreds, maybe thousands of them. There were so many pigeons that they started landing on our heads, which made us scream in delight and horror.

Monifieth had a chip shop – just the one. On an evening, Gran, Mum and I would have a 'fish supper', as they call it up there, while Tony had white pudding and chips. White pudding, a sausage made with oatmeal and suet, was a local speciality. Although it surprised no one that I wouldn't touch it, Tony loved it almost as much as he loved black pudding, which he could have eaten till the cows came home. He may have had his mother's personality, but he followed his father in his appetite for offal.

After supper, it was back to the caravan, where the gas lamps were lit and we'd play cards until our eyes began to droop and then it was time for bed. Mum said we kids never slept as well as we did that holiday, lulled by the gentle sound of the wind and the waves, knocked out by the fresh, salty air.

I think we must have been in Monifieth when *Apollo 11* landed on the moon on 20 July 1969. Since we had no electricity in our caravan, let alone television, we missed it. It might have passed me by completely if there hadn't been a boy called Neil Armstrong who lived on the corner of our street in Wakefield. Poor lad, all anybody could say to him for weeks after the *Apollo* mission was, 'Where's yer rocket?' and 'You've just landed on the moon!'

We got back from Scotland to find Dad in the living room with the TV on, intent on balancing our indoor aerial at a precarious angle on a propped-up chair.

'We're back!' Mum announced blithely.

'Don't come anywhere near,' Dad warned. 'It's taken me all afternoon to get a clear picture.'

As Mum laughed, the screen went fuzzy. Dad shouted in fury.

We were home.

Dad was a very charming man, but he had a quick temper. 'Don't worry, his bark is worse than his bite,' Mum used to say to reassure us. I often heard that particular phrase in relation to my father – he used to shout a lot, but never followed it up. Still, I don't recall him ever shouting at me. Even when he was angry with Janet and Tony for running around and creating havoc, he calmed down the moment he turned his attention to me. For some reason, I brought out his soft side.

I was a quiet child, partly because I understood what used to wind my dad up, but also because I had a really old head on my shoulders. From an early age, I felt different from the other two: I was the youngest but felt the most grown-up. Janet and Tony found Mum and Dad to be very strict, but they needed to be, because my brother and sister were little swines! Lively and shouty and full of personality, they were constantly doing things to upset our parents. I used to sit there, thinking, 'Stop doing that, Dad'll lose his temper.'

Often, I felt as if I was on the outside looking in. I used to picture myself sitting on the rim of a soup bowl, set apart from the chaos within it, watching everybody fighting for their lives. It was a weird image to have in my mind, but that was my perspective. The atmosphere wasn't helped by Mum and Dad's constant arguing. Dad was a sulker – sometimes he wouldn't speak to her for three or four days.

My mother would think, 'Well, I'm not speaking to him, either,' and then there would be silence between them, apart from Mum asking, 'What do you want for supper?' But she could never remember to keep it up. All of a sudden, she would be excited about something and say to my dad, 'Have you heard what the club are doing on the Bank Holiday?' Then, realising she'd been first to break the deadlock, she'd leave the room, muttering, 'Damn, I can't believe I've just done that!'

As well as being a sulker, Dad was a worrier, so if Mum said she was coming home on the three o'clock bus and she wasn't home, he used to pace. He couldn't stand lateness and in his book if you said you were going to do something, you should do it, so when Mum was late, there would be a blazing row. It was the same whenever Janet went out – Dad would insist on picking her up, but if for some reason he couldn't, he'd pace about endlessly until she got in.

I remember Mum saying, 'I loved your dad, but I didn't like him very much.'

You hear that said so often, don't you?

'Why did you stay with him, then?' I asked.

'In those days, Jane, you couldn't just walk away. I had three children,' she sighed. 'People used to say, "You've made your bed, now lie in it."'

It's funny, Dad was brilliant when we were on our own and

Mum was fantastic when I was with her on my own. But it was a different atmosphere when they were together – unless we were on holiday, away from the worries of everyday life.

After his accident, Dad wasn't keen on going down the pit again, so after a few weeks of convalescing, he got a job as a crane driver. He didn't take to it, though, and went back to the mine, only this time as a banksman, directing the cages that went up and down the shaft. It was much less perilous work than before, which pleased Mum, but the drop in Dad's wages soon started to bite, so he started a little chimney-sweeping business on the side. It still wasn't enough, and when Gran decided to move out into her own cottage and the police college up the road opened up its own residential facilities, there was nothing for it but to down-size. That's what Dad said, anyway. Mum said she would have been quite happy to look elsewhere for lodgers and keep on with the boarding house.

Dad put his foot down, thankfully. He wanted shot of the boarders – he'd had enough of coming home, tired out and sooty, only to hear them regaling Mum with tales of their heroic police work around the world. We started looking for a smaller place, in a different part of town, somewhere we could afford. I went along to the viewings with Mum and Gran, roaming through empty houses while they discussed whether or not our dining table would fit in the downstairs front room.

In one of the houses we looked at, we found an old piano abandoned in the corner of the front room.

'He's so blimmin' cautious. I know what he'll say, it's out of our range,' Mum was telling Gran.

Gran surveyed the room. 'Maybe he's right, love. It's pricey for what it is.'

I stared at the piano. It looked to me as if it was waiting to be played, so I ran over and started picking out a tune. Finding the notes came naturally, instantly. Soon I was playing a melody I'd heard earlier in the day.

My grandmother looked at my mum: 'We need to get a piano,' she said.

Since Dad could find anything, it wasn't too long before he came across a pub piano that was being thrown out. It was an old battered thing with ring marks on it where the pint glasses had been, but it was perfect for me. I was good at listening and could play almost any tune by ear, even before I started having lessons. Mum would say, 'Play this song,' and I would play it; my brother would say, 'Play that song,' and I would play it. Mum started asking around about a piano teacher.

I couldn't have been happier when we moved from the big house in Eastmoor Road to our small, cosy mid-terrace on Silcoates Street, on the Peacock Estate close to the centre of town. It felt like the best thing that had ever happened to me. Understandably Janet wasn't quite as delighted, especially when she saw the tin bath hanging on the wall and the outdoor toilet. Like any teenager, she was worried about what her friends would think.

'I can't have any of my friends seeing that!' she cried.

Never mind that Mum said we'd be installing an upstairs bathroom as soon as we moved in. And there was even worse news awaiting Janet: the lack of bedroom space in our new house meant she would be sharing a room with me, her annoying little sister. You couldn't help but feel sorry for her, because all her friends from the girls' high school lived in smart houses on the posh side of town and she was of an age when appearances were everything.

As for me, I loved our new house, absolutely loved it. It was warm and safe and I felt totally at home in the neighbourhood, with its close-knit community and friendly neighbours. True, it was very working-class and probably felt like a bump down to earth for my mother as well as my sister, but Mum took it in her stride and never complained – and I was too young to notice. How the heck she cooked and washed up Sunday dinner for five in our tiny kitchen I'll never know. And she was endlessly cooking and making sandwiches for Dad to have down the pit on his various shifts. Dad worked all times – afternoons, days and nights – but we mostly managed to sit down to our meals at the same time, we didn't have split shifts for dinner.

There was an ever-present smell of cooking in the house, partly because Mum would make a pan of soup that stayed on the stove from Monday to Sunday, bubbling away. She would add vegetables, lentils, water and a stock cube every now and then, maybe some ham stock if she'd made a ham joint for my dad. People would help themselves whenever they felt hungry. That soup was constantly evolving and being enriched with different ingredients.

My parents were of the generation that ate breakfast, dinner and tea – and then supper at about 8.30pm. How they weren't as big as houses, I don't know.

Whenever Mum said to Dad, 'What do you fancy for supper?' he'd always say, 'What have you got?'

Mum would go through a list of possibilities: supper could be anything from milk and biscuits to pilchards on toast with vinegar. Dad appeared to consider all the options thoroughly, then he'd say, 'Cheese on toast.'

'Oh, God!' Mum would exclaim, because he chose cheese on toast every time.

Mum never stopped. The washing was never-ending and we didn't have a tumble dryer – no one did at the time – so Dad rigged up a pulley above the coal fire in the living room. It was an eyesore, looking back on it, but it worked a treat. Still, if Mum had done a really big wash and the pulley was full, she used to put a clotheshorse by the parlour fire. The parlour was our best room and we didn't go in there much, but I used to sneak in and make a little den, hidden from view by the drying clothes. I loved to sit quietly by the fire and think, staring at the embers and dreaming, sometimes listening to records.

I'd stopped buying sweets (Tony always ate them, anyway) and started spending my pocket money on singles. Mum and I would go into Woolworths on the high street and, while Mum headed for the pick 'n' mix counter, I'd go to the records section. 'Lily The Pink' by The Scaffold was the first single I ever bought and I was keen on novelty records for a good few years after that. Meanwhile, Dad, being a heavy smoker, collected Embassy coupons by the dozen and sent off for four LPs that he gave me, including the *Show Boat* and *South Pacific* soundtracks and a selection of waltzes by Johann Strauss, including 'The Blue Danube'. I had a great time singing along to all this wonderful music, acting out the songs, copying the accents and adding my own soprano flourishes.

Home was my haven, as it had been in Eastmoor Road, but for different reasons. Whereas I didn't go out a lot before because of Dad's dire warnings about the asylum next door, now I just loved staying inside for the sake of being at home. It was a hive of activity, with people coming and going, and I loved being at the centre of everything. Mum was busy, but she wasn't always rushing off to tend to the boarders' needs as she had been before, and Dad would often be in the back yard, repairing or building something, so when I'd had enough of my own company, I had a choice between helping Mum in the kitchen or handing Dad his tools while he worked.

Dad was really good at mending stuff and there was always an engine in pieces in the yard. You could've found anything down in the cellar, where he stored his tools and boxes of stuff. There were boxes everywhere, packed full of bits and pieces he'd picked up. Although it was all chucked in and higgledy-piggledy, he knew where everything was.

Anybody in our street could have gone to my dad and said, 'Have you got a Ford Cortina camshaft?' and he would have said, 'Yes, I've got one down in the cellar.'

One day, he was passing Pinderfields Hospital and noticed builders putting new windows in. All the old ones had been thrown in a skip. Just then, Dad had an idea and, quick as a flash, he went home, got his van and loaded it up with all these windows they'd chucked out. In the weeks that followed, he used them to build a conservatory out the back of the house, and, although it looked shocking, it never fell down and it never once leaked. He was brilliant, my father, he could really make things work – they just looked terrible.

Saturday mornings when my dad looked after me while Mum went out to buy the meat and vegetables for the week were my favourite. It was such a special time for me and Dad. We used to sit watching the wrestling, and he loved the wrestling so he was always really happy. I can picture him now in his heavy green armchair; I can conjure the smell of him – a mixture of Brylcreem and tobacco – and I can hear him laughing as Big Daddy bounced off the ropes and landed face down in the ring.

'What a clown, eh, Jane?' he'd chuckle.

We still had a black and white television, much to my mother's disgust. But Dad was paranoid about debt. His whole life was about earning enough to feed the family and pay the mortgage off.

'If you can't afford it, you're not having it,' he'd say.

'But we need a colour television,' she'd grumble.

As well as wrestling, Dad liked watching snooker, which puzzled me.

'How do we know which one's the pink ball?' I asked.

37

'That's the pink ball,' Dad said, pointing at the screen.

'The grey one in the corner?'

'What are you talking about?' he laughed. 'It's pink!'

Although we no longer lived next to the asylum, I was still anxious about venturing out into the world and going to school. My nervous stomach played havoc with my insides; I was travel-sick wherever we went and the slightest worry would make me vomit. Whenever Tony took me to the fair, I was a nightmare. 'She's feeling sick again,' he used to say to anyone who asked what was the matter with his silent, pale-faced sister. 'Don't worry, she's always like this.'

It was another reason to stay at home, although, funnily enough, our new house wasn't as safe as I thought, even though Dad had put locks on everything, including the outside toilet. What none of us knew was the attic space along the entire terrace was joined into one long corridor, because when they built the houses, the builders hadn't put in dividing walls up there. This meant anybody could come into your house through your attic at any time.

One evening, when Mum and Dad had gone to the club and Janet was babysitting Tony and me, I heard a piercing scream coming from upstairs. We ran up to find Janet in the loo.

'Get in this bathroom now!' she yelled.

Without any explanation, she locked us in the bathroom for ten minutes while she waited at the door with bated breath. We were terrified, because we had no idea what was going on. Sensibly, she didn't tell us that she had seen the door to the attic lift up on her way up to the loo: someone was up there, trying to get in.

The minutes crawled by as Janet waited for an intruder to appear. But whoever was there had gone away, no doubt scared off by her shrieks.

Tony and I soon got over the excitement, but it was a scary moment for Janet. We grew up in an era when you could leave your front door open, so it was the last thing anyone expected to happen.

Janet was that much older so she was off with her friends most of the time, but Tony often got stuck with me. In the summer, we would make ourselves an equal number of jam sandwiches and tomato sauce ones and go over the fields behind our house to play with all the other kids in the neighbourhood.

You could see by the look on Tony's face what he thought of having me trailing along behind him: 'Oh no, I've got to take her again. I bet she's going to be sick.'

The upside was, if Mum gave us some sweets to take, he got my share as well, because I didn't really bother with them.

There was a beck with a little bridge that we would cross on our way to the fields. When the grass had been cut, we used to throw it in the stream to make a soft bed to land on. The bridge wasn't very high, but to me, as a kid, leaping into the beck was like jumping off the Empire State Building. Oh, the sound of my heart pumping in my chest as I hovered on the bank, gearing myself up to do it! 'Now? No, wait . . . now?'

All day long, we'd play daft games and our own versions of hide and seek and chase. Then, when dusk fell, Dad used to come and find me – Tony was allowed to stay out a bit longer, but I had to go in as soon as the light began to fade.

The other kids were frightened to death of my dad. I don't know why. Maybe it was the guttural way he called out, 'Jane!' in his Scottish accent as he loped across the fields, looking for me.

It put everybody on alert.

'Maccy, your dad's here – run!'

'All right, I'm coming,' I'd call, and tootle off.

He may have intimidated other people, but I always felt that Dad was my mate as well as my father, whether he was tenderly showing me how to tie a shoelace or teaching me to dance. The dancing came about because my mother was often up at the church on a night and my dad resented her being away so much.

In the end he gave Mum an ultimatum: 'If you won't come to the club on a Friday, I'm going to take Jane dancing in your place.'

'Fine with me,' she said breezily, 'and Jane would enjoy it, wouldn't you, love?' she added, turning to me. 'You can wear your pink and purple Whitsuntide dress. I'll put it out for you and do your hair in plaits before I go.'

That evening, I felt like a princess as I walked around the corner to the Balne Lane Working Men's Club, hand in hand with my handsome father. We arrived just as the dancing was about to begin, the air full of anticipation. I stood beside Dad and counted the coloured lights around the bar as he got a pint for himself and a glass of pop for me. Then I noticed a couple of women looking his way and smiling. Everybody was looking forward to their night of fun.

'I'm going to teach you how to ballroom dance, Jane,' Dad said, grinning down at me. 'What do you think to that?'

I grinned back at him, speechless with happiness.

The club smelled of people and beer. To me, it was the smell of pure excitement.

3

Over The Rainbow

I tended to take my grandmother's psychic predictions with a pinch of salt, especially when she spoke about all the travelling I would do in the future.

'I don't know what you're going to do,' she would say, 'but there are wheels: there are cars, trains and planes. You're going everywhere, you're going all over the world.'

It seemed unlikely, given most of the time I didn't want to leave the house for fear of being sick. I didn't even want to go on holiday. Mum and Dad could never tell me we were going to Bridlington because I'd throw up just thinking about the journey. Instead, they used to tell me we were going up the road for a picnic. Never mind all the suitcases were coming out of the attic and the contents of the food cupboard being packed into cardboard boxes – I must have believed them because I wanted to.

Brid may have been the nearest seaside town to Wakefield, but it was still more than 70 bumpy miles away in one of Dad's old bangers. I only had to look at his old green Ford Thames van to feel nauseous. Dad's vans were always falling apart: the carburettor would overheat, the gear stick would snap or the petrol cap disappear. He never bought anything new. Still, he could mend anything, so we always got there in the end, just about – but we would never have made it further than Bridlington, and for that reason we never tried. We used to chug along with a rag plugging the tank, wires everywhere, the engine held together with elastic bands; I'd be sitting on a petrol can between Mum and Dad and my dad would be smoking an Embassy Regal. Never mind the MOT, even Health and Safety didn't get a look in. We could have gone up in flames at any moment.

The journey was a living nightmare, but I recovered the instant we finally arrived at the coast. One whiff of that saltwater air and my queasiness would disappear. All that mattered was that I had a week of pure enjoyment ahead of me. Our holidays in Bridlington were always fantastic. I think of my childhood as being a rosy, beautiful place that I can happily visit at any time, with Bridlington at its centre.

Janet was old enough to go away with her friends and then, when she was 18, she got married to her boyfriend, Robert, and moved to Huddersfield. It was a bittersweet moment when Janet left home: I was going to miss my big sister but I was going to have the bedroom all to myself. I don't remember her ever coming with us on holiday because she was that much older – it was always Mum, Dad, Tony and me. We stayed in different caravan parks: as well as Brid, we went to Barmston and Skipsea, down the coast a bit. Mum always insisted on booking a caravan. Sometimes Dad used to take Tony and me camping closer to home, but she said, 'No, I'm not doing a tent.'

I suppose it wasn't a holiday as much as a change of scene for my mother, who cooked and cleaned and did most of the things she normally did at home. On our last day, she used to scrub the caravan from top to bottom until the whole place smelled of bleach and Dettol.

'I don't want people to think we're scruffy,' she'd say, giving the surfaces a final wipe.

'Heck, I wish it had been this tidy when we walked in,' I'd think.

Our days always started with a big breakfast, a full English, and then it was off to the beach until lunchtime, with bags packed with sandwiches, crisps, drinks, towels, cossies and beach games. On an evening, we'd have fish and chips out, or go to the club-house in the park. I was always begging to go to the clubhouse – it had the same exciting smell as our club back in Wakefield.

We went on a few excursions, but they rarely ended well for me. One of the worst was a boat ride we took around the harbour in a little pleasure cruiser called *Bridlington Belle*. From the moment I got on that boat to the moment I got off, I was leaning over the side.

'Never again,' I vowed as I staggered up the quay.

My brother laughed the whole way round the harbour.

'I don't see you travelling the world, Jane,' he said. 'You can't go in a car or on a boat and I can't imagine you in a plane. I reckon the only thing you wouldn't be sick on is a bicycle.'

He was wrong about that, unfortunately. I finally got a bike after Dad found a frame in the beck behind our house in Sil-coates Street. He brought it home, sanded it down, polished it, sprayed it gold, added wheels and gave it to me for Christmas. It was fabulous, the best and prettiest bike I've ever had, and I was thrilled.

'Come on, we'll go over and see my Auntie Pauline in Ossett,' Tony said, a couple of days later. We were quite close to our cousins, who lived about three miles away.

I set off behind him, wobbling. Before I'd gone half a mile, I called out to him to stop.

'What is it, has the chain come off?' he asked.

'I feel bicycle sick,' I moaned.

'Don't be silly, nobody gets bicycle sick,' he said.

I proved him wrong by vomiting over the handlebars, not once but three times on the short journey to Auntie Pauline's.

'I just don't believe this,' Tony said, slapping his forehead every time we stopped.

Despite my shy, sickly nature, I always had an answer when asked what I wanted to be when I grew up.

'An entertainer,' I'd say.

It was just something I knew I was going to do, even if I didn't know how. I was average at school, really average, but I was good at music. I lapped up programmes like *Cilla* and *Opportunity Knocks*, loved Shirley Bassey and Bruce Forsyth and the other big Saturday night entertainers. I even liked *The Good Old Days*, with its old-fashioned jokes and long words. I hadn't decided whether I wanted to sing, dance, act or play the piano when I grew up – I think I would have been happy just to paint the backdrops or help build the stage. It didn't matter as long as I could be a part of the same world as the performers I saw at the club and on the TV.

I didn't have a promising start to my musical career, though. After a few lessons, my first piano teacher rang my mother and said, 'She hasn't a musical bone in her body and she'll never do anything with music.'

My mother was stunned. 'I beg to differ,' she argued. 'I think she's very musical.'

Mum began looking around for someone else and found Francis Walker, a blind piano teacher, who was just right for me. Francis was a brilliant teacher – I was quite lazy and he was very patient with me. I could never get anything by him, even when I was sure he wouldn't notice what I was up to.

'You're not reading the music, you're making it up,' he'd say, because he knew the music so well.

'No, I'm not!'

'Yes, you are. Start again.'

There was a lot of repetition in Francis's lessons, and a lot of scales. It's not surprising that every Tuesday I used to think, 'Oh no, it's my piano lesson again!' But I stuck with it because I didn't want to let Mum down and, little by little, I improved.

I was at St Michael's Middle School now, where I was bullied something awful by a group of girls who seemed to enjoy making my life miserable. There were bullies at every school I went to and they always seemed to pick on me. I was a poor scholar because of it, and very unhappy, but thankfully, I had one good friend I could count on: Elizabeth Baxter. I often felt that Liz was the only friend I needed. When we were together, we were inseparable, like two peas in a pod, and Mum would say, 'When you've seen one, you've seen t'other!'

I used to walk to school with two other girls, Jane and Mandy, and they were a good laugh, but that was it: I didn't have any other friends. In those days there was very little awareness of anxiety, especially in children, and people couldn't understand what was going on with me or why I didn't join in their games.

'What's wrong with you?' they'd ask scornfully. 'You can't be feeling sick again.'

I was pathetic, really pathetic. When I look back at the person I was, she seems completely different to the one I am now. It makes me want to cuddle her and say, 'Come on, you can do this,' echoing the words my mother used to murmur as she coaxed me out of my nervousness.

The days at St Michael's seemed to drag on forever and lunchtimes lasted an eternity, especially if Elizabeth wasn't around. After we'd eaten, we were sent out into the playground, a huge grey expanse that was thick with menace for someone like me. I was an easy target for the girls who used to gather round me and pick on me and I would run like mad whenever I saw them coming my way. I might have been stick-thin, but I was fast.

Luckily, I had Mrs Brierley on my side. She was the music teacher, as well as being my form teacher. One dinnertime, when Mrs Brierley overheard some girls teasing me in the playground, she stopped and called me over: 'No one is playing the piano in our classroom. Would you like to go inside and do some practice for the rest of the dinner hour?'

I nodded gratefully.

'Come with me,' she said. 'I can let you stay inside every day if you want, but you have to be doing something.'

After that, I used to bolt down my sandwiches, run hell-for-leather through the playground and spend the rest of the lunch break practising the piano in our classroom. This solved two problems at once: it kept me out of harm's way and gave me time and space to practise. Since I never did my scales at home because there was always something going on to distract me, an hour of scales a day at school made a huge difference. At my Tuesday piano lessons, Francis was startled by my sudden progress.

Mrs Brierley had thrown me a lifeline and I couldn't have been more thankful. At last I had someone to turn to when I had a problem at school. She helped in other ways, too. When she started teaching us songs from the musical *Joseph and the Amazing Technicolor Dreamcoat*, I loved them so much that I begged to borrow her song sheets. A few days later, she came in at lunchtime and had a listen to what I was doing.

'Very good,' she said with an approving smile.

I think this must have given her an idea of how to bring me out of myself a little and the following day, during our Music lesson, after looking at her watch, she got up from the piano and said, 'I need to go and see the Headmaster. Can you take over at the piano, Jane?'

My throat constricted. 'Me?'

'Yes, come over here and play in my place, please,' she said matter-of-factly. 'Start from the beginning of the song.'

I got up shakily and took her seat at the piano. Although I felt privileged to have been singled out, I hated everybody looking at me. Glancing down at the piano keys and up at the sheet music, I began to play a few notes. To my amazement, everybody started singing.

Could it really be so easy?

'I could get used to this,' I thought, and by the time Mrs Brierley returned, we were halfway through the songbook.

As she appeared at the door, I stopped playing abruptly and stood up – it was her seat, after all.

'No, you stay where you are,' she said briskly before turning to face the class: 'Right, let's go back to "Jacob and Sons". Carry on, Jane.'

After the lesson, Mrs Brierley thanked me for helping out: 'I'll be calling on you to play in class again,' she said.

Pleased, I mumbled something about it being good practice for the future.

'Why, what do you want to be when you grow up?' she asked, with genuine curiosity.

I hesitated. Grown-ups usually laughed when I answered that question honestly. Still, perhaps she would be more sympathetic.

'I'd love to be a singer,' I replied at last, 'and an entertainer.'

She smiled reassuringly. 'Of all the people in this school, I think you are going to be what you want to be,' she said.

For the rest of that day, I was walking on air. I was so shy, but Mrs Brierley believed in me and somehow that made all the difference to how I felt about myself. The effect was lasting, too. Her words have stayed with me for nearly 50 years and I have drawn comfort from them many, many times.

Mrs Brierley is 90 years old now and, not so long ago, I received a card from her out of the blue, delivered by a friend, so I wrote her a letter in which I said, 'I just want to thank you for believing in me so much and inspiring me. I'll be forever grateful to you.'

School was never going to be a happy place for me, though. All the fun I ever had, even with Elizabeth, took place outside of school hours. Friday nights were the highlight of my week, when I'd be sat at home, bright-eyed with excitement, having my hair done by Mum, waiting for Dad to come in from the pit.

'Is he coming yet?' I'd ask, every five minutes.

It was the 1970s and I had a couple of long, patterned, flowery dresses that made me feel fabulous as I waltzed and foxtrotted with Dad at the club on a Friday evening. We didn't have much money at the time and Mum had bought them on the never-never. (If you needed a loan in those days, you'd go to Clegg and Huntingdon for a cheque, which you paid back in weekly or monthly instalments.)

Dad was such a good dancer that I never minded sitting out a waltz when he said, 'I think I'll go and ask that lady over there to dance.'

Although I was still small, I could tell the women thought he was gorgeous.

'Go on, make her day,' I'd say.

We had that sort of 'pals' relationship.

Saturday nights were almost as good as Friday nights because of the TV. The 1970s were a golden period of light entertainment and a time when you really felt the power of show business amid the strikes, power cuts and general turmoil going on at the time. Like a lot of children at the time, I enjoyed the power cuts. The coal fire would be lit and we'd have candles and hot water bottles at the ready and, when the power went off, we'd sit around the fire and tell stories. But then it would be great when the power cut ended, too. I remember the leccy had just come on when ten-year-old Lena Zavaroni won *Opportunity Knocks* in 1974, singing 'Ma! (He's Making Eyes At Me)'. I was on the edge of my seat, so glad I hadn't missed her – she was a powerhouse.

'Good on you,' I thought.

'I could do that,' I told Mum.

'Well, why don't you, then?' she said.

But I said nothing. I felt I couldn't have gone out and sung like that because of my nerves, but Mum, as ever, was convinced that I could, with a little persuasion.

I think it was the following year that we finally got a colour television. Mum went up to Cleggs and got into debt to buy the telly and a three-piece suite.

'Right, I'm having that,' she used to say, no matter what Dad thought about it. Needless to say, he never once stepped into Cleggs, whereas Mum was up there all the time. Still, Dad shouldn't have minded, because Mum worked and paid the loans back herself – she never asked him for money. She did all sorts of things, from sales assistant in Brentford Nylons to selling fruit on a market stall and working the early shift in a newsagent's. A real grafter, she often had two jobs on the go at one time. She was clever and somehow managed to fit them in around school hours and my dad's shifts.

Even so, we were very slow at coming in with everything and a lot of the neighbours had a colour TV long before we did. When ours was finally installed in the living room, *Emmerdale Farm* was the first programme we watched. As the orange sun set over the hill in the opening credits, we all said, 'Ah!' in unison, and for days we couldn't stop watching the TV, just because it was in colour. The only drawback for me was that it made *Thriller* on a Saturday night even scarier than it had been in black and white. Each episode told a story about a murder or the supernatural and I used to be frightened silly by anything like that. My parents would be out, my brother was babysitting and I had no choice but to watch it, unless I went to bed, so I'd be cowering behind the sofa for most of the evening – I was just pathetic.

*

Things began to improve in my last year at St Michael's, when I was nearly 13. The first big change happened when a younger girl called Julie ran up to me in the playground. I'll never forget the look of sheer terror on her face.

'Some girls are after me and I don't know what to do,' she said, her eyes flashing with fear.

My first instinct was to run, but her plight stirred up powerful feelings in me; it brought out the lioness.

'I'm not going to let her go through what I've gone through,' I thought.

Julie tensed as the group of girls appeared. Stepping in front of her, I said fiercely, 'You touch her and I'll come after you.'

That's all it took to get them to stop. I remember it plain as day: I simply had to face up to them and they never bothered me again, or Julie for that matter. She was forever grateful, but in fact it was I who should have been thanking her for forcing my hand. I felt braver and stronger now and I no longer thought of myself as weak. Life took a sharp turn for the better.

Around this time, I developed a crush on a boy in my class called Richard Tinker. Richard was blond and good at sports and the gorgeous girls were all over him, so I had no chance, or so I thought. But he was so lovely that I was content to admire him from afar. My heart leapt every time I looked at him and that's a fabulous feeling.

Years later, when I saw him again, he said, 'You had a crush on me?'

'Oh, God, yes,' I said, casting my mind back to a memory of Richard in his football kit.

'Why didn't you tell me?'

'I was too shy, I suppose.'

He gave me a pained look.

'You should have told me, Jane!'

Maybe he had forgotten how sickly I was then. My nervous

stomach continued to hold me back and set me apart. I felt anxious a lot of the time and particularly dreaded school trips. I was famous in my class for being travel-sick: nobody ever wanted to sit near me on the bus.

Our final school trip loomed dreadfully in my mind. I was so worried about the journey that I couldn't sleep for several days leading up to it. Finally, my mother came up with a plan. 'You're going to sit in the middle of the bus where there isn't as much movement,' she said, handing me a copy of the *Psychic News*.

'What's this for?' I asked.

'Sit on it and you won't be sick,' she said firmly.

Willing to try anything – anything at all – I put the newspaper in my school bag before Mum took me to school and waved me off. Inside the coach, I told myself, 'I'm not going to be sick because I'm sitting on the *Psychic News*.'

To my amazement, I got there and back without being sick. It was the first time it had happened and I was over the moon.

'It worked!' I told Mum later when I got home. Then I ran upstairs and vomited into the toilet.

I would normally have gone to bed and malingered for the evening and Mum would have come upstairs and tried to get a bit of dry bread or toast down me but today I actually felt hungry – *hungry!*

'That's it,' I thought. 'I'm fed up with this and I'm not going to let it happen anymore.'

With an air of determination, I went downstairs and ate my tea. It was Heinz tomato soup and it tasted delicious. At last I had turned a corner. I remember laughing a lot more from that day onwards.

Now that I had more confidence, you would think my studies might have started to improve, wouldn't you? But I remained an average student. My grades were stuck at Bs and Cs throughout.

Musically, though, I was growing by the day. I used to buy a single every week and listen to the radio, day and night. My tastes were very eclectic: *West Side Story* was my favourite musical and I loved all the old twenties and thirties songs in my grandmother's collection. When I went to the library after school to do my homework, I'd do about ten minutes of History and then head over to the music department to look through the huge catalogue of scores, especially in the wartime section. I used to be fascinated with songs like 'We'll Meet Again', as sung by Vera Lynn, and 'Keep the Home Fires Burning'. *Wuthering Heights* was my favourite movie soundtrack – the Timothy Dalton version, with music by Michel Legrand.

Meanwhile, I had David Essex on my wall, loved Gladys Knight & The Pips and thought Dionne Warwick's voice was magical. I have a fond memory of the day Tony and I drank orange Fanta and sang along to the Sparks' song 'This Town Ain't Big Enough For Both Of Us' in a beer garden in Scarborough, but 'Bohemian Rhapsody' was the first pop song that really hit me between the eyes. And when disco hit, a little later . . . Well, for me that was it and I became a lifelong fan of Earth, Wind & Fire.

With all those lovely melodies in my head, it's no surprise that I was always singing. One Tuesday, when I arrived at my piano lesson, Francis Walker was playing 'As Time Goes By' on the piano. I started to sing along and, since he didn't stop playing, I carried on singing, swept up in the touching lyrics and the memory of Humphrey Bogart smouldering at Ingrid Bergman in *Casablanca*.

When the song came to an end, Francis raised his eyebrows. 'What else do you like singing?' he asked.

'Everything!' I burst out, and as I started to list my favourites, he began playing 'Maria' from *West Side Story*.

After I'd sung a few more songs for him, he rested his hands in his lap and said, 'Well, Jane, I'm amazed. I think you should stop doing piano lessons and take up singing lessons.'

My heart practically stopped there and then, because I assumed he was saying there was no point in carrying on with the piano as I would never be any good. All I could think about was how my mother would react. She was going to be so disappointed, especially after what my first piano teacher had said.

'Aren't I any good? Please don't tell my mother,' I begged him.

He looked perplexed. 'No, you're good at the piano, Jane, and you work hard at it. But music lessons are expensive and, if you've only got so much to spend, I would recommend spending it on singing lessons. You have a beautiful voice and it would be a pity not to develop it.'

I wondered what Mum was going to say. She was already working two jobs to pay for my piano lessons, but considering how proud she looked when I played at family parties, I couldn't imagine her encouraging me to give up.

'Francis says I should give up piano and have singing lessons,' I told her that evening, repeating what he'd said about my voice.

Mum shook her head. 'Give up piano, after all your hard work?' she exclaimed. 'No, Jane, I'll try to find a way for you to do both.'

That was my mother. Somehow, she managed to dig deep enough to pay for singing lessons with Len Goodwin, a classically trained voice coach, and by the time he'd finished with me, I was a trained alto and soprano. Len's lessons set me up for life – they're the reason my voice is still so strong today, because I started so young and was classically trained. But they were torture at the time. They were the opposite of fun, as I told Liz and the others every Friday morning when we walked to school.

'It's so boring!' I complained. 'Yesterday was the same – nothing but scales, scales, scales! He says he won't let me sing a song until I've strengthened my voice. "You must first learn to sing from the diaphragm and not from your throat, Jane," he says.'

Mandy looked confused. 'Isn't a diaphragm something women use to make sure they don't get pregnant?'

'I shouldn't think so,' I laughed. 'My singing teacher says it's a major respiratory muscle below the lungs.'

'Oh, because I'm sure I heard my older sister talking about it . . .' Mandy said, her voice trailing off. 'Must have been something else,' she muttered to herself.

We were 14 years old and adult life remained a mystery to us, but all that was about to change now that we had moved from St Michael's to Thornes House Secondary School, where you heard about all kinds of things. Teenage love was in the air as well and, before too long, my sole reason for going to school was Michael Cornfield, a boy in my year.

Perhaps I should have let him know how I felt this time, but Thornes House was the sort of school where you kept your head down and tried not to do anything that would get you noticed. The school had a discipline problem and a bullying atmosphere prevailed: neither the pupils nor the teachers could ever really feel safe. I made lifelong friends in Wendy and Caroline, two girls in my class, but there wasn't much else at school to stop me playing truant – apart from Michael. If it hadn't been for him, I probably wouldn't have bothered going at all.

I was the original latchkey kid, with my key on a string around my neck, so I could let myself into our house any time I fancied. Often the thought of school proved too much to bear on a morning and I'd sneak home before I'd reached the school gates. Mum would be at work, Dad would either be asleep or at the pit, and that left me free to read books and listen to music in my bedroom all day. If I was sure nobody was coming back, I might even slip into the parlour and play the piano quietly, so as not to alert the neighbours to the fact that I was there. Those days alone at home were heaven and I read so many books that I probably learned more than I ever would have done at school. But then that changed too, after my mother approached the drama teacher, Arthur Starkey, at a school careers evening.

'Jane wants to be in entertainment,' she told him.

He smiled broadly. 'Well, we're putting on *The Wizard of Oz* next term. She should come and audition, or think about helping behind the scenes, if she'd prefer. We have a very good drama department at Thornes House.'

A couple of weeks later, I went along to the audition, hoping to be picked for the chorus. Brian Murrison, the music teacher, frowned as he looked at my sheet music: 'Are you really going to sing this?' he asked.

It was 'The New Moon', a classical song for a soprano voice that I had been practising with Len ever since he'd allowed me to move on from scales.

'Yes,' I said. Then I took a deep breath, swallowed hard and tried to sing it as best I could.

There was a very odd look on Brian's face when I finished the song.

'Holy . . . !' he said, stopping himself just in time. 'Are you taking singing lessons?'

'Yes, sir.'

'Why didn't you tell me?'

'Um, you didn't ask.'

I scuttled off, thinking I had probably made an awful job of it.

The following day, Brian called us all together and announced the cast. To my total amazement, he had picked me for the part of Dorothy. *I was Dorothy!* I was only a first former and I'd got the starring role in the annual musical. Suddenly I was in with the sixth formers and part of a clique. Even better, I found I was able to learn the part really quickly – and everybody else's, too. I knew every note and every word of the show.

It was fantastic, it seemed too good to be true. 'What if I mess up?' I thought. My nerves crept back, my stomach turned. I started throwing up again.

I was sick before each show, not that anybody would ever have known once I got onstage. Once my nerves had worn off, I really enjoyed playing Dorothy. And every time I launched into 'Over The Rainbow', belting it out and making sure to sing it straight from my diaphragm, Mum said there were tears and sniffles among the other parents sitting around her.

I still had a long, long way to go, but I was on my way to becoming an entertainer.

4

In The Stars

When we were 15, Thornes House School let us loose on the world to get some work experience. I applied to do mine at the Wakefield Theatre Club, a cabaret venue where some of the most famous musicians in the world had appeared. People like Shirley Bassey, Johnny Mathis, Dusty Springfield and Tony Bennett all played at the Theatre Club – it was where you went to see the really big stars. I'd watched my mother getting dressed up to go there; I'd seen the excitement in her eyes as she put the finishing touches to her hair and make-up on her way out, and I longed to go along too.

There was something for everyone in the Theatre Club annual programme: touring orchestras like the Hallé, comedians like Les Dawson, ventriloquists like Ray Alan and his dummy, Lord Charles; famous names and not so famous, anyone from the Senegal African Ballet to the amazing Marti Caine. And every so often the line-up included Harmony Blend, a trio of singers featuring a certain young songstress named Sue Ravey, who went on to become a very good friend of mine.

I was hooked from the moment I walked through the doors on my first Monday morning. The Theatre Club was the sort of fabulous place where ladies drank Dubonnet and Tia Maria, where the menu offered grapefruit cocktail for starters, followed by golden deep-fried scampi (with chips and a salad garnish) or sirloin steak, and ice cream topped with fresh cream for dessert. It was a place for fine dining and, if you fancied lighting up with your after-dinner Cointreau or Armagnac, there was a cigarette kiosk in the foyer that stocked Dunhill King Size, Havana cigars and everything in between.

'I love it here!' I thought as I stepped into the deserted club and breathed in a heady mix of beer, furniture polish, stale smoke and fried food. I studied the signed photographs of famous entertainers lining the walls of the staircase leading up to the office. 'This is it,' I thought. 'This is the world I want to be a part of.'

For the next two weeks, I worked in the office as a secretary. It was quite relaxed and I remember the manager's small son, Steven, running around in the afternoons. My job was typing letters and addressing envelopes, but I also spent a good chunk of my time dreaming about the stars who had stood on the stage downstairs. I wondered what Stevie Wonder had thought of the Wakefield crowd. To me it seemed unbelievable that he'd actually set foot in this very club.

My ears pricked up whenever I heard noises downstairs in the auditorium. 'I'm just going to the loo,' I'd say, sneaking off to see what was going on. Often, it would just be a roadie setting up the stage, but sometimes I'd be able to watch a soundcheck or an act rehearsing, and I'd look on intently, trying to commit to memory every last detail of what I saw.

On my final Friday, I hid behind a pillar and watched a full band rehearsal. It was thrilling to see the guitarists tuning their instruments. They seemed totally at home on the stage, so slick and synchronised.

'A-one, a-two, a-one, two, three, four . . .'

As the band launched into the old sixties hit 'You've Got Your Troubles', a song I knew inside out from hearing it on the radio, I suddenly realised who they were.

'It's The Fortunes!' went the screech inside my head as the guy at the mic began to sing.

My skin began to prickle with a sense of how lucky I was to be behind the scenes, privy to a sight few others would ever see. The Fortunes were such big stars! Peeping out at them from behind a pillar increased the intensity of my ambitions a hundredfold. It was like a stroke of destiny that I was there, unseen, unknown, to witness this incredible moment.

'I *really* need to be in entertainment,' I thought, my heart pumping fiercely.

After that, it was just a question of how quickly I could get through my O levels and out into the world. I wasn't very interested in my exams – I tried to be studious but the world was full of distractions and I only really shone at Piano and Singing. I worked hard at Music, but by now subjects like Maths and Science had lost any appeal they'd once had.

I only passed my Art O level because of a boy in my class called Chris. Now, Chris was lovely and we got on really well. He had a slight crush on me and there was a little frisson going the other way, too, if I'm honest. Nothing ever happened, but we really liked each other.

Since Chris was a superb artist, the best in the class, I couldn't help but play on his soft spot for me when I turned to him in Art one day and said, 'Can you help me with this?'

I was hoping he might be able to provide the magic touch that would make the difference between passing and failing, but it turned out my paintings needed more than a bit of extra brushwork. Chris practically repainted them all – and thank goodness he did! It's a terrible thing to admit, but I only passed because of him.

I did just about enough to get a few more O levels along with Art. Far more beguiling – for me, at least – was the Drama department open evening at the end of term. Mum and Dad came to watch and Mum couldn't believe what she was hearing when I sang 'The Boy I Love Is Up In The Gallery' in my best London accent. Apparently, I sounded like a proper Cockney, without a trace of my Wakefield roots.

Mum turned to Dad and said, 'That's Jane, that's our daughter, singing that!'

'Blimey, that was good!' she said afterwards. Many years later, she said this was the moment she knew for sure that I was destined to be a performer.

Meanwhile, Francis Walker and the old pub upright – the one that Dad had found me all those years before – saw me all the way up to my Grade 7 Piano in the London College of Music exam syllabus, after which he declared me to be an accomplished piano player. He also taught me to play the accordion, which was hard to get the hang of, in more ways than one. At 16, I had a very big bust, so the accordion sat awkwardly on my chest and, for some reason, it used to eat the shirt or jumper I was wearing, slowly yanking it up to reveal my midriff as I was playing. Believe me, it's not easy to concentrate on a Ukrainian polka when your top keeps riding up and getting caught on the back of your accordion.

I kept at it because there is something about the sound of an accordion that I find really uplifting, even more so when several are played together. As I improved, Francis invited me to join The Wakefield Accordion Band, adding that I would need to buy my own instrument. This was a huge obstacle, but then, by some miracle, Dad found me a second-hand accordion, although I don't know how or where, because it's not the sort of thing you come across for tuppence on a market stall. He found everything for me, my father. He had a knack for it, and I'm glad he did, because I loved being in the accordion band. We rehearsed once a week and put on charity concerts, in and around Wakefield.

At one of our shows, Francis said, 'Can you get up and sing this evening?'

Perhaps because I was used to performing for him, this request didn't strike me down with nerves and sickness. It was more a case of thinking, 'Wow, this is my big moment!' That night, I sang the folk song 'Nobody's Child', and had a regular solo spot after that, thanks to my music teacher.

'It almost feels like fate, doesn't it?' Mum used to say. 'If your first piano teacher hadn't been so rude about your musical abilities, you might never have met Francis Walker.'

Mum was right, and one thing leads to another, and my appearances with the accordion band gave me the confidence to think perhaps one day I could become a professional singer. Mum and Dad were as encouraging as ever and used to come along to support me. One night, after a concert, as I was going upstairs to bed, my father called out to me.

'Have you got a kiss goodnight for your dad?' he said, pointing to his cheek.

So I went over and gave him a hug. I could tell he was feeling proud of me. At the concert that night, I'd sung 'Early One Morning' and he and Mum had beamed with pleasure at the compliments I'd received afterwards. Now, his expression grew serious.

'I believe you're going to be the best singer the world's ever seen, Jane, but you should always have a plan B,' he said.

'You mean, "Don't put all your eggs in one basket?"' I said.

Dad squeezed my arm. 'You can do anything you want, you can be anybody you want – you've just got to work for it.'

Those were wise words and I took them to heart, because Dad never said anything he didn't mean. As far as I was concerned, he was the best and most dependable dad in the world. My experience of him was different to Janet's or even to Tony's, because he had mellowed as he'd got older. Nothing could have made him happier than when he paid off the mortgage, around the time I left school.

'Now I can go to bed at night, put my head down and not worry,' he told me.

It was his whole reason for living. He wanted a nice life and to look after his family, whereas my mother always wanted more. 'But we need this,' she'd say. 'Why can't we have that?'

'I've paid off the house. As long as I live, I'm never going into debt again,' he'd reply.

He didn't have to worry about me, though, because I intended to work hard and make something of myself, whatever I did, and what's more, Mum had impressed on me the need to be independent. 'Earn your own money,' she used to tell me, rolling her eyes in Dad's direction. 'Then you can buy what you want.'

In those days, women either went into shop work, office work or nursing and so, the week before I left school, Mum went up to Wades furniture store to see if there were any jobs going. Wades had bought out Clegg and Huntingdon – Cleggs – where Mum drew her cheques to buy things on the never-never. She had a good relationship with the two company bosses, because she always paid back her loans on time, and they took her at her word when she said that her daughter would be an asset to the firm. It was all very simple: there happened to be a vacancy for a clerk and she got me the job.

It was the summer of 1979 and I was 16 years old: I left school on a Friday and started at Wades on the following Monday. I'll never forget how fantastic it felt to get my wages in a brown envelope at the end of the week. I used to peep inside and think, 'I've got money!' I gave a third to my mother straight away, for my bed and board, and put a little bit in the bank, then I hit the shops. Before too long, I had an account at Lady at Lord John, where they had all the best trouser suits. I waited for the sale, mind: I would have my eye on something for a while before I bought it.

I loved my job at Wades and was determined to work my way up the company. Remembering my father's advice, I went to night school to learn shorthand, typing, how to write formal letters and do accounts; I worked hard and passed with honours. Within a year, I was secretary to both my bosses and beginning to get a business grounding.

I was a lightning typist. In fact, the only person who could type faster than me was Wendy, one of the few friends I had made at Thornes House School. Wendy was lovely and had a terrific sense of humour, and it hadn't taken us more than five minutes to find out that we had a lot in common. She was a day older than I was and, like me, would run a mile if anybody picked on her, but if they picked on somebody younger, or a mate of hers, she wouldn't think twice about getting out her proverbial fists and laying into them. We were the same in that way – our fellow feeling for the underdog gave us the courage to fight their corner.

I didn't see much of Wendy after I left Thornes House – I was busy working during the day and my evenings were packed. I went jiving at the Mecca on Mondays with Elizabeth Baxter; I went ballroom dancing with my dad on Thursdays and Fridays. Saturday night was family night at Balne Lane Working Men's Club with Mum and Dad – and maybe Tony – and sometimes we'd even go to watch the turn on a Sunday night as well. But then one Thursday, when I was out ballroom dancing with my dad at Alverthorpe Club on the outskirts of Wakefield, I bumped into Wendy and some of her family.

'We've decided to take a leaf out of your book,' she said, her green eyes twinkling. 'Mind you, I'm not sure my lot will keep it up,' she added, 'so perhaps I'll start coming with you and your dad instead.'

I saw her there regularly after that and sometimes we'd take it in turns to dance with Dad. Occasionally, Tony dropped in for a drink, but their paths didn't cross until a few months later, when Wendy arrived to find Tony and me at the bar, laughing our heads off about Dad's latest patch-up job on his car. All our lives Tony and I had shared a daft sense of humour and we were always joking about something. Tony is a giggler and his giggle is infectious, so when he starts to laugh, it's not long before everyone else is laughing too.

Dad had been dancing with someone he knew from his days living in the Piccadilly area of Wakefield. Now, he came over to see what was so funny and he and Tony got talking about cars. Wendy glared at me good-humouredly.

'How come you always get the best-looking blokes?' she asked in a tone of mock resentment.

'What are you talking about?' I said.

She nodded at Tony: 'That guy is just gorgeous. Trust you to have all the luck!'

'Him?' I said, incredulous. 'Ugh, that's my brother! You can have him.'

Well, to Wendy it was as if the sun had just come out on a wet, windy day. She lit up and began to make eyes at my brother like there was no tomorrow. There was no denying he was a stunning lad and his dark looks, inherited from Dad, were enhanced by the telltale line of coal dust around his eyes that marked him out as a miner. There was always a trace of soot around a miner's eyes, however hard he scrubbed his face after work, and that sweep of occupational guyliner looked fabulous on someone as darkly handsome as Tony – he looked like an Italian matinée idol.

Four years previously, and against Dad's wishes, Tony had decided to follow his father down the mine.

'You're not going down there!' Dad had said, genuinely upset when Tony broke the news.

Remembering the day they brought Dad home in an ambulance, Tony listened to his warnings and didn't spend much time at the coalface, where the worst of the pit dangers lay. Instead, he became an all-rounder, someone who could work on the cages, the trolleys and in the office – his mates at the pit used to call him 'Tony Ten Jobs'.

Tony asked Wendy out the night they met at the Alverthorpe Club. He was her very first boyfriend and they went on to get married in 1983. They're really close to this day and still have a huge amount of fun together. It's how everybody wants their marriage to be, isn't it?

As for me, I wasn't too bothered about boyfriends. That sort of thing was never a driving force in my life. I didn't go out to pick up a bloke, I went out to have a good laugh and a dance with my friends. Dad insisted on collecting me afterwards, which my sister Janet had hated, as a teenager, but I loved.

'I can go in, I can dance, I can do what I want, and then my dad's there to meet me,' I thought.

It was a lovely safe feeling – and we'd all have fish and chips on the way home.

Everything changed when I met Richard, who became my first proper boyfriend. Richard was a carpenter and I met him through Janet, who worked with his sister in Huddersfield. He was a really nice fella and very family orientated, which I found attractive – as much if not more so than his thick brown hair and chiselled features. Being the oldest sibling, it was in Richard's nature to look after people and I really liked the way he looked after me. Never mind all the kids in the family came with us everywhere we went, even to the cinema, because he was looking after them too! I wasn't bothered and this delighted Dad, who was naturally wary of the new presence in my life.

Mum and Dad were as protective of me as ever, so it helped

when Janet said, 'I can vouch for Richard, he's a lovely lad.' Since Dad approved of anyone who was good with their hands, Richard's carpentry skills were another mark in his favour. He even built my father a new shed up at the allotment, so he was all smiles until I mentioned that Richard had asked me to go on holiday to Menorca with him.

It was a straight 'no', no matter how much I pleaded. When pushed, all Dad could say was, 'You're 16, Jane,' by way of an explanation.

Luckily, Janet came to my rescue. 'The whole family is going,' she explained. 'There'll be that many kids and people that Jane and Richard won't be alone for a single minute.'

But Dad shook his head, his expression grim – he wasn't budging.

'Tell you what, I'll go too,' Janet said.

There was a pause. All the while, I was hovering outside the living-room door, in an agony of suspense, willing Dad to give in.

'If you're going, she can go,' he said at last, and I nearly screamed with happiness from my hiding place out in the hall.

We had a great holiday in Menorca, just amazing. The hotel was lovely, the weather was great and every five minutes I caught myself thinking, 'It's so warm!'

Not only was it my first trip abroad, but I was also on holiday with my first boyfriend. What could be better? Even if we were protected like mad, because Richard's family were the type of family that went everywhere together. We had kids with us all the time, there was no escaping them – we took them swimming and to the beach, we ate our meals together and bought them ice creams. I loved it because it made me feel part of the family – I liked everything that came with Richard.

Richard and I had a lot of fun together until I started to get jealous, once we'd got back from holiday. It was difficult living in different towns. I'd ring him up and ask, 'What are you doing? Where are you going tonight?'

If he so much as mentioned a girl, I'd jump in and say, 'Who's she, then?'

I didn't understand the feelings I was having, all I knew was that I didn't like them, and neither did Richard. The clingier I became, the less he liked it, and the worse I got. I was constantly asking, 'What's up with you? What's wrong?'

A year into our relationship, he told me it was over. I was devastated, but I had no one to blame but myself. 'It's your own fault,' I told myself, vowing never to be clingy again. You learn something from every relationship and this was the lesson I learned from Richard: jealousy pushes people away, it doesn't make them like you more.

As my mother always said, 'Don't chase after a man or a bus, because there's always one behind.' She was a very wise woman, Mum, and I'm a quick learner – I've never been jealous since.

There was a gap in my life without Richard and I started looking around for a way to fill it. I was still enjoying my day job, Dad was happy I had a plan B and it felt good to be able to give some money to Mum for my keep. But I still wanted to be a singer, or at least something in the world of entertainment. With this in mind, I scanned the local paper and newsagents' windows for opportunities.

My first break seemed to come out of the blue. I was still with The Wakefield Accordion Band and it just so happened that one of their main accordion players also played the organ at the Working Men's Club in Kirkburton, about half an hour's drive from Wakefield. She was the organist and her husband the drummer: they were known as Rex and Wynne.

'Would you like to sing with us in Kirkburton one night?' Wynne asked me after an accordion rehearsal.

'Do you mean, just me, onstage, singing alone?' I asked, completely taken aback.

'Yes, would you like to try a half-hour set?'

I must have looked alarmed, because she added, 'We'll rehearse first, don't worry.'

Although I felt sick to my stomach at the very thought of doing a whole gig on my own, I said, 'I'd love to!'

'Great, we'll get you some charts together,' she said.

Charts was the term we used for sheet music that was written out and notated for an individual singer or musician. The other word we used was 'dots'.

In a fizz of nerves and excitement, I went home and flicked through the latest Kays Catalogue feverishly. My first ever solo gig required a special outfit, something glitzy that would make me stand out. I wanted to shine on that stage at the Kirkburton Working Men's Club. I wanted people to forget about their troubles as they watched me sing, as my family and I did when we watched the turn at the Balne Lane Working Men's Club on a Saturday evening.

Mum and Dad would sometimes be arguing up until the moment we left to go to the club. She'd be saying we needed new curtains, he'd be telling her we couldn't afford any. And then one of them would suddenly announce, 'That's enough now! Forget it, let's go and see the turn at the club.'

It was time to put everyday concerns away and go out and have some fun.

My throat was bone-dry on the way to Kirkburton in the car with Mum and Dad. I was close to exploding with nerves and there was a whooshing in my ears that set me off worrying I wouldn't be able to hear the backing music when I was onstage.

'Let's go home, Mum. I can't do it, please don't make me,' I whimpered. 'I'm going to let everybody down.'

'You'll be fine, love,' she reassured me. 'It's going to make my year to see you up there on that stage tonight.'

Rex and Wynne were already at the club when we arrived.

'If you can sing as well as you did in rehearsal, we'll be fine,' Wynne said, when she saw how nervous I was.

Wearing my new multi-coloured boob tube matched with a pair of silver satin trousers, I walked onto the stage trembling with fear. Rex and Wynne started to play the intro to 'Don't It Make My Brown Eyes Blue' by Crystal Gayle. I took a shivery breath and began to sing.

Half an hour later, when I'd finished my set, I felt fantastic – and I seemed to go down all right, judging by the clapping in the audience. I'd watched enough Saturday night turns with Mum and Dad to know when a crowd was happy or not. Rex and Wynne said I did very well for my first performance. We all have to start somewhere and I will be forever grateful to them both for their encouragement. As Dad drove Mum and me home, I was filled with wonder at how my life had led me to this point.

It was a huge confidence boost, and a couple of weeks later, when I saw an advertisement in the local paper for a singer in a band, I decided to apply. The band was the Brian Gordon Sound, a well-known cabaret ensemble who used to tour the working men's clubs of the North, and the auditions were being held in a dusty hall in Ossett. Without telling anybody, I went along, waited my turn and got up and sang 'You Light Up My Life', a seventies ballad filled with emotion that I happened to know was a part of their repertoire. I started off a bit shaky, but the musicians were so experienced and the band so tight that I felt supported as I reached for the high notes and belted out the chorus.

As the song's final notes died away, Alan Cobett, the band's compère and trumpet player, stepped forward, his eyebrows raised.

'Where did you learn to sing like that?' he asked.

My nerves, which had disappeared as I sang, whooshed back.

'I've always been able to sing,' I said, with a tremulous smile.

'And how old are you, Jane?'

Now I hesitated. I had thought everything through – my song, my outfit, my make-up – but I hadn't thought about how I would answer this question.

'I'm 16, but I've left school and I've got a job, so I'm legal age,' I babbled.

A ripple of laughter went around the band and I wondered if I'd said something stupid.

'We'll let you know,' Alan said. 'We've got a couple of other people to see yet.'

I got the bus home feeling desolate, wishing I had said I was older. I'd sung well at the audition, so why had I gone and blown it by being honest about my age? The band was made up of middle-aged men, chances are they wanted someone more mature than I was and I should also have factored in the probability that you had to be 18 to work in some of the bars where they played.

Two days later, I was having a cuppa with Mum after work when she said, very casually, 'Oh, I forgot, you had a phone call today.'

'Who from?' I asked, my heart leaping.

She pursed her lips and I could see that she was trying not to smile. 'Someone who said he was the trumpet player in the Brian Gordon Sound,' she announced airily. 'Does that ring a bell?'

'Yes, I auditioned for them, and . . . ?' I said.

She started giggling.

'He said to tell you to ring him back today, because there's a show this Saturday and you're the singer.'

In my excitement, I jumped up and sent my cup of tea flying.

'I got it!' I yelled.

'What's all this about?' Mum asked, her eyes sparkling with mischief, as I rushed off to get a cloth to mop up the spill. Of course, I didn't have to explain a thing, because she had already extracted every last detail out of Alan Cobett on the phone.

It was great singing with the Brian Gordon Sound and it was a bit of an adventure at first, because the gigs were quite far and wide and they were booked for private functions as well, so Mum and Dad didn't come and see me very much. The saxophone player, Mike, used to pick me up and drop me off, which made me feel very grown-up and independent. As well as being fun and good experience, I was on a decent £5 a night, which I put aside in savings. And Dad was happy because I was picked up and dropped home every time we had a gig, and we never stayed away, no matter how far we travelled, because the musicians wanted to get home to their families. All the same, after I turned 17, I started to think there might be more to life than spending my weekends travelling across the Pennines with a group of home-loving dads, nice as they were. I was brimming with energy, mad about disco and wanted to buy myself a car, so I decided it was time to branch out.

On my lunch break one day, I popped into the Wakefield Theatre Club, which had recently been taken over by a couple of savvy businessmen called Philip Colloby and Kees Van Der Merwe. Philip and Kees owned clubs all over the North, from the famed Amsterdam Bar in Huddersfield to Antonio's in Barnsley and the Barcelona in Leeds.

Times had changed in the three years since I'd done my work experience at the Wakefield Theatre Club. It was still the place to go, and it still had all the top acts, but people no longer swanned about in evening dress there, sipping brandy. Kees and Philip had renamed it Pussycat, the barmaids wore leather shorts and it was a thumping pop and disco heaven. On a Friday and Saturday night, it was packed to the rafters with 2,500 people all out to have a good time.

'I love being here,' I used to think. 'Why don't I just work here?'

I was over the moon when the manager agreed to give me a trial shift.

5

Dance Yourself Dizzy

If you were good at what you did, you could be a success – that's what I learned at Pussycat. I took my job at the club seriously. My glasses were spotless, my section polished and I was conscientious about getting everyone the right drink. The rule was that you were only allowed to take a pound in tips all night: you were limited to 10p a tip from ten customers. By eight o'clock in the evening, I had all mine – maybe I should have stretched it out a bit.

I started off working at the very back of the club because I had no previous experience, but I learned fast and worked hard, hoping if I was good enough at serving, I would be rewarded with a place at the centre bar, which was *the* bar, the focal point of the club, where all the beautiful people worked. When I finally made it there, I joined a group of people who wore weird and wonderful outfits and did pre-planned dance routines when certain songs were played. It was like being in Patrick Swayze's clique in *Dirty Dancing*: as soon as we heard the intro beat to 'Baby Hands Up' or 'Oops Upside Your Head' we'd stop what we were doing and slide into a routine behind the bar, cheered on by a sea of clubbers.

Earth, Wind & Fire were at their zenith and tracks like 'September', 'Boogie Wonderland' and 'After The Love Has Gone' take me straight back to those fantastic Pussycat nights, when you jumped up to dance the moment you heard a familiar guitar riff or bassline. Every once in a while, our group did a routine on top of the bar and I'd be shaking my stuff, wearing a pair of red leather shorts, a gypsy top and cowboy boots, with my hair wild and bushy – because I always had a perm – looking for all the world like Wakefield's answer to The Supremes.

I still worked at Wades every weekday until five o'clock. On Thursdays and Fridays, I went home, had my tea and went straight back out to Pussycat, where I served drinks until midnight. I loved working there and did the Saturday night shift there too, but I also had one eye on Casanova's, the posh club in town, which had recently been bought up by a couple of entrepreneurs.

One day, I sneaked into Casanova's to have a little nosey. It was just my luck to bump into Michael Craig, one of the owners.

'You're from Pussycat, aren't you?' he said.

'Hmm,' I replied, annoyed with myself that I'd been caught spying.

But instead of sending me away with a flea in my ear, Mike said, 'I've seen you in action behind the bar. You're good at what you do. Would you like a job here?'

I thought about it for a moment – Casanova's was a great club, and I still wanted a car.

'Yes, okay,' I said.

I started waitressing at Casanova's on Monday, Tuesday and Wednesday nights. The uniform was a brightly coloured body stocking and cowboy boots, which sounds daft, but wasn't offensive, even though it showed off every contour of your body. I was more likely to attract unwanted attention in my leather shorts at Pussycat, and there was always a bit of that, but nothing I couldn't handle. Those days in the clubs taught me how to let people down nicely and, fortunately, I never got myself into a situation I felt uncomfortable in. You had to look after yourself – you didn't have security guards watching out for you as you might have today; in fact, no one batted an eyelid if they saw someone coming on too strong to you because it was more acceptable in those days – and since I didn't want to offend anybody, because they were customers, I tended to make a joke out of it if someone got too close. I'd say, 'Come on, now, what are you doing? I'll give you a slap if you do that again!'

Now I had three jobs and the hours I was putting in were ridiculous. I didn't stop, except to have a sunbed in my lunch break, which turned into a 30-minute power nap, and I'd walk out of the salon feeling refreshed – and tanned into the bargain. (Sunbed salons were all the rage at that time: we had no warnings about how dangerous they were. These days, you would have a spray tan to get the same effect.) On Sundays, I'd have a good old lie-in and that seemed to be enough for me, I never ran out of energy. After leaving school I'd taken on a new lease of life and was making the most of my opportunities.

As soon as I started working in the clubs, Dad said to Mum, 'We need to find Jane a car so that she can drive herself about at night.'

Tony and my dad taught me to drive. They shied away from teaching Mum – probably because she would have been off in a trice and never come back – but they were insistent that I had the freedom to do what I wanted in life.

My brother took me over the fields in his Hillman for my first lesson. He always had great cars, did Tony: they were his pride and joy, so I was terrified of breaking something, or losing control and hurtling into the beck. Luckily, Tony had a lot of patience.

'You'll be fine,' he reassured me. 'I'll tell you exactly what to do.'

He turned out to be an excellent driving instructor.

'Right, put it into first. Let your foot off the clutch . . .'

And I was off! Soon, I was driving round the fields like mad.

'There you go. See, it's easy, isn't it?' he said.

Dad started taking me out on the roads and I really got into driving, but I failed my first driving test when I swore at a bus driver who pulled out on me. You should always let buses out first – I certainly learned that. I felt like I'd let Dad and Tony down, but Dad said, 'Put in for another test right away,' and I sailed through the next one a couple of months later.

'Well done,' Tony said, when I told him the good news. 'Tell you what, I'm going away with Wendy for a few days and you can borrow my Vauxhall while I'm gone.'

So, I took a night off work and drove Mum to see a musical at the local amateur dramatics in Tony's red Vauxhall Viva. Beautiful, it was, and very shiny too, because he waxed it every week.

'Isn't this nice?' Mum said. She was looking forward to seeing the play.

'Wait until you see me trying to park,' I joked, because, although I was really good at driving forward, my reversing skills were shocking.

I shouldn't have said anything, because the next thing I knew I had reversed into a truck. Not a scratch on the truck, mind, but the back of my brother's beautiful red Vauxhall Viva was a crumpled wreck.

I have never felt so sick in my life. I can't remember anything about the musical we saw, I just sat in my chair, thinking, 'My brother's going to kill me.'

'Dad, I've crashed the car,' I wailed, once we were home.

'Jeez!' he said. 'Don't worry, lassie, we'll fix it.'

First thing the next morning, Dad went to a scrapyard and

found a replacement boot, which was almost an exact match. He took the car to Silcoates Garage, where they beat the panel out and fitted the new boot. Still, it wasn't quite right and I was dreading Tony's return.

The following day, Tony pulled up outside the house with Wendy.

'There's my car,' he said, glad to see I'd returned it in one piece. 'Oh no, it's not my car,' he went on. 'Wait, it is mine. No, it's not, it's got a blue boot. Oh my God, that IS my car!'

I had locked myself in my bedroom while this was going on. All I can remember is Wendy saying, 'Don't shout at her, there's obviously a reason why. Just don't shout at her.'

Luckily, Tony saw the funny side when Dad explained what had happened.

'These things happen,' he said, after Wendy had persuaded me to come out of the bedroom. 'It's just a car,' he added magnanimously. 'A red car with a bloody great blue boot,' he muttered under his breath.

Tony had the paintwork resprayed and the car looked good as new again, but he got rid of it soon afterwards, as it was never the same in his eyes. He didn't bear a grudge, though, and so I decided to forgive him for the time he'd 'borrowed' my precious collection of singles when he'd started his youth club DJ business some years earlier – and then sold them to the lad who took over from him, without checking with me.

Meanwhile, Dad bought me an old banger, a gold Vauxhall Viva. 'But you're going to have to pay for the insurance, road tax and petrol,' he warned, 'so you'd better be sure you can afford to keep running it.'

He was good at teaching me how to afford things, whereas Mum would say, 'You'll be fine, go into debt.' Although, saying that, Dad did pay my car insurance for that first year.

So now I had a car and three jobs: I felt very grown-up. And

I was fast falling in love with Mark, a gorgeous barman at Pussy-cat. Mark had bundles of charisma. A girl magnet, he was one of those guys who make you go weak at the knees when he smiles at you. When he asked me out, I was on cloud nine. I loved telling people he was my boyfriend. It made me feel special to think that he could have had anyone he wanted and had chosen me. Only, it turned out I'd slightly misjudged the situation, as I discovered when another barman, a guy named Colin, asked me to go to the cinema with him on our day off.

'I can't go out with you, I'm with him,' I said, nodding in Mark's direction.

Colin frowned. 'So, it's okay for him to see someone else, but you can't?'

It took me a moment to register what he was saying and then my mind went blank.

'Oh, I . . .'

'I've said something I shouldn't have,' Colin murmured, sidling off. 'Sorry, I thought you knew.'

I went straight over to Mark and dragged him off for a heart-to-heart. When I told him what Colin had said, he didn't deny it. He just shrugged and said, 'I'm really sorry, but that's how it is. I've never promised you anything.'

It felt so unfair, because it was true: he hadn't promised me anything. And yet his eyes were full of promise, and so was his smile; everything about him was full of promise when we were together.

He absolutely broke my heart. I remember sitting at the kitchen table with my mum, crying my eyes out over him. I half-expected her to tell me to stop bawling and pull myself together, but she was really sympathetic: 'It's an awful feeling, isn't it?' she said.

What made it worse was that I found I couldn't give him up, even though it was like a stab in the heart to see him with another girl. Things were very on and off between us after that, but I kept going back to him. 'This guy is completely wrong for me. Why do I keep going back like a moth to a naked flame?' I thought. I never bothered with any other lads, I was hooked on Mark. Then, one Saturday night, Kees Van Der Merwe came over to the centre bar and beckoned to me.

'What have I done? Why is the boss coming to see me?' I thought in a panic, as I made my way through the crowd.

The place was heaving that night, because the disco group, Liquid Gold, were playing in the club. They were riding high on the popularity of their single 'Dance Yourself Dizzy', which had got to No. 2 in the charts. I'd seen them perform and they were great.

Kees gave me a friendly smile. 'The drummer of Liquid Gold would like to have a drink with you,' he said. 'He really likes you. Are you happy to talk to him, maybe have a dance with him?'

Since Mark and I were on a break at the time, I said, 'Yes, bring him over.'

A couple of minutes later, I saw this guy walking towards me and – oh my God – he was an Adonis! He was beautiful, he was stunning, he was gorgeous . . . And I was speechless.

'He wants to talk to me?'

I glanced over at Mark, thinking, 'Hah, look at what I've got now.'

Mark's eyes were boggling, as if to say, 'Hang on, what's going on here?'

'Yes, you've not promised me anything, so you can go off with your other girlfriend now, thank you very much,' I thought.

The drummer introduced himself as Wal, short for Walter: he was tall, blond and built like a god. We hit it off straight away and spent the next two hours talking mainly about music, from Genesis and Yes to Bobby Womack.

Wal couldn't stop smiling and laughing at the things I said.

'You're so funny!' he kept telling me.

'Am I? I don't mean to be, it's just that I see the lighter side of everything, I suppose,' I said.

At the end of the evening, Wal told me that he was staying at Kees's house while the band did the Northern circuit.

'I really like you. Can we see each other again?' he asked sweetly.

'I'd like that,' I said.

We went out quite a lot after that and, one night, Wal asked me to come to a party at Kees's house after the club closed.

'I don't know, I'll have to ring my dad,' I said.

Kees let me into his office to make the call.

'Dad, I've been invited to a party at the boss's house. Can I go?' I asked.

'Yes, but I need to know the address,' he said. 'Ring me when you want to leave and I'll come and get you.'

The party was fantastic, full of beautiful, freaky-looking people wearing crazy outfits. It was very rock and roll, but Wal was a nice guy and looked after me, and I tried not to appear too amazed by it all.

By four o'clock in the morning, I was starting to flag, so I rang my father and said, 'Okay, I'm ready to come home now.'

'Right, I won't be long,' Dad said cheerily, not at all fazed by how late it was.

He must have put his foot down, because he was there within 20 minutes, ringing the doorbell. A few moments later, the front door opened up to reveal a guy in a leather cap, wearing a leather shorts and bib ensemble so skimpy it looked like a mankini. Dad didn't bat an eyelid – at him or any of the other bizarre people walking round in outlandish outfits.

'I've come for Jane,' he said simply.

I left the party and got in the car.

'Did you have a good night?' Dad asked.

'Yes, I had a great night, Dad. Thanks for coming for me,' I said, relaxing back in the passenger seat.

'It's fine,' he said. 'I don't mind what you do, as long as I know you're all right and I can come and get you.'

I loved my father for that. He was protective, but also happy to give me my freedom.

A few weeks later, Wal was gone – off to Europe, where Liquid Gold were massive.

'I'll be back soon, so don't go away,' he said, as he kissed me goodbye.

'Don't worry, I'm not leaving Wakefield,' I said cheerfully.

That evening, I felt wistful as I played back our last kiss in my head. Was it my destiny to live in Wakefield all my life? I thought about what Gran had said about all the travelling I would do. Her words looped around my head: 'I don't know when or why, but I see travel, travel, travel for you, Jane.'

Maybe her prediction was going to come true one day, but for the time being, I was the girl back home while Wal toured the world, living the very definition of a rock and roll lifestyle. I knew he really liked me, but I wasn't under any illusions about being his only girlfriend. Anyway, after what happened with Mark, I was learning that maybe fidelity didn't have to be the most important thing in the world, if you could just enjoy the moment for what it was, when it was. I couldn't wait to see Wal again, but in the meantime, I'd get on with my life – he wasn't the only one with things to do.

When Michael and Tony at Casanova's headhunted me for their PR team, a whole new world of horizons opened up to me. Michael's wife, Janice, instigated it, as she saw something in me – I'm not sure what! – and had plans to put me to work in several areas of the business as it expanded. I started in the PR team, promoting the revamped club, which was a really swish place now and branching out into new ventures. It was an exciting time, because the owners gave us free rein to try out new ideas. We were a young team, all Zodiac fire signs, fizzing and sparking with ideas, and the owners trusted us to get on with our jobs. Before too long, I gave in my notice at Wades and then at Pussycat.

There was only one wobbly moment, when I asked Mike, 'Can I have next Saturday off? It's my eighteenth.'

'You what?' he spluttered.

'It's my eighteenth birthday. Can I have the night off?'

He looked stunned. 'You mean, you've been working here all this time and you're not even 18?'

'Yes,' I said.

I didn't understand what the problem was. I'd been doing a day job since I was 16, so why couldn't I do a night job? I didn't drink, so I wasn't consuming alcohol illegally, I was just working.

'Don't come in again until you're 18, please,' said Mike. 'And yes, you can have that Saturday off as well.'

Since the customers seemed to love it when the bar staff got up and danced on the bar at Pussycat, I suggested going one step further at Casanova's and having podium dancers above the dance floor. Mike and Janice thought it was a great idea and asked me to put together a dance troupe, so I advertised for dancers and models, designed their outfits and rehearsed them. When we launched them on the club, a few weeks later, I was up there on the podium, dancing with them. Just like that I became a club dancer.

'You've got such a future ahead of you and you don't even know it,' said Janice, admiringly.

'Are you for real?' I said, laughing. 'In Wakefield?'

I must have had itchy feet without realising it, because a few weeks later, when one of my dance team said she'd got an audition in York for a dancing job abroad, I agreed to drive her there. While she was waiting to be seen, I took her through her routine and the dance captain happened to see me rehearsing her. Before I knew it, we'd both been offered a job with a dance troupe in Italy – it seemed like an amazing opportunity.

'Why not go?' I thought. 'I'm a free spirit, I can do whatever I want.'

First, though, I had to get Mum and Dad's approval. On my way home, I gave Mum a call: 'Shall I get us a takeaway for tea?' I said. 'From that new Chinese that's opened up?'

'No need to, love. I've made shepherd's pie,' she said. 'Just how you like it.'

The shepherd's pie was delicious and I waited until I'd cleared my plate before I brought up the subject of the job offer.

'What sort of dance troupe?' Mum asked suspiciously.

'Er, exotic, I think. We'll be wearing feathers and sequins.'

'And not much else, if I'm not mistaken!' Mum huffed.

You couldn't get a thing past my mother.

I assured Mum and Dad that the troupe belonged to a legitimate dance company and we'd be well taken care of. What I didn't realise was that we would be so closely chaperoned we would barely get to see outside our *pensiones* and the nightclubs we danced in, let alone get up to any mischief. There was no danger of mixing with any gorgeous Italian men, or anyone else, for that matter. We weren't allowed to have any spending money either, so it was worse than being on a school trip.

Although it was fun being with the other girls, I couldn't help thinking that I was in the wrong place. I wasn't a very good dancer either – I was untrained, a freelance – and I thought to myself, 'Why am I dancing?' There was a singer among us and she was being paid an awful lot more than we were. I used to watch her onstage, thinking, 'I could do that, I should be doing what she's doing instead of dancing.'

Already I was starting to feel desperately homesick when the troupe manager decided that I needed to go on a diet and lose weight. I couldn't understand it. After being skinny for most of my life, I was now a size 12–14 and quite curvaceous – and I liked that. I never once thought about my weight and had a good appetite; I ate anything and everything my mum made me.

The troupe manager was adamant: 'You must lose weight, you're the biggest girl in the line.'

After that it was torture because I was only allowed tiny portions of food at every meal and not even a crumb in between, so I was hungry all the time. Everywhere I turned, I smelled gorgeously aromatic Italian food – rich Bolognaise sauce, garlic and onion fry-ups and creamy tiramisu – but it was all out of reach because I was being closely monitored and had no money of my own.

'This is definitely not for me,' I thought miserably.

I suffered in silence because I didn't have a return ticket and I was locked into a contract. Then one night a guitarist in a French band asked me to write out the lyrics of 'Billie Jean' by Michael Jackson for him.

'I'll try, but I'm that hungry, I don't know if my brain is capable of remembering them,' I said.

'Why don't you just eat something?' he asked with a wry smile.

I explained my situation: 'They're not letting me near food and it's making me dizzy.'

'Well, I'll give you 1,500 lire if you write out the lyrics,' he offered. 'I know it's not much, but . . .'

It was the equivalent of 50p, and 50p meant the world to me at that moment, so I racked my brains to remember the words to the song, wrote them out backstage and gave them to him at the end of the evening.

'Now I can nip out and get something to eat,' I thought as he handed over the money.

Back at the *pensione*, I couldn't risk being caught in the corridor by the manager, so I climbed out of my bedroom window, slid down a drainpipe and ran off to get myself a Mars bar. Now, if you've ever had a Mars bar when you've been really, really hungry, you'll know how good every chewy, chocolatey mouthful of it tasted to me that night. I wolfed it down in seconds and immediately felt overwhelmed by guilt.

On my way back to the *pensione*, wishing I was anywhere but there, I suddenly realised that I was going to have to climb the drainpipe leading up to my room. It was one thing coming down, quite another going all the way up again.

'Oh, heck,' I thought in dismay. 'What am I going to do?'

I probably used up every guilty Mars-bar calorie struggling up that pipe to get back into my room.

The next day, I rang my father from a phone box: 'It's not for me, this,' I told him tearfully. 'I can't stand it, I'm so hungry. Can I come home?'

'Course you can,' he said. 'Get back here now. Just tell me where you are and I'll sort everything out.'

Relief washed over me: Dad was coming to the rescue. Then the phone suddenly went dead.

'Dad?' I said in a panic. All I could hear was a dial tone. 'Dad!'

Time stood still. We'd been cut off and there was nothing I could do about it, as I didn't have any more money to call back. I put the receiver down, desolate.

'Oh, God!' I thought.

Then the phone started ringing. As I picked it up, my heart leapt.

'Hello?'

'Jane, I've got you back!' Dad exclaimed.

'How did you do it, Dad?' I asked, stunned.

'I don't know! I just thought, "I need to get back to her," and pressed loads of numbers.'

To this day, I don't know how my father managed to ring me back in a phone box in Italy without knowing the number. It was a physical impossibility and we were both completely baffled by it, but Mum and Gran had a simple explanation: divine intervention.

Dad didn't waste any time after that call. He got me a plane ticket, paid off the dance troupe and took the train to London to meet me off my flight at Gatwick Airport. As I came through the arrivals gate, he handed me a packet of sandwiches, which brought tears to my eyes – I was that hungry and grateful.

My seven weeks as a dancer in Italy had taught me two important things: firstly, that I'm a real home girl and I don't like going away; secondly, I had the most caring, dependable father in the entire world. I was so pleased to see him and he was so pleased to see me that we laughed all the way back home on the train.

As we were pulling into Wakefield, I said, 'Can we go on holiday somewhere other than Bridlington this year, Dad?'

'But we all love Brid,' he said, puzzled. 'It's got everything.'

'It has, but it might be nice to take Mum somewhere different, for a change.'

'Where were you thinking, lassie?' he said. 'Not Italy?'

I couldn't help but laugh.

Back in Wakefield, I was welcomed back to Casanova's, where I became the bar manager of a new VIP lounge within the club, which opened every night at 11. The lounge was for people with money who wanted to get away from the bang, bang, bang of the club and enjoy a good brandy, an exotic cocktail or a nice cup of coffee in more sophisticated surroundings. It was where Wakefield's elite came to party in private and many of the members were rich and powerful, including top brass at the council and the police.

Being a good organiser, like my mother and grandmother, I made sure everything in the lounge was perfect in every way. I used to go into work during the day, check the tills and do the stock, go home for my tea, get a bath, get dressed for work and go back again. My role was as much hostess as manager, really. As it was a private club within a club, we were able to keep it open after the main doors closed and as time went on we had quite a few late nights.

The club-owner Janice was pleased with how things were going, but she was always thinking of ways to improve. 'Can you sing?' she asked me, although I honestly don't know where she got that idea from, because I had never mentioned it.

'I can, actually,' I replied, 'and play the piano.'

'Let's get a keyboard for the lounge,' she said, quick as a flash, and after that, we started having sing-songs: I'd sit down and play and get everybody singing into the early hours.

'You really should take it further,' Janice told me when she heard that people had started asking me to their houses to play and sing at parties.

'I'm fine doing what I do,' I said, partly because I wanted to go on learning the business side of entertainment, but also because I wasn't ready to take on that role yet.

Janice was clever and gradually drew me out, though. She organised a charity pantomime and got me performing in that, then asked me to cover for her as a DJ in Central Park, another club within the club. It meant working from seven thirty until ten thirty and then getting changed in time to open up the VIP lounge, but I liked a challenge and always wanted to keep moving forwards.

'Yes, I'll take over while you're away,' I said, not quite sure what I was letting myself in for.

'You'll be fine,' she insisted. 'Just be yourself.'

*

I approached being a DJ in the same way I did being a barmaid: it was another lesson in knowing what people like and giving them what they want. Just as I never forgot people's drinks, I made sure to know everybody's favourite song, so that I could play it when I saw them coming up the spiral staircase into the club.

It worked every time.

'How does she do that?' they'd think, bouncing straight onto the dance floor.

Part of the job was talking between the records, which seemed to come naturally right from the start. I'd see something funny happening at the back of the room and say, 'Ooh, hello, what's going on over there?' It could be anything from a bloke coming back from the bar carrying too many drinks – 'Careful, there!' – to a woman scouring the floor for a dropped earring – 'It's the new dance craze, everybody!'

I'd make a joke about everything and, after a few weeks, nobody dared move when a song finished because the moment anyone stood up, woof, I was in! Without knowing it, I was in training for the next stage of my career.

Eventually, I wore Dad down and persuaded him to book our summer holiday somewhere other than Bridlington.

'Come on, Dad,' I said, 'I can pay my way, you're working, Mum's working, we can afford to go somewhere really special this year. Let's give Mum a break and find a lovely hotel to stay in, so she's not cleaning the caravan and cooking from morning to night.'

We went to Jersey and had an unbelievable time; it was probably the best holiday I've ever had. The weather was sunny, the beaches golden, and we went to see all the shows. I loved spending time with Mum and Dad. They weren't just my parents – I actually liked their company – and my mother used to make us laugh all day long. She had a right sense of humour, Mum, and that's where I get it from, I think. We were so alike and so close; we even had the same laugh.

God, we laughed on that holiday in Jersey. The only time a cross word was spoken was when we were watching a turn in a club and I leaned over to Mum and whispered, 'I could do that.'

'Why don't you do it then?' she asked, sounding exasperated. She was that sick of hearing me say those words.

Usually, I would have annoyed Mum even more by saying, 'No, I don't need to.' But as I watched the singer shimmy across the stage in a glittery backless dress, belting out 'Big Spender' to an enraptured audience, I thought, 'Maybe I will, actually.'

6

Lessons In Love

When she looked to my future, my mother never brought up the idea of me settling down. She didn't say, 'One day, when you get married . . .' or even 'When you have children of your own . . .' Janet and Tony had gone down that road, but Mum saw something different for me.

'You've got so much else ahead of you,' she said.

I wasn't bothered about boyfriends and marriage – I was too busy working and having fun. I had my two jobs at Casanova's and I was singing again, doing occasional gigs as and when the opportunity arose. I didn't think I was good enough to get an agent yet, but had enough confidence to do a warm-up slot here and there.

Wal was constantly on the road, so I tried not to have too many expectations of our relationship. Having learned my lesson from my experience with Mark, I just took things as they came. I knew that being in a successful band meant you could click your fingers and a girl would appear, especially so for someone as stunning as Wal, who was the life and soul of the party. People gravitated towards him. Still, I was Wal's girlfriend when he came up to the North and I was enthralled by the idea of being the girlfriend of the drummer in Liquid Gold. I had to pinch myself as I watched him onstage: 'That's my fella,' I'd think.

Wal liked the fact that I came from a really close family, maybe because he had lost his own parents. He had two brothers, Tony and Franz, and a sister called Helga. He liked the fact that my relationship with my dad was so strong as his father had left when he was just four years old. His mother passed away in 1977. I was good fun, but prim and proper at the same time, and he liked that too and was grateful that I didn't ask too much of him. You might look at me and think, 'high maintenance', but I'm not high maintenance in any shape or form and never have been – I'm very happy left on my own. So, Wal could go off, do his stuff and, when he came back, I'd be there, doing my stuff.

The summer after I turned 19, he rang me at home to say the band were on their way up to Yorkshire.

'How long will you be around?' I asked casually.

'About ten days,' he said. 'Then I've got a couple of months before I go off to Mexico and I was thinking maybe we could spend some time together. I've just bought a house down in Buckingham and I'd like you to see it.'

My heart skipped a beat. 'Sounds good,' I said, trying to keep my voice steady.

'Do you think you'd be able to take some time off work?' he asked. 'It'll be fun, you can come round some of the clubs with us.'

'I could probably persuade Mike that I've got some holiday owing to me,' I said, my excitement levels soaring.

'Oh, and one more thing,' he added. 'Isn't it about time I met your parents?'

I made a rollercoaster-scream face at the other end of the line.

Dad was passing as I put the phone down.

'He's coming up North again!' I said.

'Is this the boyfriend, the drummer?' Dad asked. 'Is it getting a bit serious?'

I gulped. 'Well, yes, I think it might be.'

*

Two weeks later, Liquid Gold headlined at Casanova's on the Saturday night. Afterwards, Kees and Philip from Pussycat joined us for a drink and I found myself sitting in a booth with my boyfriend, the rest of the band, the bosses from Pussycat and Janice and Mike from Casanova's too. Talk about kudos!

'I like this,' I thought.

I had such a fab night. Wal was the beaming light at the centre of things, making us all laugh with his stories of life on the road. He was such a confident man, loved by everybody, and it was great to be by his side.

'He's so vivacious and beautiful,' I thought longingly. 'I'll never be able to hold on to him.'

The band were spending the night in a hotel next to Casanova's.

'Would you like to stay over with me this time?' Wal asked, squeezing my hand.

'Oh, things *are* moving on a bit,' I thought.

I rang my dad: 'Can I stay out tonight?' I asked.

'Hmm,' he said. 'The drummer?'

'Yes.'

'Okay, but only if you bring him for Sunday dinner tomorrow.'

The next morning in our hotel room, Wal got dressed for lunch with my parents in a pair of leather trousers and a vest top. With his long, blond hair flowing to his shoulders, he looked every inch the pop star.

'This could go one way or the other,' I thought to myself.

Meanwhile, at home, Mum was saying to Dad, 'Peter, don't say a thing! Just let it fizzle out. Don't put your foot down, because she'll go against you. You know what she's like.'

When we arrived at Silcoates Street, I introduced Wal to Mum and Dad with my heart in my mouth.

'Good to meet you, lad,' Dad said. 'I was just off up the allotments to pick some veg. Would you like to come along?'

'That would be great,' said Wal.

For the next three hours, Wal rolled fags while Dad showed him all his plants on the allotment. Since the way to my dad's heart was to roll him a fag, they got on like a house on fire.

'What did you talk about?' I asked Wal later.

'Everything, but nothing,' he said. 'We just had a good old natter.'

At home, Mum emerged from the kitchen, her cheeks flushed from the heat, and said to me, 'Right, go and get Wal and your dad. Dinner's ready.'

It was a boiling-hot day, and as I walked up to Silcoates Garage, I could see them in the distance, my boyfriend and my father, ambling along side by side, making their way back home for dinner. I would have recognised Dad from a mile off in his old trousers and vest, carrying his shirt like a sling over his shoulder, as he often did when he was bringing veg home. The smell of his shirt comes back to me the instant I think of it. But it was something else altogether to see Wal loping alongside him, tall and rangy in his leather trousers and vest top, his flowing blond hair silhouetted against the bright sky.

'Well, that's a sight you don't often see,' I thought.

At home, we sat down to one of Mum's fantastic Sunday dinners. There was an appreciative silence as we ate. Mum made the best roasties and Yorkshires I've ever tasted and her gravy was out of this world.

Halfway through the meal, Wal said, 'Can I take Jane back to Buckingham with me next week for a holiday? I'll take good care of her, don't worry.'

My mum gave my dad a look as if to say, 'Just let her go.'

There was a pause while Dad chewed his food.

'Okay, as long as you look after her,' he said eventually.

The following Friday, I was booked to sing at a club in Leeds. I wasn't expecting Wal to be able to make it, but the early timing of my gig allowed him to get to his late gig afterwards, so he came along with Mum and Dad. I was a wreck beforehand, afraid that I'd mess up my set and Wal would go off me. All kinds of disaster scenes went through my mind. Backstage, I threw up, as usual, and my throat was so parched by the time I went on I'm amazed I was able to sing a note.

I was nearly sick again – with relief – when I saw the expression on Wal's face afterwards. 'That was really good, Jane,' he told me, gripping my shoulders enthusiastically. 'You're a fantastic singer.'

Years later, Wal told me that, when the band picked him up to go to his gig afterwards, they asked him, 'So, what was she like, then?'

'Really good,' he said, and nobody said another word, because they'd all been expecting him to say, 'Oh, God, she was dire!'

Two days later, I drove us to Buckingham in my gold Vauxhall Viva.

'It won't go over 50, so don't even try,' Dad warned as I set off.

I'm sure it wasn't true, but I believed everything my father told me in those days.

As Wal and I sped down the motorway with the music on, at a steady 50 miles per hour, I couldn't help thinking, 'Hey, I'm all grown up!'

Eventually, we pulled up outside Wal's new house, which was a gorgeous three-storey townhouse in the centre of Buckingham. They say an Englishman's home is his castle – and Wal's house was clearly his pride and joy. All his money had gone into buying it and now he was doing it up. 'It's going to be amazing when it's finished,' he said, leaping out of the car to open the front door for me. 'Hope you like it.'

I must have a nose like a ferret because I can still recall the smell of that house to this day: a mixture of old beams and floorboards, dust, sawdust and paint. There were so many alterations going on that you had to be careful where you stepped, but right at the top of the house, up an old wooden staircase, Wal had made his bedroom into a haven among the eaves. With its sloping roof and thick oak beams, dark wooden floorboards and brass bed, it felt like a deliciously romantic hideaway, a refuge for eloping lovers. When Wal opened the windows, the church bells were going and the room filled with the scent of fresh air and summer.

It was our little sanctuary, and what a time we had there. You remember moments, don't you? – and I have a snapshot in my mind of Wal in the early-morning light as he got out of bed to make us a cup of tea. Watching through half-closed eyes as he walked naked across the room, I couldn't get over how beautiful he was, from his long legs and tiny hips to his wide shoulders and muscular drummer's arms.

'Wow, that's a body!' I thought, and it was the first time I'd thought of a man in that way.

We spent hours lying in bed, listening to music playing on Wal's reel-to-reel tape – an impressive state-of-the-art gadget in those days. Even better, he had one of my favourite songs on it – 'Ripples' by Genesis – and every time it came on I'd lie there, thinking, 'He's the coolest guy in the world! I love him.'

But while everything in the bedroom was rosy, things didn't go quite so well in the kitchen, unfortunately. I think because he'd had such a great Sunday lunch in Silcoates Street, Wal naturally thought I was going to be a good cook. But I couldn't cook and I had no idea how to look after a house either, because

I'd always had everything done by my mum, bless her. Now, I was wishing she'd taught me about keeping house instead of doing it all for me.

Wal and I went around with the band to gigs and parties and, when we got back to the house, there would be an expectation of food. I was constantly ringing Mum and saying, 'How do I make gravy? What do I do?'

'Oh, just go out,' she said, which was the best advice in the circumstances.

But interest rates were high and, while Wal was paying everything he had into his mortgage and house renovation, we soon found ourselves surviving on my meagre wages, which began to dwindle. Eating out was expensive and we took to having cheese on toast for breakfast, lunch and supper, because it was all I could make. Things got so desperate that we literally jumped for joy the day we discovered smoked cheese on sale at a stall in Buckingham market – a delicacy when you were eating nothing but Cheddar.

Wal was waiting for a royalties payment and promised me fine dining galore the moment it arrived. He was very affectionate. At 28, he was nine years older than me and sometimes talked about settling down in the future.

'Maybe you should learn to cook, because I'm not going to be touring the world for ever,' he'd say and I could tell he was only half-joking.

It got me wondering. As far as I was concerned, he was the one. Was he starting to think the same way? I couldn't help hoping.

One day, while we were shopping in town, he called me over to the jeweller's window to ask my opinion on a ring. 'See that one, third row back?' he said, pointing to an antique diamond cluster. 'Do you like it?'

'It's gorgeous,' I said lightly, 'I'm a big diamond fan, me.'

A few days later, he pointed out another.

'Why are you so interested in rings all of a sudden?' I asked.

He grinned cheekily. 'Why do you think?'

'I don't know,' I said, taken aback. 'What do you mean?'

'Isn't it obvious?' he said, laughing.

We could probably have gone on asking each other oblique questions all day if his brother, Franz, hadn't suddenly bounced up and started talking about going to a party later. Franz and Wal were close in age and they got on really well, but they were like chalk and cheese: Wal was blond, blue-eyed and always smiling, Franz had dark hair and smouldering looks – he was the cool one. They were both stunners and I used to feel fabulous walking down the street with them: 'I'm with these,' I'd think happily.

Now, I barely heard a word Franz was saying because my head was buzzing with questions. Was Wal thinking about asking me to get engaged? Why else would he be looking at rings for me?

Franz broke into my thoughts. 'We'll need to take some bottles to the party,' he said, stopping outside a wine shop.

'Got any money?' Wal asked him.

Franz shook his head.

Wal shrugged. 'I haven't either.'

'Nor me,' I said.

Franz looked pained. 'What are we going to do? We can't turn up without any wine.'

We looked at each other helplessly.

'I could write a cheque, I suppose,' I said eventually. 'Although it seems a bit daft to waste a cheque on a bottle of wine.'

Wal and Franz shrugged.

'Well, let's go into the shop, at least,' I said, and I ended up writing out a Yorkshire Bank cheque for two bottles of wine: one white, one red.

Goodness knows what my bank manager would have made

97

of it, but I know what I was thinking: 'At this rate, I'm going to have to go back home and earn some money again.'

Sometimes I like to take myself out of a situation, sit back and watch what's really going on, and that night, I went along to the party in a pensive mood. People were flocking around Wal, as they always did, and I thought, 'I'm never going to be able to hang on to this, I'm a barmaid from Wakefield.'

Ellie Hope, the lead singer of Liquid Gold, came and sat down next to me.

'Is everything all right with you and Wal?' she asked.

'Really good,' I said, trying to look happy. 'I think he'd like me to move down, actually. He's been talking about getting a ring and stuff.'

Her face fell.

'What's wrong?' I asked.

'You can't do it to him, Jane,' she said reproachfully. 'He's in a very successful pop group, don't hold him back.'

'Hmm,' I said, shocked by her bluntness.

'What about you?' she went on. 'I can't see you sitting around in Buckingham, twiddling your thumbs while he's off round the world, can you?'

I smiled wanly and went off to find Wal, but as the days went on and my savings disappeared, Ellie's words echoed in my mind. She was right, I realised. Even though it hurt to acknowledge it, I had things to do in my life, and Wal probably needed to get all that rock and roll out of his system.

We didn't fall out, we never had a big row – I just got up one day and left, without telling him I was going. We'd had five wonderful weeks together, but now I needed to get back to work.

Wal was gutted, apparently, but he didn't get in touch or try to persuade me to come back. Liquid Gold were off to Mexico, so what was he going to say? 'Come back, but I'm off to Mexico and you'll be on your own'?

'I can't believe you've let her go, you idiot,' Franz said to him, as I learned many years later.

But Wal felt he couldn't ask me to give up everything, move in with him and then go away, leaving me behind. He just didn't have enough to offer me.

When I got home to Silcoates Street, Mum was in the kitchen. Her face lit up when she saw me. 'What are you doing back here?' she asked.

'Well, he's . . .'

I shrugged.

Mum smiled as if to say, 'I knew she'd come back.'

It was my decision to leave, so I wasn't upset in the way you're upset when you've been dumped. At the same time, I had been in love with Wal and we'd come that close to making a permanent commitment. What I didn't realise was that a pattern of behaviour was beginning to emerge in my life: of subconsciously picking men it wasn't going to work with because, deep down, I knew that I had something else to do.

Although I missed Wal, at least I was somebody in my own right in Wakefield, albeit a big fish in a little pond. I went back to work, saved my money and bought myself a TR7, which I look back on as quite an achievement for a 19-year-old. Yet something had changed in me: it was almost as if I'd been in training for marriage and commitment with Wal and, the moment a replacement came along, I fell in love with him on the rebound. Paul was a drummer in a band on the same circuit as Liquid Gold and I had met him a couple of times when his band played at Pussycat. The similarities are weird. It's a bit like *Groundhog Day*, when I think of it, only with a different fella. I've always gone for a drummer – I don't know what that's about.

When Mike Craig asked me if I could recommend a band to play at Casanova's the following winter, I remembered Paul and his crew and suggested them. Paul was a good musician, blond and gorgeous; he was also a very nice guy and, before I knew it, we were in love and I had moved into his flat in Sheffield. I grew up quickly over the next couple of years. It was a shock to be living away from home, playing house and paying the bills. I was used to giving my board to my mother and leaving her to do everything, but now I was the one having to budget. And I wasn't the only one. Times were hard for a lot of people in Yorkshire and they got much worse when the National Union of Mineworkers (NUM) called the miners out on a national strike in 1984, after the National Coal Board (NCB) announced a massive raft of pit closures across England.

The strike was an awful, painful time, not just for the miners and their families, but for the whole community. Until then, the miners had good money coming in, which funded the clubs, the pubs, the butchers, the builders and all the other businesses in the community. But when the mines went down, everything else went down too: suddenly rentals weren't being paid, electrician's shops collapsed. Everywhere you looked, there were places boarded up because there was no money going in.

There was a lot of in-fighting and it was upsetting to see son go against father and brother against brother. People were torn between solidarity with the NUM and their guilt over not being able to support their families. They needed to work, but if you worked then you were branded a scab, so they were in a complete bind. The women stepped up, rallying round to set up soup kitchens and take food and fuel parcels to the miners' families who found themselves with next to nothing, but times were really hard. You saw people so desperate they would kill themselves because they couldn't look after their loved ones.

Mum and Dad didn't suffer as much as everybody else because my father had paid off the mortgage and spent his life avoiding debt. Yet with Dad and Tony on strike, it was left to Mum and

Wendy to keep their households afloat with their wages. They had just enough to survive, but we saw the whole community around us die, which was devastating.

That year definitely shaped me: it was when I realised what a vital role entertainers play in keeping the working man going. Despite the slump, Casanova's and Pussycat were always full: people needed an escape, even if they were skint and only having one pint while they watched the band. I'll never forget that: it really brought home to me the power of entertainment and the huge effect it can have on people's lives. Giving an audience an uplifting evening is a lovely thing to do at the best of times; at the worst of times it can be a lifesaver.

Paul was quite traditional and I was that mad about him I somehow let him talk me into giving up work at Casanova's. He wanted his woman at home in the evenings when he wasn't out working himself and I can't say I blame him. Practical as ever, I went out and got myself a nine-to-five job as a call dispatcher at Nixdorf Computer AG, sending out engineers to fix computer glitches and breakdowns across the North of England. It couldn't have been more of a contrast to working in the clubs, but I stayed at Nixdorf for the next two years and enjoyed the challenge of working under pressure. I had a great group of friends in the office and used to spend my lunch breaks with a lovely girl named Kelly Charles, who I'm still in touch with to this day, so I was happy enough, although I could see that Mum wasn't altogether pleased by the direction I had taken. She believed that I was destined to do something else with my life; Dad felt the same and, in my heart, I did too.

When Paul and I discussed the future, I often said that I fancied being a singer, yet the pull to go a more conventional route was stronger. I said yes when he asked me to marry him after two years together. It seemed like the right thing to do, because everyone I knew got married in their early twenties. So, I had a beautiful, traditional wedding in the Spiritualist church, just as my sister Janet had all those years before. I wore your typical meringue dress and my father walked me down the aisle. All our friends and family were there, including Mike and Janice from Casanova's, and Paul's mum and dad, who were lovely. It was a very happy day.

Being young and headstrong, I was surprised when Dad said, 'It's not too late to change your mind,' in the car on our way to the church.

'Why has he said that?' I wondered.

I didn't acknowledge it really. 'No, it's going to be fine,' I assured him, and I really thought it would be, because Paul was such a lovely fella.

At the reception I got up and sang a duet with David Charles, a friend from Casanova's who had joined me at the VIP lounge keyboard for many a sing-song into the early hours. David and I sang 'How Do You Keep The Music Playing?' by Michel Legrand, which turned out to be an apt choice, considering how things turned out.

'Those were such great nights, weren't they?' David said as he hugged me onstage. 'You must miss them, Jane. Don't lie to me and say you don't.'

'I do,' I said, suddenly nostalgic for my days at the club.

'You've got such a gift,' Mum said proudly, when I went to sit with her. 'You don't seem to realise what you're wasting,' she added, unable to resist having a jab.

Paul had heard me sing in the lounge at Casanova's, but he'd never been to one of my gigs, so he was astounded to see his bride get up and belt out a stunner on our wedding day.

'That was amazing!' he said. 'I had no idea . . .'

Right then and there, he started taking my singing more seriously and, when we got back to Sheffield, he left his band, I sold my car and we set up as a duo. We couldn't find anyone to play bass guitar so I taught myself the basics and improvised. I was never going to be a great guitarist, but I sufficed until Mike Craig offered us a spot at the new club he was setting up in Leeds, when we were able to afford to employ a bass player, Tony, to take over from me.

We had a great few months at Mr Craig's and I think I would have been back on track had my marriage to Paul not fallen into difficulties. They say a leopard can't change his spots. Well, a tigress can't change her stripes, either. We wanted different things and I couldn't live up to his expectations. I loved him, but not enough – I wanted more out of life. Six months into our marriage, I could see my life panning out in a certain way and realised it wasn't for me.

'I can't do this,' I thought. 'I'm not going to make him happy and he deserves to be happy.'

The guilt was overwhelming. 'What a stupid thing, Jane. You shouldn't have got married. How could you do this to him?' I asked myself again and again.

I felt really bad for Paul. He deserved much better than me, because I was destined for other things. I had to go, though – I felt I had no choice. Eventually, I rang my brother Tony.

'Can you come and pick me up?' I said.

Tony didn't ask questions, he could always tell when I needed him. The next day, he drove Dad's van over to Sheffield and brought me and my belongings back home to Silcoates Street. He said little as we drove back to Wakefield, giving me space to gather my thoughts. Finally, I started talking: 'I haven't got one bad thing to say about Paul, but that chapter's closed,' I told him. 'I just wish I hadn't upset him. I hope he meets someone who can make him happy one day.'

Mum and Dad didn't question my return or the fact that I was getting divorced six months after I'd got married – they were always open arms at home.

'Welcome back,' they said.

'What are you going to do now?' Mum asked, smiling expectantly.

'Get a job, because I'm skint,' I said.

Her smile faded.

'And once I've got myself on my feet,' I went on, watching her face light up again, 'I'm going to be a singer.'

7

Queen Of Clubs

I started saving up for a PA system to take on the road: a good one, with a high-quality microphone, amplifiers and speakers – I wanted to sound the very best I could onstage. But the system I wanted was expensive and saving up for it was an uphill struggle. I also felt slightly concerned about going out on the road on my own: the clubs could be rowdy so I needed someone to keep an eye on me and help carry all my stuff. Since I couldn't afford to pay anybody, the answer would be to get a boyfriend to do it – but a boyfriend was the last thing I wanted.

My father came to the rescue – his own as much as mine, I think – when I talked it over with him. He had recently taken voluntary redundancy at the pit and was planning to give Janet, Tony and me a small share of his payout. It wasn't much, just a little bit of help.

'Tell you what,' he said, 'instead of giving you money, I'll buy you that PA.'

'Really, Dad? That would be amazing!'

He smiled, and there was a twinkle in his eyes that I hadn't seen for a while, maybe because he'd been feeling slightly aimless since stopping work.

'Come on, I'll be your roadie and we'll go out together,' he offered.

It was the perfect solution: Dad began to fizz with a fresh sense of purpose and I had someone to drive me around and do all the heavy lifting. I never looked back. He took me to an open night at a club in Leeds, where booking agents came to audition new artists and acts. I got up and sang and straight away two agents took me on. All of a sudden, I had a load of work coming in.

'Right, we're off on the road,' my dad said.

'This is serious,' I thought. 'I'm a proper singer now.'

It was time to devise a setlist. I didn't bother to go and watch any other singers because I had already decided that I wanted to do things my way – I couldn't see the point in comparisons, I just had to be the best that I could possibly be.

'That's a good song, I could sing that,' I thought, jotting it down on a piece of paper. Within no time I had my setlist.

I practised in the church: I set up my PA, put on a backing tape and belted out each song. The acoustics were fab, so everything sounded good. 'Yes, I can sing this. Yes, that's fine,' I thought, ticking them off on the list. I kept it current and tried to perfect the crowd-pleasers, songs that would make people think, 'I love this.'

As I started earning money, I got into the fashion side of it. I went shopping in theatrical shops and upmarket dress shops and my mother would come with me. We found that the smart boutiques always had something elaborate that no one would ever wear, marked down to sale price or even cheaper. I used to clean up. I liked to surprise the shop assistant by saying, 'I'll have that one, please.'

One day, Mum and I went to a boutique in Leeds called French Dressing, which was very much for races day and posh charity balls. It had some amazing sparkly outfits and I wanted to try them all.

As I went in and out of the changing room, swapping one

fabulous dress for another, the other shoppers grew curious and began to gather around. I couldn't help playing to the crowd.

'She had an audience and she was only trying things on!' my mother told my father later – she loved it.

'Which one, the gold or the silver?' I asked her, as I began to narrow down my choice.

The onlookers were divided: half of them said gold, the other half silver.

'What'll it be, Mum? You decide,' I told her.

'Get 'em both,' she said, with a dismissive wave. She was always saying things like that. She would spend my money, would my mother.

The clubs, for me, were Yorkshire RADA – they taught me everything. After the almighty disruptions of the miners' strike, in 1984, the North was thriving again. We had industry and money and it was a great time to be a singer in a club, although, saying that, I never thought I was good enough. There were far better people in the clubs than me, so I learned to be an entertainer too and that's what set me apart. Between songs I'd talk and get everybody onside by making them laugh. One of my agents started promoting me as 'Jane McDonald: personality vocalist'.

The clubs were a tough gig because the audiences didn't care who was on, especially in the North. For the miners, the mill workers, the factory workers and their wives, this was their time to come together, in their club, in their community, and have a drink and a right good laugh on a Saturday. It was irrelevant who was on that stage. As far as they were concerned, there was going to be a turn on, and there would be someone else on next week, and the week after that. The challenge for me was to make an impression, so that people thought, 'I'm going to look out for her next time.' Or they might say to a committee member, 'Ooh, can we have her at Christmas?' When that happened, you knew you were getting somewhere.

It was an incredible training – you went along with your charts, your PA and your dress over your arm and played with whoever happened to be the backing musicians. In Manchester, we used to do three clubs in a night and they were all packed to the rafters. It was a battle every time. At the start of a show, I'd look out into the audience and think, 'Right, what do you want?'

It was up to you to create the atmosphere and it wasn't always easy. If you showed any weakness in a club, they would kill you. They'd be, 'Nah, not for me,' and go back to what they were doing. It's something I had to learn the hard way; I had to die onstage a few times.

At one of my first gigs booked by an agent, there was a group of guys playing pool right in front of me. I found it impossible to perform when they kept saying to each other, 'Champion! Whoa, that's a good shot!'

'Just have a bit of respect,' I thought to myself. 'There's somebody dying up here.'

I was young, I was green. It was one of my first gigs as a pro. During my final song, I snapped and said, 'Do you think you could just possibly—'

The committee instantly paid me off. I was so upset; I felt I had failed miserably. But I learned from it: no matter what's going on, don't let it get to you and keep singing. You have to get a thick skin in this business. Not everybody's going to like what you're doing – that's the first thing you have to remember – but if you've won over the majority, then you're fine. You can't please everybody all the time and don't take it personally if someone doesn't like you. If they've had a bad day, it's not you they're having a go at, it's just that you're there and they can direct their bad mood at you by saying, 'I can't stand this.'

And I've done it myself. I've had something going on in my life and thought, 'I can't deal with this, I'm going.'

It's hard for the artist to see someone walk out, but whenever it happened to me, it made me determined to improve my show and be better. My mother always had good advice for me when she came to watch me. I'd say to her, 'God, they're hard tonight!'

'No, it's you. Have a sherry,' she'd reply, quick as a flash.

'What do you mean, it's me?'

'Change your vibration. It's not them, it's you. They've been working all week, it's up to you to make them feel good.'

As time went on, I learned once you've got the women onside, the men will come so I never actually addressed the guys – mostly, I didn't even acknowledge that there were men in the audience. I just imagined that I was talking to people like myself, who wanted to have a laugh and let off steam on a night. It was always, 'Oh, girls . . .' and it was a natural position for me to take, because I'm a woman's woman and would rather go out with the girls anytime.

'Oh, girls, what a week, eh? What a week! Did you see *Emmerdale*?' I'd say and, as soon as I mentioned a soap, heads would jerk up. Then I'd have the women's attention.

Now, you've either got that funny bone or you haven't, but I don't think I could have stood on that stage and talked if I hadn't had the experience of chatting between records while I was DJ-ing at Casanova's. That was vital training for me. It gave me the confidence to yack about the soaps, something in the news – anything, as long as they were all familiar with it – and for some reason, it sounded funny when I said it onstage. That was my saving grace because I was just wittering on about everyday things.

If in doubt, there was always a story to tell about the journey to the gig: 'Oh, I had a right time getting here . . .'

Something always happened. I remember stopping in a village with my dad, winding down the car window and asking the nearest man impatiently, 'How do you get to the Working Men's Club?'

'My brother takes me,' he replied.

'I don't care if your brother takes you. Where is it?' I said.

'I don't know, my brother takes me,' he repeated.

Nuggets like that went straight into the set and got everybody going.

If a place was difficult to find, I'd come out with something like, 'Flipping heck, if there's ever another war, I'm coming here, because the Russians will never find us!'

That was all it took to get people's attention. They'd smile at each other, as if to say, 'I know, it's in the middle of nowhere, isn't it? Everybody gets lost!'

Once I had something in common with everybody, boom, I'd give them a big song so that they'd think, 'Wow!'

I made sure my first number was something familiar that they could all sing – and nothing too clever, so the organist could play it. Years of singing with an organist and drummer really teaches you your trade. I used to have two sets of dots, or notated-sheet music: one set was really easy, in case the organist and drummer were a bit sleepy; the other set included all the latest chart songs, which I'd hand out at the clubs where I knew there was really good backing.

If you had good backing, you were guaranteed a great night. But bad backing wasn't always a disaster, because it so often led into comedy. The organist would bungle a chord and I'd think, 'I've got to say something funny here. I can't just pretend everything is fine.'

'Flipping heck!' would often be enough to make people laugh.

One night, a guy turned up and he had a glass eye and a

funny leg. He said, 'Organist is off tonight, but I'm here and I can play anything, as long as it's in C.'

'Oh great!' I thought, and for some reason I just couldn't stop laughing when I went on.

'Give me that note again. No, can't get it?' I said. 'Give me a G – that's the note down from A!'

Everybody started laughing. 'I'm struggling up here tonight,' I told them, with a deadpan expression on my face. In the end, I gave the bloke a fiver and said, 'Look, just go and get a drink at bar, love. Get me one and all, a double!'

With my musical accompaniment gone, there was nothing for it but to launch into some stand-up – and I went down a storm and got booked again. You just had to fly; you had to entertain that crowd, come what may.

I don't know how it happens – something takes over – and my mother used to love it. She'd say, 'Third song in, people were swapping their chairs round and paying attention, thinking, "Ooh, this is different," because of the chat.'

As my confidence grew, I learned to deal with the hecklers and then I actually began to welcome a heckle, because you could put someone down without being offensive and get a laugh at the same time.

'Who said that?' I'd snap. 'Stand up, let's have a look at you because you must be gorgeous!'

When they stood up, I'd say, 'Yeah . . . Anyway, ladies and gentlemen . . .'

You didn't have to do much. It was just a way of saying politely, 'Shut up, I'm trying to do something here.'

I grew to love the challenge of a new club: 'Right, I'm going to get you,' I'd think.

If I went down really well and they liked me and booked me again, it made me want to be even better the next time. My constant aim was to keep progressing, so I ploughed my money back into the show, making sure I had the best of everything: I had the best PA system, I was the first woman to have my own lights, my dresses were fabulous . . . I did everything to be the best I could be.

There wasn't much trouble in the clubs, but when there was, you had to know how to handle it. It's funny how you can actually feel something happening before it happens; I was very sensitive to what was going on in a crowd. One night, a sense of unease crept up on me halfway through my set. I couldn't put my finger on it, I just knew something wasn't right. The next moment, somebody got up and punched somebody.

'Oh, hang on! What's going on?' I said.

As the turn, you're not supposed to react or even acknowledge trouble in the crowd. You've just got to stop singing and let them get on with it, because, although there may only be two people fighting, there are always about six who want to get involved as well, and if you join in, they're going to go for you. Fights didn't happen very often, but when they did, you had to learn to back away.

I stopped singing and waited for a little bit, but then it really started to kick off and the club erupted into a brawling mass of fists, legs and arms. My dad ran up onstage: 'Quick, Jane, get in the dressing room!' he yelled, and I scurried off just as someone leapt up behind me and started smashing up my precious lights.

I was lucky not to get hurt, but then I had my minder with me. Dad was really protective and I appreciated it. There were never any locks on the dressing-room doors at the clubs and he would stand outside while I was getting changed, so that the odd committee man couldn't 'accidentally' come in, looking to pay me. Dad was very, very astute. He had this look as if to say, 'I know what men do.' Only when I said, 'Right, I've got my clothes on,' would he go and get the gear down off the stage.

He protected me so fiercely that I never got into trouble and I always enjoyed his company. We had many hours together on the road, rattling back and forth to gigs across the Pennines in his old van, talking and laughing about anything and everything. Dad was really stern, but he used to love going out for a pint or to the club. Even when I was in my twenties, he'd say, 'Do you fancy going up to the club?' and off we'd go ballroom dancing. We often had a drink and played bingo after a show, although woe betide you if you won, because if the turn won the bingo, they'd let your tyres down! When people have worked all week, hoping to win at bingo on the weekend, it's bad news for everyone if the turn gets the prize ticket.

I could usually hear Dad laughing in the audience, but he never said, 'That was good.' Never in a million years. Instead, he'd say, 'Right, come on, let's get the gear packed up.'

I knew he was proud of me, because he used to tell all his mates down the allotments, 'She were brilliant the other night.' But he never told me.

My dad was my roadie all through the club years. Mum had a job in a newsagent's and had to be up at four in the morning so she didn't come with us. Of course, with Dad as my minder, I couldn't cop off because he was always there. Luckily, I didn't want to. At the time I wasn't interested in men, I was far more focused on my career. Instead of boyfriends, I had good mates – and a couple of the people I met in the clubs during this time went on to become lifelong friends.

There was a group of people who came to a club specially to see me, just as my dad and I followed certain bands when we went dancing, and sometimes we'd have a drink after I'd been on. One night, a guy named Steve mentioned that his dad had been the manager of the Wakefield Theatre Club.

'I did my work experience there,' I said. 'You must have been that little boy running around the office and causing havoc.'

'Yes, I'm Steven Holbrook,' he said.

There was another link between Steve and me, but we didn't discover it until a few weeks later when my mum said, 'We've got a really good speaker on at the church tonight, why don't you come?'

So I went along and, when I walked in, the first person I saw was Steve.

'What are you doing here?' he asked.

Since I hadn't gone to the church while I'd been living in Sheffield, I didn't know that Steve was spiritualistic, or that my grandmother was training him.

'Well, that's my gran and that's my mum,' I said, pointing them out.

'Oh my God!' Steve gasped. He couldn't get over the coincidence.

Later, the speaker said, 'I've got something to tell you, in the red coat.'

I looked down at my coat, which was red. 'Here goes,' I thought, crossing my fingers that it would be something good.

'I don't want to say it here, because it's a bit personal,' he went on.

At this point everybody turned to look at me.

'Oh no, how embarrassing!' I said to Mum.

The speaker came to find me afterwards. 'You've just split up from someone,' he said, referring to Paul. 'Don't go back, because it's not your destiny and it's not his. He needs a different life to the one you'll have.'

'Different in what way?' I asked.

'You're going to be a big star,' he said.

My eyebrows shot up.

'But you'll be 33 when it happens,' he added.

I was in my mid-twenties and 33 seemed an age away.

'Thirty-three?' I said, then went home and forgot all about it.

*

I was far from being a big star, but I was starting to become a name on the club circuit. I had one main agent now, who was good for getting gigs, but insisted I had to perform at the pub he owned, for free. All the acts on his books had to do it, including Too True, a duo of girl singers, June and Sue Ravey, who were sisters. Some friends had told me they were really good, so I went to see them one night at the pub – with my dad, obviously, because Dad went with me everywhere in those days.

After the gig, my agent introduced us to June and Sue. They were great and I was especially drawn to Sue, who was confident, funny and a brilliant singer. What a voice! She oozed an aura that made you want to be around her. More than that, I wanted to *be* her.

That night, June gave me a load of charts and said, 'We don't use these anymore, they might come in handy for you.'

It was a generous gift because charts are a vital part of any singing act and you can't just buy them. They have to be made for you and a lot of work goes into them: finding the right key, having them written up in your key, rehearsing them with the person who has written them. They were all handwritten. Things have changed with computers, but in the old days somebody had to write out every single note.

June and Sue's charts were good for me because we were all girl singers and sang at roughly the same pitch. I was thrilled to have some new songs to put into my show.

'What a nice thing to do,' I thought. 'These are nice people.'

It was hard to keep up with friends in the industry because you were always out doing your own gig, but Sue and I kept in touch through a couple of friends, Neil and Anthony, who used to follow us both.

'Sue says hello,' they'd say.

'Is she all right? Tell her that agent of ours is getting on my nerves again!'

Our agent irritated me with his demands for free gigs at his pub, but he was good for the work and got me on something called the Bass Roadshows, which gave me a lot of shows. He took his cut, though: he would pay me for all the shows at the end of the month, when he took his 17.5 per cent and gave me what was left.

One night, unusually, it was a 'pick-up', where you got paid on the night and gave your commission to your agent later. My fee was £80, minus my agent's commission, so when the club manager handed me £100, I said, 'I think you've made a mistake . . .'

He looked down the list on his clipboard: 'No, you're definitely on 100 quid,' he insisted.

It turned out he was right: only the agent was taking £20 off me on the sly and giving me £80 a gig, less his percentage.

'You mean to say that I was on £100 all this time?' I screeched.

I was furious, and felt very hurt too. The following day, I went to see the agent and went mad at him.

'I don't know what you're complaining about,' he said airily. 'You've got all this work. If you don't like it, don't do it!'

'You cheeky sod!' I thought.

On the spot, I decided I wasn't having it. 'I'm leaving you and I'm not doing your pub anymore, either,' I told him. 'You can give the roadshow to somebody else.'

My mum was aghast. 'Look at all the money you're giving up,' she said when I told her.

But I wouldn't budge: 'I'll manage, but I will not be cheated,' I replied.

I know it sounds daft, but if he had been honest with me and said, 'Look, I'm going to take £20 and give you £80, because that's my little cut,' I wouldn't have batted an eyelid. I'd have said, 'Yes, I see your point there.' But to do it behind my back was unforgivable and, after that, I wised up to the way agents operated.

*

With eyes wide open, I signed up with a bigger agent, who paid more money and took my career to another level.

'Best move I ever made,' I told Sue the next time I saw her. 'Don't be afraid of change.'

'June and I have refused to do his pub, an' all,' she said with a giggle.

I worked hard on improving my act and started to win the clubland awards for Best Club Singer and Female Vocalist of the Year. I played big clubs like Dial House and the Arundel Club in Sheffield and then I got to Blackpool, which was the ultimate for an entertainer coming up through the ranks. When you got booked in Blackpool, you'd made it, and that's why Blackpool is so special to me: for club singers, it was the Mecca of the North. But the moment I got there, I began to think about where I was going next. That was me: constantly looking to move forwards. It was great to get the good gigs and recognition but I wanted to go as far as I possibly could in my career; I couldn't bear the idea of sitting back and resting on my laurels.

I still did local gigs and was singing at a club in Wakefield when an old friend, Vicky Calvert, came to see me. I knew Vicky from the clubs but hadn't seen her for a while because she'd been away working as a singer and dancer on the cruise liners. That night, I was feeling a bit flat. I was bored and couldn't help thinking that it was time to move on. Still, I gave it my best, as I always did.

During the interval, Vicky said, 'That was great! I can see why you're winning the top awards. Are you still enjoying it?'

'To be honest, Vicky, I could do with a change of scene,' I admitted. 'The club circuit is becoming monotonous.'

Her eyes lit up. 'Oh, you'd be brilliant on the ships! Why don't you think about giving it a try?' she said.

I didn't need asking twice. 'Please! Just give me a number.'

I'll always be grateful to Vicky. 'Right, this is the number of the company that I work for,' she said. 'Ring them.'

And I did.

I arranged an audition with Matrix Entertainment in London, an agency specialising in producing shows for the ships. I did a good audition – I sang 'Somewhere' – and they were very complimentary about my voice, but I'm sure I got a job because I was a size 12 and all the outfits fitted me. It was like being back in French Dressing in Leeds again: I was in and out of that dressing room like a yo-yo in sequins, chatting away and making everybody laugh. When they'd seen all the dresses fitted like a glove, they signed me up to a three-month contract on a ship called the *Black Prince*.

I rushed home to tell Mum and Dad the good news.

'I've got a job on a cruise ship!' I shrieked.

Mum started laughing.

'You're doing what?' she said.

'I'm going to be a cruise singer,' I told her.

'I can't wait to see this,' she giggled. 'You can't go on a bike without being sick! Now you're going to work on a ship?'

8

Rock The Boat

I felt more anxious about being homesick than seasick as I flew to Tenerife to join the *Black Prince* in the spring of 1990. If working on the cruise ships turned out to be anything like touring with a dance troupe in Italy, I knew I would be heading straight back to Silcoates Street.

My mother waved me off. 'You'll be back before you know it,' she said reassuringly.

But I needn't have worried: I was so busy that I didn't have a chance to miss home and, although the *Black Prince* wasn't great in choppy seas, I soon found my sea legs. You just took a couple of tablets and you were fine.

I loved being at sea: the sights, the sounds, the food, the sunshine, the people and the work. I even loved my tiny cabin down in the bowels of the ship, near the engine room, where the smell of industrial diesel filled the air. Everything was new and exciting. Each morning, I sprang out of bed and rushed up on deck to look out at the horizon. The sky seemed eternally blue, the sea shining and salty fresh, and in the distance I'd catch sight of whichever volcanic island we were sailing towards on our tour of Gran Canaria.

'This is heaven,' I thought, as the sun warmed my face.

I used to write to my mother every week: 'Oh my goodness,

Mum, I've woken up in La Gomera! It's a beautiful island and there are trees and flowers everywhere.'

After rehearsing in London with a singing coach and a choreographer, I slotted easily into a four-handed jazz vocal group called Atlantic Crossing, a sort of cruising Manhattan Transfer. I had the luck to be put together with my friend Vicky and two guys called Graham and Peter, all great singers, and we gelled instantly. The ships were good for teaching range, from the top end to the bottom, and, although at first it was strange to be sharing a stage after years of performing solo, it was fantastic to hear our different voices come together in harmony. I was singing soprano again and I silently thanked my mother every day for the tuition she had paid for when I was younger. I realised that I had got into lazy ways while working in the clubs. I'd avoided singing anything difficult because I'd thought, 'Backing won't be able to play that.' Now, I was having to push myself much more. It was hard work: we rehearsed daily, did a show every night and were on duty looking after the passengers during the day, yet being among people who were on their holidays created a real buzz throughout the ship and, in the evenings, you were guaranteed a happy, appreciative audience.

I made friends among the crew, but was so grateful to have Vicky to lark around with on that first cruise. We visited as many tourist attractions as time allowed, giggled our way through colourful markets and guided tours and sampled every seafood dish on the menu: giant prawns, lobster, whitebait, squid and octopus – you name them, we ate them. A whole new world of taste opened up to me and I put on at least one dress size, if not two, during my 12 weeks on the *Black Prince*. I also took advantage of occasional invitations to the captain's table, where the food was superb, and thanked the heavens that my grandmother had shown me which knives and forks to use at a formal dinner – the soup spoon was safe with me!

One day, a frisson went through the ship because the Royal Yacht *Britannia* had come alongside. I went out on deck to take a look. Unsurprisingly, it was a very elegant vessel. Some of the crew came onboard to watch the show and I got chatting to one of them in the bar afterwards. It was my own show that night, singing alone with the band, and this guy from the *Britannia* seemed very taken with my performance.

'You were fantastic! You should definitely have your own show,' he said.

One thing led to another and I sold the *Britannia* crew quite a few of my tapes.

'Would you write to me?' my new friend asked, because you were always looking for someone to write to in those days.

'Yes, of course I will,' I promised.

A few months later, he wrote and asked for another tape because Princess Anne had snaffled his copy and it had become quite a favourite with her.

When I got back to England, I thought people might have forgotten me after three months at sea, but it seemed the opposite was true. Sometimes less is more, and when the clubs rang my agent only to be told I was unavailable, they became desperate to book me: 'When will she be back?' they demanded.

Suddenly I was seen as a much bigger act, which meant that I didn't have to do the pubs and small venues anymore. Since I was already booked to do another cruise in a few months' time, I felt I could pick and choose my gigs.

Soon, I was earning a good living travelling the world for six to seven months a year and going home to work in the best clubs, which at the time were on the Manchester scene. After the awards I had won, I was finally getting a sense of my worth as a singer and entertainer, but then one night after a show, when I saw the manager paying the other performers, I noticed the guys were being given more money than me: there was a guys' rate and a girls' rate, it seemed.

I had an agent who dealt exclusively with that circuit and so I rang him the following day.

'Hello, Jane, how can I help you?' he said. 'Did everything go all right last night?'

'It went fine, but from now on I'd like to be paid the same rate as the men,' I said. 'I watched them being paid last night, I saw what they were getting.'

There was a pause. 'Sorry, we don't pay girl singers that kind of money,' he said eventually.

'Well, I think you should start thinking about paying *this* girl singer that type of money,' I shot back.

'No way!' he blustered. 'Who do you think you are? You either take the job or you don't.'

'Fair enough, then,' I said calmly, 'I will do the two shows I've already booked with you and then I will go somewhere else.'

When I told my mother about it, she said, 'Oh, Jane, don't rock the boat.'

'Always know your worth, Mum,' I replied.

I knew I was good at what I did and was prepared to walk away, which gives you strength in any situation. There's power in saying no.

At the next show, one of the barmaids had a word in my ear: 'You've just had boss's son in,' she whispered furtively.

'Ooh, blimey,' I joked, 'I wish he'd seen me on a good night.'

'He never comes in. I don't know what you've been doing,' she said, grimacing.

'Oh dear, you might not see me again!'

The next day, the agent rang me back.

'Okay, we *will* give you what you're asking for,' he said.

His son had come home from the gig and told his father, 'Just pay her the same.'

'Thank you,' I said briskly.

Still, I was never happy. I was always on to the next thing.

'Gosh, I hope you find contentment in life,' Mum said when the dust had settled.

'I know what I'm worth and I'm going to make sure I get paid accordingly,' I insisted. I stood my ground and, by the age of 29, I was the highest-paid girl singer in the clubs.

When I came home from a cruise I often went to visit Gran, who was now living happily in sheltered accommodation. We used to reminisce about our holiday in Monifieth at least once a visit and sometimes that led her on to talk about her childhood. Gran still couldn't get over the idea that her mother had left her behind to go around the world with the Darlings.

'How could she leave me?' she asked, again and again.

'You must let that go, you know,' I told her gently. 'If I had a baby and left her with you while I went off and still did my job around the world, would it be that bad?'

She looked thoughtful.

'No, I suppose it wouldn't.'

'So, it would be all right for me to do it, not for your mum?'

'Oh my goodness, I've never thought about it that way,' she said.

I poured her another cup of tea.

'So, where are you off to next, love?' she asked.

'First, I'm flying to New York for rehearsals,' I said. 'Then I'm going to work on one of the really big cruise liners.'

'Are you, love?' she said approvingly. 'I always knew you were destined for something special.'

*

The *Horizon* was one of a fleet of big ships owned by Celebrity Cruises, based in Fort Lauderdale, USA, and it dwarfed the likes of the *Black Prince* and the other ships I'd worked on before. Celebrity Cruises put on big, glitzy American shows and I was really excited about taking part, but my goodness, it was hard work! I was singing, I was dancing . . . I was practically swinging from a trapeze and juggling during my time on the *Horizon*. As well as being an intensive lesson in discipline and how to work as a team, it was good fun and I sensed it would stand me in good stead for the future.

The *Horizon* was a happy ship and I made a couple of good friends, but as my contract drew to a close, in early 1993, I experienced a strong pull towards England and home. It felt as if fate was on my side when I heard I had been offered the gig of compère and headline singer at a huge caravan park just outside Skegness for the upcoming summer season. The summer season at the Maid Marian in Robin Hood Park was a massive gig. The clubhouse was enormous and, some nights, I was on in front of 2,500 people.

'Holy cow!' I thought, the first time I went onstage.

The audience weren't in seats facing the stage, either: they were sat at tables or milling at the bar, yacking away to their families and friends, and all the while their kids ran riot and Auntie Margaret fell asleep in her chair. Confronting this vast, restless sea of activity was scary at first, but I soon relaxed into it and enjoyed the challenge of trying to win people's undivided attention.

One of my lines was: 'Ladies and gentlemen, I know you hate it but I'm doing it anyway. I'm going to sing "Blanket On The Ground".'

'Blanket On The Ground' was a big club anthem and the crowd had heard it at least a hundred times – 'Oh no, not this!' they'd say.

My musicians, John Hope and Chris Merry, would then

make a big show of not wanting to do it. They would rip up pieces of paper and say, 'No, we're not playing it!'

It used to bring the house in.

I'd say, 'I'm singing it anyway,' and off I went.

Everybody loved it and sang along.

'Give the people what they want,' I'd say to John with a big stage wink.

'Beautiful Sunday' was another anthem on my setlist, along with songs by anyone from Dorothy Squires to Whitney Houston. The slower songs and ballads always went down well, the faster numbers were more of a problem. You had to do a fast song for the last spot, so everybody could get up and dance, and it was difficult to get that disco sound with just an organist and a drummer. Somehow, I managed it, although I'm not quite sure how.

The season lasted for 26 weeks. Since I was hosting as well as singing, it was fabulous for sharpening my funny bone and learning the gift of the gab. One day, just after we opened, our musical director, John Hope, rushed up to me backstage and asked frantically, 'Can you go out and fill for ten minutes, please?'

'What?' I said.

'We're running under. Just get out there and fill the time, somehow!'

Like a rabbit in the headlights I went onstage but then they couldn't get me off because I started laughing, telling jokes and talking about *Emmerdale* and *Coronation Street*. I enjoyed improvising and I'd have conversations with people from the stage: 'Have you seen her in that caravan down there . . . ?' While I was wittering on, I'd hear a hiss from the wings: 'Get off! We're running over now.'

Having to think on my feet honed my skills as an entertainer and I noticed that my singing was improving as well. The coaching I'd had for the shows on the ships had paid off and people were really starting to sit up. One hot Saturday night in August 1993, I decided to tackle the Dolly Parton song 'I Will Always Love You', which had recently become a smash hit for Whitney Houston.

The place was heaving that night. Everybody was talking and laughing – they had just arrived for the weekend, full of holiday spirit, raring to go.

I took a deep breath and started singing: 'If I . . .'

It was as if a spell had been cast. All of a sudden, the whole place went from yack, yack, yack to silence; nobody spoke or made a sound.

Tingling from head to toe, I sang the verse in silence and then reached for the top note: 'And I . . .'

As I hit the note, the crowd went berserk, roaring, cheering and leaping to their feet. It was an overwhelming outburst of emotion and I had never experienced anything like it. I was astonished that I could have that power over so many people.

'What just happened?' my father asked me in the next interval.

Dad was at the show selling my tapes, which I had recorded in a studio with a top arranger and producer before the season started. My father was brilliant: since he couldn't be my roadie while I was doing a residency, he came down at weekends to man a stall for me instead.

'I don't know, but it was amazing,' I said, breathless with excitement. I could sense my career shifting up another level after just one song.

'I think you sing "I Will Always Love You" better than Whitney,' he said quietly.

My mouth dropped open. I'd hardly known my father to remark on my singing before, let alone lavish me with that kind of praise.

'You what?' I said.

'I just think you really sing it well.'

'Thank you very much,' I said, still not quite able to believe what I was hearing.

I had decided that I wouldn't go back on the ships after the summer season – I wanted some time at home with Mum and Dad. It felt like I hadn't seen them properly for ages, what with my stints on the *Horizon* and then at the Maid Marian. I had let my club agents know and already had loads of bookings in; I was all set to base myself in Silcoates Street and tour the North again. My only worry was taking Dad along. He didn't seem as fit as he had been, even a year before, and I was concerned the heavy lifting would be too much for him.

'I've just sold ten of these in a row on the back of that song,' Dad said, reaching into a box under the table to get out some more Jane McDonald tapes. As he bent down, a packet of ten cigs fell out of his shirt pocket. I picked them up.

'Are these yours?' I asked.

I knew he was trying to give up. He was such a heavy smoker that people kept saying, 'You're going to kill yourself if you carry on like this.'

'Oh, Jane, I just love a cigarette,' he sighed, taking them from me and tucking them back in his pocket.

'Who am I to say?' I thought.

Dad insisted he was still going on the road with me.

'Are you sure?' I asked – I didn't want him to feel obliged. 'I can find someone else, you know.'

'No, Jane, I'm your roadie. No one else knows the ins and outs of working with you,' he insisted.

'I know, Dad, and it wouldn't be the same without you, anyway.'

My father would normally have come and driven me home at the end of the season, but Mum had a word on the side.

'His eyes are terrible, Jane,' she told me. 'Talk him out of it, because I don't want him to be driving at that time of night.'

'That's okay, Dave can do it,' I said.

Dave was my boyfriend at the time. Come to think of it, he might have been another reason why I had decided to stay in England for the winter.

On my final day off before the season ended, I went home to drop off my car and pick up Dad's van to bring all my stuff back from Skegness.

'How's it running?' I asked him.

He frowned. 'Playing up a bit.'

'Nothing's changed, then,' I said.

He laughed and a look of relief washed over his face.

'I can't wait for you to get back,' he said. 'I've been so bored. Thank God we're going out on the road again!'

I can still see Dad at the garden gate, watching me go. As I walked towards the van, I stopped and hesitated. A few weeks earlier, he had complimented me on my singing for the first time in many years. Now I turned and said something I had never said to him before: 'I do love you, you know.'

Dad smiled. 'Yes, I know you do.'

I drove back to Lincolnshire thinking how lucky I was to have the best father in the world.

We had a great last night at the Maid Marian and it was well after midnight when Dave and I loaded up the van and set off for home. But then disaster struck. Just over an hour into the journey, as we were chugging through the middle of nowhere in almost total darkness, there was an almighty bang and the engine stopped dead. I looked at Dave in horror.

It being Dad's van, I knew it was probably being held together with a bit of old wire and some elastic bands, which meant one thing: the only person in the world who could fix it was my father.

I sighed. It was two o'clock in the morning and I just wanted to go to bed.

'Try starting it again,' I suggested in desperation.

I didn't hold out any hope of the engine firing up again, but there wasn't a phone box in sight, nor anything else for that matter, and I wasn't ready to admit defeat.

Dave turned the key in the ignition and the van started.

'Go!' I yelled at him, just in case it changed its mind.

Off we went with a rattle, and eventually we turned into the back lane behind Silcoates Street. Just as we pulled up, the engine blew again.

'Look at that! I can't believe we made it,' I said, looking blearily at my watch (it was by then four in the morning). 'We'll have to push it to Silcoates Garage in the morning.'

I went inside the house, flopped into bed and slept through until nine o'clock, when I heard Mum knocking at the bedroom door.

'Jane, I'm really sorry to bother you,' she said softly, 'but I think your dad has died.'

It took a moment for her words to sink in.

'What?' I yelped, jumping out of bed.

I ran downstairs naked, in a blind panic.

'Are you sure, Mum?' I asked.

I was confused because her manner had been so apologetic, as if my dad dying wasn't a good enough reason to wake me up. Or maybe he hadn't really died, and that's why she was being so hesitant.

Mum gave me a helpless look.

'Will you go into the bedroom and check?'

'Okay.' I caught a glimpse of my reflection in a window pane and realised I didn't have any clothes on. 'Wait, I need my dressing gown!'

I quickly got dressed. Dave came with me to check on Dad, but when I reached Mum and Dad's bedroom door, I froze.

'I can't,' I thought. I must have known in my heart that Dad had passed. 'Can you go in?' I asked Dave.

A few moments later, Dave came out of the bedroom saying, 'Yes, he's gone. He's dead.'

I couldn't take it in, and neither could Mum.

'I don't understand it. He was at the club last night,' she said. 'He seemed fine, came home full of the joys, because you were on your way . . .'

'I was on my way home,' I said, echoing her thoughts. 'I wish . . .'

'You came in the back door and he went out the front,' Mum said thoughtfully.

It was such a terrible shock. Neither of us knew what to do. In a daze, I rang Tony. He was at work, down the pit, and Wendy answered the phone. Knowing how devastated my brother would be, she drove over there to break the news in person. It was very dramatic: they pulled him out of the mine so that she could tell him, and he was in bits.

Our sister Janet was on holiday in Tenerife and even harder to get hold of. 'I'll get the next flight back,' she said, but it took some arranging.

I didn't know what to do after that, except make cups of tea. I kept getting flashbacks to Dad lugging my heavy speakers and lights up and downstairs in the clubs.

'I've killed him,' I thought.

The coroner arrived. He estimated Dad's time of death at 2am, exactly the time the van broke down. I shook my head in disbelief – it seemed uncanny.

'Thank goodness he wasn't driving you home, Jane,' Mum said with a gasp. 'If his heart had given up on the journey, I could have lost you both.'

When Mum and I went to see Dad's doctor the next day, she explained that Dad had died peacefully in his sleep of a heart attack.

'Why would his heart just have given up like that?' I asked. 'He was only 69.'

'He had an enlarged heart, and of course he smoked heavily,' the doctor replied, 'so when his lungs filled up, his heart wasn't strong enough to pump them out.'

I thought about how Dad had been trying to give up cigarettes: 'But he didn't know about his heart, did he?'

'Yes, he's known about it for several years,' the doctor said. 'He was very ill, but didn't want any of you to know or to worry.'

Mum and I looked at each other in bewilderment.

'He knew?' I said. 'Then why was he planning to come out on the road with me this winter?'

'Because it kept him going, I imagine,' the doctor said with a kindly smile. 'He would probably have gone a lot quicker if he hadn't been going out with you all these years. It was good for him to be getting out, lifting and exercising. It was exactly what he needed.'

Mum nodded. 'It certainly gave him something to live for,' she said. 'He loved his garden, but he needed a purpose in life and nothing gave him more pleasure than getting the maps out to plot a route to where you were going next.'

I swallowed hard. It was a relief to know that I hadn't contributed to Dad's death. Suddenly, I felt a stab of grief.

'If only he'd managed to give up smoking!' I cried out.

The doctor gave me a resigned look. 'But who's to know whether the stress of giving up might have killed him quicker than carrying on?'

I have no idea whether this might have been true or not, but it made me feel better. Dad had been smoking 20 to 40 cigarettes every single day since he was 14 – and he'd been a miner for years, too. I could see that his lungs might have packed up at the first sign of a break from all of that congestion.

Back at home, I opened up the bureau to look through Dad's papers.

'Where do I start?' I thought, leafing through piles of bills and documents.

I took charge, registering the death with my mother and going to probate. That's when I started to look after Mum, really. I took over from my father as the head of the family.

What was strange was that in the days that followed everything in the house started to fall apart. The electrics went. The fire broke. The electrician nearly had a stroke when he saw the state of the wiring in the basement – 'The whole lot could have burst into flames at any moment!' It was as if Dad had kept things ticking over with his make-do-and-mend approach – but only just – and as soon as he was gone, it all collapsed.

It made Mum furious: 'I can't believe he left the house in this state! Why didn't he think about me and how I was going to get along without him? How *could* he? And his papers . . . he didn't sort anything out, he's left it all to us to do.'

Her anger was a stage of the grieving process, but I'd never seen anything like it. She was bursting with rage.

'I don't think he knew he was going yesterday,' I said, trying to calm her down. 'Stop being so angry.'

Mum didn't cry – not in front of me, anyway. She didn't know what to do, nobody did. I didn't really get a moment to grieve, I felt I had to be strong for my mother and there was so much to think about.

A few days after Dad had died, while we were discussing the funeral with Janet and Tony, Janet asked Mum what she was planning to do now.

'You can't still live here, it's falling apart,' Janet said, looking around the room. Her gaze swept over the shabby, worn furniture and Dad's various patch-up jobs, from the chipped tiles around the fireplace to the back door that wouldn't shut.

Janet's question got Mum thinking, 'What *am* I going to do? Where are they going to put me?'

I think my sister was assuming, with Mum being 62, it would be sensible to sell the house, split the money and move her into sheltered accommodation, like Gran. I knew my mother wouldn't take to that plan, though.

While Mum was out of the room, I said, 'Why don't we all put £5,000 in? We can do the house up and she can stay here.'

Tony and Janet shook their heads – they didn't have the money.

'I don't have it, either,' I said, 'but we could get a loan? Just to make sure our mother is all right?'

But they couldn't do it, and that's when I knew it would be me who looked after our mother, because they didn't have the income.

Mum came back into the room and started serving up tea.

'So, what do you think you will do?' Janet pressed.

'Jane's going to buy this house,' Mum said.

It was the first I'd heard of it, but I said, 'Yes, I am,' just like that. 'This is my responsibility now,' I thought, and I took it very seriously.

'Right, this is what we'll do then,' I said. 'I'll buy the house and we'll put the money you get from the purchase into doing it up.'

Still, I couldn't help feeling curious about where Mum had suddenly got this idea from. After the others had gone, I said, 'What made you say that at teatime?'

'Well, you're the only one in the family who doesn't own a house and you need to start putting roots down,' she told me.

'I'll give you a good price as long as you make sure I've got a roof over my head.'

'Good girl,' I thought – Mum was a canny woman.

The first thing I got rid of was the coal fire.

'That's going,' I said.

It was all very well having a coal allowance with Dad's pit pension, but we were up and down those flipping stairs to the cellar like pit ponies in slippers and the dust got everywhere.

Mum was so happy, she practically gurgled with delight: 'I won't have to get up and do the grate every morning!' she said.

With the money we got from the mortgage company when Mum sold the house to me, combined with my savings, we got new central heating, a new boiler, new curtains and carpets; we had a new conservatory built and a beautiful gas fire installed with real flames. It took a good few months, but the house was absolutely beautiful by the time it was finished.

In the meantime, Tony came with me to get the van mended. The mechanic at the garage took one look and said, 'Engine's blown. You can't have driven this.'

'Well, we did. We got home from Skegness,' I said, describing how it had stopped dead and then started again.

He gave me a funny look. 'That bang you heard was the big ends going. The engine is completely seized up, you can't have driven it,' he declared adamantly. 'It's impossible.'

Now that got me thinking and I mulled it over with my mother later. At the time we broke down, I had thought only Dad could have fixed the engine. Now I was convinced that he must have somehow got it started remotely: 'He was making sure I got home safely,' I said.

'He needed to come and get you after all,' Mum said with a laugh.

It was a strange time for all of us and I have some vivid memories of the days and weeks that followed.

'I had a dream about your dad last night,' Mum said at breakfast, about three weeks later. 'He was with his father on a farm and there were horses in the fields – in particular, a white horse.'

'What a lovely dream! He's obviously passed over and met up with his dad,' I said.

It was comforting to think of Dad in a countryside setting. He loved the land and, with this in mind, Mum decided to scatter his ashes on his allotment. We all went up there with her after the cremation, but when we arrived, it was so long since anybody had been there that, at first, we weren't sure which allotment was Dad's.

'It's definitely the one with the shed,' I said.

My ex-boyfriend Richard's shed was still standing and I have no doubt it would be to this day if the allotments hadn't been cleared to make way for houses.

'Oh good,' said Wendy. 'Can you imagine if we scattered them on the wrong allotment?'

I looked at her and started to giggle. It was the thought of Dad's ashes blowing over somebody else's carrots, I think. Wendy's got a right sense of humour and the moment she caught my eye, she was giggling as well. Well, once we'd started, we couldn't stop: it was supposed to be this really sombre moment and we were on the floor because we were laughing that much. Eventually, Mum turned around and said, 'Will you two shut up?'

It was the only time I let off steam in all those weeks after Dad passed. I was still in shock, I think – I had to look after Mum and be strong for her and now I had the responsibility of getting a mortgage so I bottled my emotions up and kept going. I told myself that I couldn't stop: I had to carry on as normal, there was so much to do and I had to make sure Mum was all right.

It's funny how life goes on and the wheels keep turning, no

matter what. You think the world will come to a halt when something momentous happens in your life, but it doesn't, not for a second. It was very hard going back to work. People were used to seeing my father with me everywhere and now they were constantly saying, 'Where's your dad?'

Sometimes I couldn't bring myself to explain that he had died: 'He's not here today,' I'd say.

The grief caught up with me one night during a gig. Onstage at the Albion Road club in Rotherham, my voice dwindled to a grating rasp halfway through the song. I felt my throat constrict and a lump form near my tonsils.

'Excuse me,' I croaked, leaving the stage.

I rushed into my dressing room and sat with my head in my hands.

'I'm ill,' I thought. 'I'm going to die.'

I went to the doctor, who said it wasn't a physical problem, but an emotional reaction to the loss of my father. I only half-believed her, but I felt very listless and wasn't interested in going out or seeing anybody. Dave and I broke up. The days passed and still I couldn't sing. Worried I'd lost my voice forever, I stayed at home and read books for days on end. I've always loved reading: if it's a good book, I get completely swept up into the story as if I'm actually experiencing it myself.

One of the novels I read had a scene between a little girl and her father. There was nothing to it, really, but it touched something within me and a flood of memories came rushing back: of Dad teaching me to tie my shoelaces, of feeling like a princess as I danced the waltz with him, of telling him to shush when he boomed 'Delilah' out in the club sing-song on a Saturday night. As I thought about my lovely father, I felt a surge of gratitude that we'd had such a close relationship and one minute I was smiling, the next plunging into the depths of darkness and loss. Overcome by grief, I started to cry and couldn't stop.

Jane Ann Fenton, my great grandmother, the daughter of a French nobleman.

Mum, tickled pink, with her big sister, my aunt Nancy.

Dad looking thin in his paratrooper uniform, the only evidence of his wartime experiences.

Mum and Dad looking slightly stunned on their wedding day in 1953.

Aunt Nancy, Mum,
Aunt Barbara and
Gran in the middle,
at a family party.

Antony, my Lithuanian
grandfather on
Dad's side, with Janet.

Dad, my brother Tony
and sister Janet, before
I came along to
annoy them.

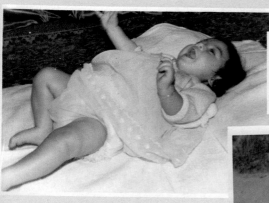

With Gran and Mum on the beach in Monifieth: our best holiday ever.

Singing the Petula Clark hit 'Downtown' when I was one – I started young!

Me aged 5.

Posing in front of Dad's old van wearing my new dress for the holidays.

Uncle Harold, Mum,
Uncle Stan, Gran,
Auntie Wynn and Dad.

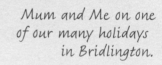

Mum and Me on one
of our many holidays
in Bridlington.

Junior clerk at Wades:
it felt fantastic to be
earning my own wage.

1981: Me and Ed – the
barmaid from Wakefield
and the drummer from
Liquid Gold.

New Year's Eve knees up
at Gran's. I'd just finished
working at Pussycat.

Garry, Dad, Mum, Janet, Me
and Aunt Nancy raising a
glass of Christmas bubbly.

As my roadie, Dad came everywhere with me on the Northern club circuit.

Me and Dad off ballroom dancing at the club.

On stage, wearing a dress from the bargain rail of an upmarket Leeds boutique.

Singing 'Bali Ha'i' during 'The World Goes Round' show on the Zenith.

Our wonderful holiday in Jersey, where my mother made us laugh all day long.

Me and the cast onboard the Zenith.

Mum's first cruise and she was hooked!

Celebrity Cruises

MV CENTURY
CREW ID

Name: MC DONALD JANE

Birthdate: 04-04-63 Expiry Date: 01-03-96

Position: VOCALIST

Every night was party night onboard the Century.

Mum heard me sobbing from outside the bedroom door: 'At last!' she thought, as she told me later. 'Now she can start to heal.'

I cried for hours and hours, letting out great racking, howling sobs.

Mum was right, as always: after I had let out all that pent-up emotion, my voice began to improve and, within a few days, it was back to normal. But I couldn't go back out to the clubs again. The idea of people asking me about Dad was bad enough, the thought of drying up onstage even worse – I was terrified it might happen again.

I wasn't sure what to do next. I'd had an offer of work on the *Horizon*'s sister ship, the *Zenith*, but felt I couldn't leave my mother to cope alone. I needed to work, though; I felt torn in two. When Mum suggested going over to Rotherham, where my mate, Steve Holbrook, was holding a psychic demonstration, I agreed to go, even though I wouldn't really call myself a spiritualist. I'm more of a humanist than anything, yet at the same time I know there is something out there because I've had a lot of proof – so much of what has happened to me has been predicted.

Steve was a renowned psychic by then and, when we arrived for the demonstration, the hall was full and there were people queuing round the block.

'We'll never get in,' Mum said. 'Let's go home and have a cup of tea.'

We were just walking back to the car when Steve came out the back door to enjoy a fag before he went on.

'Jane, what are you doing here?' he said.

'We've come to see you, but it's sold out, so we're going home for tea,' I explained.

'Come in,' he said, ushering us through the back door. 'I'll find you a seat somewhere.'

We were sitting up in the gods, looking down on the proceedings, when the speaker said, 'I'm looking for a lady who has just lost her dad.'

Mum started nudging me; I didn't move.

A few hands went up.

'No, it was very early in the morning that he passed,' the speaker said. There was a pause, then she looked our way: 'It's you with the red coat on up there.'

She came straight to me.

'You've just lost your dad.'

I nodded.

'You've just lost your voice as well, haven't you? He's saying to me here, "It's just emotion."'

'Okay,' I said, biting my lip.

'There's definitely something about a ship, and there's nothing wrong with your voice. He says you have to go on a ship, because you need to let your mother grieve and you have to grieve yourself.'

'Right.'

'Is this your mother beside you?' she asked. 'He's saying, "I'm really sorry for everything I did, and I apologise, but I'm with my dad now, on the farm with the horses."'

My mother went pale. 'Oh, my God!' she gasped.

We were both shocked to the core.

'I can't believe you told me about that dream,' I said, on our way home in the car.

'So, it's back to the ships for you,' Mum said.

'But what about you? Will you be all right?' I asked.

She smiled. 'Yes, I will,' she said, all of a sudden seeming happier. 'I want you to go away and travel the world and write me letters, telling me about all the wonderful things you see.'

The need to escape overcame me in a huge rush of feeling: I

was 30 years old, new worlds were beckoning. 'That's me finished now with the clubs,' I thought. 'That time is over.'

The next day, I took my PA to the place where I bought it and sold it back to them. 'Right, that's me done,' I thought.

A few weeks later, I packed up my things and ran away to sea.

9

What A Wonderful World

When you spend time on a ship, there's a certain place you will always go to read a book or have a drink or a coffee. Often you find it on your first day and then you'll revisit it every day after that, because it's your space. I had a favourite chair up on deck, where I'd go with my book and quietly bask in the sunshine. It seemed I was living a charmed life, travelling the world, making new friends and singing every night.

I was constantly writing to my mother in Wakefield and saying, 'You will never guess what I did!' There were so many amazing experiences to tell Mum about. As we cruised through the turquoise waters of the Caribbean, I explored tropical islands, sunbathed on palm-fringed beaches, swam with dolphins and learned to scuba dive in fantastical underground landscapes. Back onboard the ship, living in a melting pot of nationalities and cultures gave me an endless supply of eye-opening stories and dramas with which to entertain her. They could have filled a book, let alone my letters to Mum, who looked forward to weekly instalments of tales from the *Zenith*.

The job was fantastic: the productions on the *Zenith* went from intimate, informal piano bar recitals to all-out Vegas-style spectacles. The big shows were my favourite – they dazzled audiences with glitz and glamour. The theatres were always full, which was great for the performers, and the acoustics were fabulous, as good as any West End venue so you could really give it your best. While my time in the clubs had been good for learning how to capture the attention of an audience, the ships were a crash course in different genres of music and how to expand my range.

The cast of the main shows included 20 dancers and two singers: myself and a male vocalist, Mick Mullane. Mick and I got on well from the moment we were put together. He had years of experience on the ships and had once been a member of a harmony group that I'd seen on telly countless times during the 1980s.

'Stutz Bear Cats?' I said, when I first met him. 'You're joking, aren't you? My mum and I used to watch you on Jim Davidson and Des O'Connor.'

Mick was an amazing singer and generous with it. He would let you shine. Our voices blended well and we brought the house in with songs like 'A Whole New World' from the Disney film *Aladdin*. The audience loved the idea of cruising to new places while Mick and I serenaded them with lines like, 'I can show you the world . . .'

Things got even better when the production company, Matrix, were brought in as the owner, Al Radcliffe, put on the best shows in the business. Al seemed to know exactly what people wanted. My favourite show, still to this day, was called 'The World Goes Round' and featured songs from all over the world, crowd-pleasers like 'Hernando's Hideaway', 'One Night In Bangkok' and 'Bali Ha'i'. When we were sailing from Bermuda to New York, with an audience mainly made up of US citizens, we'd finish the show with 'Coming To America' – clever thinking on Al's part as it instantly made people feel patriotic. Our outfits were always fantastic and, for the finale, we wore an all-American combination of short white skirts, red sequinned boots and Stetsons. They looked sensational under ultraviolet light, especially when we started swinging our lassoes. It tore the balls off the audience – the whole place would stand up and go berserk.

We worked incredibly hard. You could never slacken off because of something known as the show ratings, which were designed to keep everybody on their toes. Passengers gave their feedback on our performances by filling out forms that were left in their cabins and then the production team calculated each performer's overall ratings based on their scores and comments. If you got less than 7.6 out of 10 points, three times in a row, you were out. You had to leave the ship immediately. I dreaded the days the show ratings came out, even though Mick and I consistently scored over 9.5 and the audiences clearly loved us. Terrified of a dip in popularity, I worked hard to make every show better than my last.

Like the *Horizon*, the *Zenith* was a happy ship and everything was done to make sure that the passengers had a great time. But things weren't always rosy below stairs. There were rules that didn't make sense, because the bosses hadn't thought them through properly. For instance, the dancers always went to bed late after a show, so it was crazy that they had to get up at the crack of dawn to be on the gangway to greet people as they got on and off the ship. They had a curfew that was set to ensure they got to bed in time to have a good night's sleep, but nobody seemed to take into account the huge adrenaline rush that comes after doing a rehearsal and a show, sometimes two shows – you can't just go to bed and sleep after a performance, it takes time to wind down.

After weeks of rehearsing with bleary-eyed dancers, I took it to the captain.

'They're half asleep most of the time,' I told him. 'Why on earth would you put them on early duties?'

'Because the passengers have seen them the night before, so they know who they are on their first morning,' he said.

I wasn't convinced. 'And what about their curfew?' I went on. 'You're not going to get the best from your people if you try forcing them to go to bed early. Trust me, the adrenaline rush after a show means they're going to be up late in the staff bar anyway. If they go on like this, they'll be fit for nothing.'

'I can extend their curfew,' he said, 'but they'll still have to get up early to do the gangway.' He paused, and his eyes twinkled with amusement. 'Unless you've got a better suggestion?'

'Well, I've been thinking,' I said. 'Why not swap the duties with the childcare people who've gone to bed at nine o'clock?'

He tried it and it worked much better, so I started suggesting other changes. I felt I was really helping to improve life for the cast until I had a warning from the bosses in London to stop telling the captain what to do. I had too much power on the ship – if I didn't watch it, I'd get the sack.

The captain seemed oblivious to all this and every few weeks he would come and find me and say, 'Do you fancy coming up for some fish?' He enjoyed angling and used to catch all sorts of weird and wonderful creatures off the side of the ship.

'All right,' I'd say, because you got the best food on the captain's table.

Towards the end of dinner, he'd say, 'Have you had any more thoughts about how things on the ship could be improved?' and he'd have that twinkle in his eye again. I think he was interested in my ideas because I saw things from a business point of view.

'Well, why don't you let the dancers go out into the disco after the show?' I said one night.

He frowned. 'Why would that be a good idea?'

'It would transform the disco!' I exclaimed. 'The officers will come in because the dancers are in and, if the officers are in, the women will come in and the men will follow. It will be heaving. Think of the extra drinks revenue.'

The main shows were staged on formal dining nights, so people were already dressed up. After going to dinner and watching the show, they wanted something else to do. Nobody was keen to go to bed, least of all the dancers, who were also dressed to the nines and raring to go.

So I staked out the disco a couple of times. I saw passengers wander up for a dance, look across an empty mist of dry ice and flashing lights and think, 'No.'

'It's completely dead,' I told the captain. 'The dancers need to be in there, boogeying with the passengers and creating an atmosphere.'

'Okay, we'll give it a go,' he said eventually.

He tried it, and hey presto, everybody went to the disco after the main shows. It was fantastic, the place was absolutely buzzing. The officers looked fabulous in their white suits, the dancers worked off their adrenaline high on the dance floor and the passengers had the time of their lives. Rules on ships have tightened up since then and officers aren't allowed to dance with passengers, but nobody was worried about that sort of thing in those days. When I remember those nights, it makes me think that I've lived through the best of times: when things were slightly un-PC, but not offensive. At least, *I* never found anything offensive, although perhaps that's because I chose to live in a rose-tinted bubble.

It was party central on the *Zenith* and we had a lot of fun. We used to stay up every night and still go on and do 12 shows a week.

'I didn't take a year off to go backpacking, I worked my passage,' I used to joke. 'I went on a gap year for eight years, but got paid for it.'

*

Every week on the dot Mum would send me out packages from home: videos of *Emmerdale*, *Coronation Street*, *EastEnders* and anything else she thought I would like, along with a newsy letter packed with Wakefield gossip and a copy of *Take A Break* magazine. It was all very well seeing the world and meeting different people, but the home girl in me longed for a couple of hours in the living room at Silcoates Street, watching television with my mum, and I couldn't help missing my family and friends at times like Easter and Christmas, on birthdays and anniversaries. Mum's packages were very special to me: she was sending me a little bit of home each week to keep me going through my patches of homesickness.

'I've got *Coronation Street*, do you want to come and watch it?' I'd say to the other Brits and we'd get big bottles of wine and have girly nights in my cabin, giggling about what Ken Barlow was getting up to.

Onboard romances thrived and people were constantly getting together, splitting up and going off with someone else; half the time you couldn't keep up with all their comings and goings. I was surrounded by friends – I was everybody's mate, and a shoulder to cry on when their affairs hit the rocks – but I must have given out a 'no' when it came to romance because I didn't get that sort of attention, or not much, anyway. Whether I was wary after my divorce or still grieving my father, I don't know, but I think people sensed not to even go there.

I couldn't understand it because I'd always had boyfriends. Late one night, when I was sitting in the bar with the ship's photographer, saying goodnight to the girls as they coupled up and went off to their cabins, I took a sip of wine and asked him, 'Why doesn't anybody come on to me?'

'Because you're different,' he said.

'What do you mean?'

'You're not the sort of person to have a fling with, you're marriage material.'

I was mortified. 'I'm not! Why do you say that? I don't want to marry anyone. I've tried that, it wasn't for me.'

He shrugged. 'That's just how it looks to me.'

In my cabin that night, I thought about what he had said. Was it true? Were my defences up because I secretly wanted to settle down again? There's a part of every woman that longs for a Prince Charming to sweep her off her feet, yet none of my dreams were about meeting handsome princes. I was far more intent on furthering my career than walking off into the sunset with a man. I wanted to develop my act, get a headline spot on a ship, win more awards . . . my ambitions were entirely focused on my work.

I didn't dwell on it – I've always had a firm belief in things working out for the best yet something shifted in me that night. The dancers were all in their early twenties, but I was in my thirties now and I decided that it was time to take a fresh look at the future. I was fiercely independent, but perhaps it would be nice to have a man come along who would look after me?

'I can't do this forever,' I thought. 'Maybe it's time to change.'

Mystical books were popular then and we went through a phase of passing round *The Celestine Prophecy* and other books that looked into ancient beliefs about enlightenment. A lot of them developed the idea that, if you adjusted your attitude and energy vibration, you could get what you wanted from life once you had recognised and visualised it.

One of my friends, a Canadian girl, was a firm believer in all of this.

'Write down what you want in a man and put it out there,' she advised me. 'If the universe doesn't know what you're after, it won't come along.'

I didn't take it particularly seriously, but one evening in my cabin, I wrote a list of my ideal man's attributes: 'Tall, blond, blue or green eyes; strong, protective, good job . . .'

Putting the list in a drawer, I turned my attention back to my career. By now, Mick and I had a really good reputation as a duo and, when we received yet another score of 9.7 on ratings day, I said to him, 'I think we've proved ourselves here. Isn't it about time we stepped up a level?'

The timing seemed right, especially when Celebrity Cruises, the company who owned the *Zenith*, announced they were building two gigantic new cruise ships, the *Century* and the *Galaxy*. Everything about these ships would be bigger and better than ever before, we were told – including the shows, which would be Broadway style and standard. We were thrilled when the company's entertainments director approached us about working on the *Century*'s inaugural cruise, offering us headline status and a lot more money than we were currently earning, as long as we agreed to leave Matrix and work directly for Celebrity. Also included in the package was a passenger cabin, which was a massive incentive for me: after years of living in cramped conditions, it was something I really longed for.

When Mick and I told Matrix we were leaving them because we wanted to move up to the next level, Al Radcliffe tried to lure us back with an offer of work with Silversea, a first-class, round-the-world cruising line. Silversea were the ultimate company to work for if you were a cruise ship entertainer because they treated their performers really well. Passenger cabins, free booze . . . the works. Now, we had two amazing offers and didn't know which to choose, so after a lot of discussion and agonising, we decided to go with whichever contract came through first. There was to be a wait of several months in either case, for various reasons, so Mick went off to do some recording and I flew home and signed up to the summer season at the Maid Marian.

It was always wonderful to go home to Silcoates Street. I experienced such a strong sense of comfort and belonging as I stepped through the front door and smelled Mum's cooking. With my father's passing, I had become much closer to my mother and hated being away from her for too long, especially now that my contracts tended to last six months rather than three. I would be a couple of hours from Wakefield while I did the summer season, but at least I could see Mum every week.

It was strange to be back at the Maid Marian. Although I loved the gig and felt happy to be among the Northern Working Men's Club crowd – the audiences I regarded as 'my people' – I didn't like the feeling of going backwards in my career. That summer of 1995, I had some cracking nights on the stage and it was all grist to the mill for what was to come later, but I could feel myself straining to move onwards and upwards to face new challenges.

As the season came to an end, Mum and I dropped in on Gran for a cup of tea on my day off. My grandmother was growing a little frail now, but she still loved a natter and to hear about my adventures at sea. I'd spent long enough in Skegness to be looking forward to going away again, I told her, even if I didn't know where I was going. I was hoping for the job with Silversea, because I fancied seeing Asia and Australia.

'No, that's not your destiny on that one,' Gran declared. 'You've got to stay on the one with the cross.'

'Oh, please don't say that,' I said, dismayed. 'That's Celebrity, the company I'm with at the moment. I've decided it's Silversea I want to go with.'

'No, don't go to the other one, Jane,' she insisted. 'Don't want what you can't have, because you're meant to stay on the ship with the cross.'

I was really miffed. I didn't take Gran's predictions all that seriously, but it wasn't very often that she spoke with so much certainty.

'And you're going to meet a man called Henry,' she continued.

'Henry?' I looked at Mum and started to giggle. 'I don't think so,' I said. 'Henry? No, that doesn't sound right.'

I had to wonder at Gran's words in the weeks to come when delays with the Silversea job meant that Mick and I decided to accept Celebrity's offer, as she had predicted. After I'd finished the summer season, we flew to New York to start rehearsals for our shows on the *Century*. I soon forgot about the Silversea job. Celebrity treated us very well in New York and it was clear from the number of staff they were employing and the show's high production values they had made a serious investment in their new venture. I felt like I was progressing again.

The next eight weeks were a whirlwind of activity and hard work.

'We're taking Broadway to the high seas,' the director told us, 'and you're the stars of the show!'

It was really exciting, but the level of investment meant that every single aspect of our performance had to be perfect in the eyes of the production team, who kept changing our songs and introducing more complex harmonies. A perfectionist by nature, I sympathised with their attention to detail, but felt they could have put more trust in Mick and me as artists to know what we were doing. And no matter how hard they tried to fine-tune our performances, they couldn't fix the show, which was where the real problem lay.

The first show we rehearsed was part of a repertoire that had been devised by a group of creatives who didn't seem to have your typical cruise audience in mind. The concepts and themes were just that bit too clever and obscure; they didn't have the escapist element of Al Radcliffe's productions, and the humour was sometimes a bit too close to the bone. A few of the jokes seemed to be unkind to older people and bigger people. Mick in a fat suit, anyone? Me in curlers and slippers, moaning about being old and ugly? Certain segments were fantastic, especially one section we worked on with Disney, but many others didn't gel and there were lots of things that didn't make sense.

Mick and I made allowances for the fact that this was the first time Celebrity's production team had worked directly with performers. It is hard to put a show repertoire together, even for the most experienced producers; things can go wrong, and usually do, and some of their people were new to it and bound to make mistakes.

I didn't feel so forgiving, however, when a few weeks later, we joined the spanking new, 70,000-ton *Century*, the ship that was to be our home for the next year, and I was shown to the tiniest crew cabin I had ever seen.

Immediately, I went to find the entertainments director: 'Where are the passenger cabins you promised us?' I asked.

He shrugged. 'I'm afraid the ship is overbooked, we had to give them to the doctors.'

'You're telling me you've overbooked a ship that has the capacity to take on 1,800 passengers?'

Having a nice cabin was a big deal for me. It had been promised as part of my package and it was a mistake on the part of the production company to go back on their word. As a rule, when you're not looking after members of the cast on a cruise ship, the problems start to pile up, especially when you're creating a new show. They just needed to fix that one thing, but they didn't, and so it put us on a negative footing, which had a domino effect because I was less inclined to sort things out when they went wrong – and things went wrong all the time once we were on the ship.

It didn't take a genius to see that the show wasn't working well. Soon we were putting in long hours of overtime to cobble together disaster plans for setbacks or malfunctions. Many things about the show were too complex, from the musical arrangements to the staging, and we had our fair share of technical problems: the trap door broke, the special effects computer froze, the state-of-the-art revolving stage only revolved twice during the whole contract. So we spent our ever-decreasing rehearsal time trying to pick up the pieces.

Our saving grace was that we had a great cast – and a great cast will make anything work. Our dance captain, Katie Foura-cre, was only teeny, but by God, she was good! Katie and I became firm friends and she brought out my sense of humour to such a degree that, whenever we shared the stage, I'd be told off for giggling. We'd give each other a look as if to say, 'I can't believe we're doing this,' and I'd be off into gales of stifled laughter.

Production staff came and went and I took over as the sing-ing captain on several shows, because I could read music and play the piano. I was put in charge of a very young cast and enjoyed being a mother hen to them. They used to come to me for things they didn't want to go to the doctor for, because everybody knew everybody. I kept a supply in my cabin that they could come and get discreetly, saving embarrassment.

I'd hear a knock at the door: 'Can I . . . ?'

I used to sort them out. I was a terror!

If the cast hadn't been such a good group of people, I don't think I would have lasted on the *Century* as long as I did. We partied hard and had a lot of laughs, which helped offset the pain of trying to meet the producers' constant demands. But our free time was very limited, because every few days we were having to learn new routines and, in some cases, whole new shows. As our opportunities to escape the ship for a few hours diminished and the technical problems mounted up, tempers became seriously frayed. What made matters worse was that our popularity seemed to plunge with every new production and the show ratings suffered through no fault of our own.

There was a 50-minute magic section that would have been an amazing spectacle if the props hadn't been too big to fit backstage. Eleven props became three props, and then those went too, because there wasn't enough room on the ship to store them. All this at a reputed cost of a quarter of a million wasted dollars – and I was still sleeping in my tiny, cramped cabin down in the depths of the ship. The magic show ended up as a weird hotchpotch of scenarios depicting the battle between good and evil, with dancing skeletons, exploding coffins and multiple references to torture. Mick and I played wizards and, as I stood in a box at the front of the stage, waiting to spring out in a puff of smoke at a sign from him, I couldn't help thinking, 'I'm a singer, what the hell am I doing in here?'

Hell was a central theme and it was too dark for our audiences, the final straw being the appearance onstage of dancers wearing striped suits that bore an unnerving resemblance to concentration camp uniforms. It visibly upset many of the elderly Jewish people watching, who were no doubt haunted by memories of the Holocaust, and sometimes there wouldn't be anyone left in the theatre by the end of the show. We all longed for the simple glitz and glamour of the Matrix productions.

It was infuriating at the time, but I see it from a more sympathetic point of view now. It is hard to put on a show and take risks. Sometimes a creative vision doesn't work in reality and naturally, you have to make mistakes to go forward. But I wish the production team had consulted the cast a little more, because shows never work when they are produced by money men and accountants. Managers are not artists and sometimes the artists know better, yet nobody listened when we tried to offer up answers and solutions.

*

On 14 February 1996, I decided I'd had enough of the *Century*. It wasn't tripping over honeymooning couples that finally did it – although it wasn't helpful to be reminded of my eternally single status, aged 32, on Valentine's Day – it was the sinking feeling that my career had come to a standstill. Several months earlier, I'd pressed the production team to give me my own show and they had reworked my schedule to allow me a few solo slots, but it wasn't enough. I wanted to be the ship's headline act and felt confident that it was the role I deserved.

A few days earlier, I had been standing by the side of the stage with the cruise director, watching the star act, when I'd muttered, 'Why isn't she going for the audience? What's she doing over there? I could do better than that!'

'Just stop whingeing and go and do it then!' he snapped, sounding exactly like my mother.

'You're right,' I said. 'I'm going to do it.'

Spurred on by a mixture of anger and ambition, I went back to my cabin and wrote my letter of resignation there and then. I slipped it under a book by my bedside, intending to give it in to the office the following day, and picked up my pen again. Next, I wrote to my old mate from the clubs, Sue Ravey. I'd heard that Sue's sister, June, had passed away at the age of 52. She died of bone cancer.

'I'm going to come back. Do you want to team up?' I asked her.

Sitting back in my chair, it struck me that every day some-thing happens in your life that presents you with a choice and it's up to you what you do with that choice. It's easy to play safe and stick with what we know.

'But I'm wild,' I thought. 'I refuse to play safe.'

At the end of Valentine's Day, as if sensing the waves of frus-tration and claustrophobia coming from the cast, the captain decided to give us the whole of the following day off, which was practically unheard of. To say that we needed to flop on a sun-soaked tropical beach makes us sound like spoilt brats and actually a freezing-cold stroll along the front at Blackpool would have been just as welcome if it had distracted us from our tired bodies and whirring minds. Anything to get away from relentlessly running through new routines to replace routines that had been reworked and replaced several times already.

When I'm feeling low, it doesn't usually take long for me to bounce back. At the end of a day spent lazing with the dancers on the beach I felt refreshed and renewed. 'I'm definitely going to resign,' I thought as I showered and dressed for the evening. It was the right decision and I vowed to deliver my letter in the morning.

I ran my fingers through my hair and winked at my reflection in the mirror. Then I went up to the bar and my whole life changed in an instant.

10

The Way You Look Tonight

The night I met Henrik Brixen I was ready for a bit of romance in my life. I hadn't had a serious relationship in years, it was time.

'I'm looking for the man of my dreams,' I confided in my friends. 'He's got to be tall, blond, handsome, strong and ambitious . . .'

They laughed. 'Not asking much, then?'

My friend, Günter Boodenstein, was on the lookout for me. Günter oversaw the ship's engines and I often had a drink with him and his wife, Angelica, when she came aboard; they were lovely people and we became very pally.

I bumped into Günter on the gangway as I was leaving the ship to go to the beach with the dancers on my day off. 'Waiting for someone?' I asked him.

His face lit up. 'Jane! You're just the person I wanted to see. I have someone called Henrik Brixen coming onboard to have a look at the boiler.'

'Oh, yes? Up my street?'

He smiled. '*Right* up your street.'

A boiler man didn't sound very promising, but I was prepared to keep an open mind. Günter and I agreed to meet up in the bar later and I went off to the beach.

*

When Henrik arrived, Günter told him, 'There's a girl you should meet.'

Was there something in the stars that night? There was definitely some kind of magic, because the air seemed to glitter as Günter introduced me to Henrik. We liked each other instantly, and when we met up again at midnight, after I'd finished the show, we liked each other even more. He stayed on the ship for two weeks, which gave us time to get to know each other a little. Relationships onboard ship were frowned upon by the bosses, so we had to sneak in and out of each other's cabin when we weren't working and steal kisses in dark corners when we thought nobody was looking. For me, this just added to the excitement of falling for someone after so long on my own. It was wonderful! I had butterflies in my stomach day and night.

I felt powerfully drawn to this tall, handsome Dane. He seemed to possess every single one of the qualities on my wish list, from good looks to drive and ambition. By the time he left the *Century* at the end of his two weeks aboard I was completely besotted and, when I noticed that people saluted him as he walked on and off the ship, it only added to the attraction.

'Ooh, he's got some power,' I thought.

I soon realised that Henrik wasn't your ordinary nuts-and-bolts boiler man. Originally, he had gone to sea as a first engineer on an oil tanker and had a raft of salty tales to tell of pirates in the South China Seas and icebergs in the Antarctic. He and his business partner, Ken, had met as colleagues in a company that specialised in troubleshooting ships' boiler systems. Henrik was so bright that he became one of the youngest engineers in his field. Known as 'The Kid', he was in such demand that his company flew him all over the world to trace and correct boiler system faults. After a few years, he and Ken took a risk and branched out on their own, moving to America and setting up a company to focus their expertise on cruise ships, which is why they based themselves in Fort Lauderdale, a hub for the cruising industry. I couldn't get over how brave and driven Henrik was. Not content with the success he had already achieved, he was now looking to expand internationally.

All of a sudden, the *Century*'s boiler started going wrong quite a lot. I ripped up my letter of resignation and decided to work out the final seven weeks of my contract.

'What's happening on that ship?' one of the girls in Henrik's Fort Lauderdale office asked him. 'Have you got a girlfriend on there or something?'

Henrik stared blankly into the distance. He wasn't one to discuss his private life with his friends, let alone work colleagues.

'Oh no, I shouldn't have said that,' she thought. 'I've over-stepped the mark.' She'd been worried that he might fire her, as she told me some months later at his company's staff party.

It wasn't serious at first but, over Henrik's next few visits to check on the boilers, things blossomed. We courted the old-fashioned way, which was lovely, really. Yet while I couldn't hide my delight that I was dating this gorgeous man, Henrik played quite hard to get. The *Century* returned to Fort Lauderdale every week and sometimes he was waiting for me, sometimes not, depending on his work schedule. It wouldn't occur to him to let me know because we weren't in a serious relationship. But I would be up on deck looking out for him as the ship approached the quay, straining to catch a glimpse of my handsome engineer, my heart going like the clappers.

Still, I got used to his ways.

As I fell headlong in love, I tried to ignore the possibility that Henrik wasn't so sure of his feelings for me. 'Would you like to see me sing?' I asked him, when my next solo show came up.

He didn't know what to expect as he sat down with Günter before the show. 'Please make her be okay, because I can't go out with her if she's rubbish. And then you started to sing,' he told me afterwards, 'and I thought, "Thank God for that. She's pretty good." '

'Oh, thank you,' I said happily.

'Is that a compliment?' I thought later.

I would probably have liked Henrik to be more demonstrative with his feelings, but his reserved manner didn't worry me as much as it might have bothered someone else, because it reminded me of my father. My dad's abrupt ways had disguised his loving nature – when it came to me, at least – and I suspected maybe Henrik had a similar kind of personality. He was a few years younger than me and had been on his own for almost as long as I had, all through moving to America and setting up his business with Ken. It was up to me to encourage him to be more forthcoming and expressive. Still, I took care not to rush him in case it made him turn tail and bolt.

As we got to know each other better, Henrik said, 'I've just got a new apartment in Fort Lauderdale. Would you like to come and have a look at it?'

'That would be nice,' I replied, trying to hide my excitement.

Henrik was quite hard to read, but I took this invitation as a sign that we might be getting more serious. The following Saturday, he was waiting for me on the quayside, leaning on the bonnet of his Mustang.

'He's here!' I shouted, waving frantically from the deck. My heart was in my throat as US Customs made their usual time-consuming checks before we could disembark. 'Hurry up!' I willed them. Eventually, we were given leave to go and I bounded down the gangway towards Henrik like an overexcited puppy. He was much more restrained, but I could tell he was enjoying my enthusiasm as he drove me along Fort Lauderdale's palm-lined boulevards to his apartment. As we sped along, I chattered about the passing sights like a first-time tourist. Suddenly I was seeing the city through fresh eyes, as somewhere I might, hopefully, live with Henrik.

Henrik's apartment wasn't big or grand, but it was well designed and nicely furnished. When you walked inside, you entered an open-plan space with a leather sofa and a black and Crome (Danish) leather recliner, which was very comfortable and great for reading. It was very much a modern bachelor pad. There were blinds at every window, not a curtain in sight, and the kitchen was done out in grey, black and Crome. Best of all, his block had a private pool.

'This is fabulous,' I thought.

I sensed that Henrik could tackle anything, because he was so focused on what he wanted to do. I found this attractive in the same way that I found his power attractive; I liked the idea of being with someone ambitious. When he told me that business was booming and he and Ken were hoping to expand, I thought, 'I could help him. I could push him forward to even greater success.'

I rang my mother and told her all about him. 'He's handsome and he's got great taste and he's got his own company and drives a Mustang . . .'

'Hang on, did you say his name was Henry?' she interrupted.

'Henri*k*,' I said.

'Didn't Gran say you were going to meet a man called Henry?'

Time seemed to stand still for a moment. I thought back to having tea with Gran: yes, she *had* said Henry.

'I'd forgotten all about that!' I burst out.

'So, you're on the ship with the cross and you've met Henry,' my mother said delightedly.

'Oh, Mum . . .' I said, lost for words as the significance dawned on me.

As my contract finally came to an end, I began to feel anxious. I had vowed not to work on another ship unless I was the headline act, which meant that I would shortly be heading home to Wakefield. Where did that leave me and Henrik? I would have moved in with him in an instant if only he'd asked me. He didn't ask me, although there was a moment, as we were having lunch in our favourite restaurant, when I thought he might.

'Are you going to rush back to England?' he asked.

My heart leapt. 'I'm in no hurry, no,' I said.

'Do you want to come and stay for a couple of weeks before you go? I won't be there all the time, as I have to go away to work, but you can just chill and have a nice time,' he said.

It wasn't much more than a stay of execution, but I told myself that Henrik was cautious by nature.

'I'd love to,' I told him.

Taking comfort in the thought that he was taking things a step at a time, as any sensible person would, I started to feel excited about the prospect of staying in his apartment.

'Will you be okay letting yourself in on the first day?' he asked, giving me his spare front-door key.

'I'll be fine,' I assured him.

'If I want, I can go to the quayside on Saturday night and watch the ship leave,' I laughed to myself.

It was a massive relief to say goodbye to the *Century* at last. During the vodka-fuelled leaving party that the crew threw for me the night before I left, people kept saying, 'She'll be back!'

'No, I won't,' I declared defiantly. 'I will never do a day's work on another ship unless I come back as a headliner.'

The following day, I hired a car and drove to Henrik's apartment. I let out a deep sigh of satisfaction as I opened the door and walked inside his airy, open-plan apartment. It was a wonderful feeling to have enough room to stretch out and relax. At long last, I was free to do as I wanted.

It was a hot day – the perfect day for a swim – and so I reached for my book and my swimsuit. Down by the pool, I found an oasis of calm and beauty, enclosed by rustling palm trees and fragrant tropical flowers. The sun shining on the surface of the pool made it sparkle invitingly. 'This is the life!' I thought, as I dived in and swam through the cool, aquamarine water. I felt fresh, alive, in love – and ever so slightly amazed, because here I was, a working-class miner's daughter from Yorkshire, splashing around in a sunlit pool at her boyfriend's apartment in America.

The next two weeks were the happiest of my life. I woke up smiling every morning, over the moon to find myself in Henrik's bedroom rather than my cramped cabin onboard the ship. Everything about Fort Lauderdale exhilarated the Yorkshire lass in me, from the scent of jasmine that seemed to follow you down the street to the gorgeous outdoor restaurants, where we ate seafood and drank cocktails in the warm evening air while we got to know each other better. During this time Henrik went away twice for three days to work, which was perfect as it took the pressure off a new relationship and gave me time to explore Fort Lauderdale and shop – I loved having the freedom.

I decided that if Henrik didn't ask me to stay beyond these two weeks – and there had been no mention of this possibility, so far – I definitely wanted him to miss me when I was gone. It was clear that he needed a partner to nurture and support him as he worked and grew his business so I hatched a plan to impress him that I was the perfect candidate for the role.

I rang my mother. 'I need your help, Mum, like never before.'

'Why, what's happened?' she said, sounding alarmed.

'I want Henrik to ask me back to live with him, so I've got to learn to cook, and fast!'

She sighed. 'Look, if you can read, you can cook. Just get yourself a cookbook, choose a simple recipe and follow the instructions to the letter. That's all there is to it. Oh, and don't skimp on the meat, remember.'

I followed Mum's advice and made curries, rice dishes and pork chops in gravy, all of which Henrik ate with relish.

'What else, Mum?' I asked.

She laughed. 'I don't know if this will help, but when we were courting, your father arrived early to take me out one day and found me ironing shirts. "That's the one for me," he thought, and before long, he had asked me to marry him.'

'He married you because you were good at ironing?' I said.

When Henrik came home from work that evening, I was carefully pressing his shirts. The effect was instant.

'I was thinking, Jane . . .' he began.

'Hmm?' I said, looking up from the ironing board with a contented smile.

'. . . Why don't you come back here after you've been to England?'

I pretended to consider this idea for a few moments.

'I'd love to,' I said happily, as if it had never occurred to me before.

'Well, it's just a thought . . . maybe . . . let's just see . . .' he said, a little too hesitantly for my liking, as if he was suddenly trying to backtrack. 'Go home and see what you feel like, first,' he added cautiously.

'Okay, my love,' I said, keeping my tone bright.

'That's it, I will definitely be coming back,' I thought.

During my last few days in Florida, Henrik took me to a party at a very posh house belonging to some business associates of his. I was no stranger to smart parties as I'd sometimes been asked to sing for the Greek family who owned the Celebrity line at their private soirées for VIP guests in their luxurious suite on the *Century*. This was different, though, because now I was one of the guests myself. Wearing a little black dress – classy and plain in style – from my favourite Fort Lauderdale boutique, I stood tall beside my good-looking beau in his tuxedo, feeling like I had arrived.

Henrik and I were shown into an enormous, airy conservatory, where staff in black-and-white uniforms were serving champagne, cocktails and canapés to the guests. There was a gorgeous grand piano in the middle of the room and, as the evening wore on, somebody said, 'Can anybody play the piano?'

'Yes, I can,' I said, because you can take the girl out of the clubs, but you can't take the clubs out of the girl.

'Oh, please play, will you?'

'I'd be happy to,' I said.

I sat down at the piano and soon I was hosting the party from my seat. A crowd of people gathered round, asking, 'Can you play this?', 'Can you play that?', and we had a lovely sing-song into the early hours.

Out of the corner of my eye I could see Henrik watching me all the while from across the room. I have a feeling that was the night he thought, 'She's for me.'

He admired my ability to fit in. 'You're a chameleon,' he told me, on our way home. 'You could blend in anywhere.'

It was agony saying goodbye to him at the airport. Henrik was a man of few words: 'Come back if you want to,' he said as he kissed me goodbye. As I walked towards the departures gate, I felt as if my heart was being ripped from my body. After months of being apart I couldn't wait to see my mother again, but leaving Henrik felt like the end of the world. I was tormented by the fear that I would never see him again.

'Don't worry, absence makes the heart grow fonder,' Mum said in an effort to cheer me up once I got home to Silcoates Street.

'Out of sight, out of mind,' I murmured, with a heavy heart.

It was lovely to see Mum again, but those two weeks with Henrik in Florida had taken the shine off being back in England for me. I tried to stay busy and catch up with friends and family to take my mind off the fact that I was longing to go back, but the simple fact was that I loved America, and Henrik was there. Why would I want to be anywhere else?

Curious to know what my friend Steve Holbrook thought of it all, I arranged to meet him for lunch. After we'd caught up with each other's news, I couldn't hold myself back any longer.

'So, this guy in Florida I'm mad about . . . ?'

'Wait,' he said, 'there's a film crew coming on a ship . . .'

'Oh, yes?' My head was too full of thoughts of Henrik to acknowledge what he was saying. 'And the guy in Florida . . . ?'

'Never mind that, something else is coming your way. There's a film crew coming, you've no idea what's ahead of you.'

'Okay, but what about this relationship . . . ?' I persisted.

'Will you stop?' he said. 'Yes, you are going to marry him, but something else far bigger is going to happen.'

'So, we're definitely going to get married?' I pressed.

Steve laughed. 'Well, this makes a change. Usually, you're only interested in your career.'

I regularly spoke to Henrik on the phone, hoping he would say, 'I miss you, Jane. Please come back to me.'

Eventually, I blurted out, 'I want to be back in America with you!'

'You want to come and live with me?' he said. 'Come on, then, let's make a go of it.'

No sooner had the words escaped his lips than I had packed my bags, booked my flight and started saying my goodbyes.

'But we haven't even met him!' my brother Tony protested.

'Believe me, you would definitely approve,' I assured him.

'All that matters is he loves you,' said Mum.

'And I believe he does, in his own way,' I told her.

Back in Fort Lauderdale, I set about perfecting the art of being a corporate wife. I wanted to be the hostess with the mostest, so I became a really good cook. Danish food was one of my specialities, which meant lots of pork, done every which way, from sausages to patties and meatballs. I made every kind of sauce for pork going and also became a dab hand at making a traditional Danish dish called risalamande, a rice pudding made with vanilla, cream, chopped almonds and hot cherries.

While Henrik worked hard and grew the business, I looked after everything else. I had time to meet friends and sun myself by the pool, but my priorities were an immaculate house and great food. I didn't feel the need to go out much and only occasionally met up with people I knew from the ships who lived in Fort Lauderdale. Mostly, I was content to be alone, pottering around, making sure that everything was just how it should be.

I had chunks of real happiness with Henrik and this was the best of times, partly because I felt so carefree. It was fantastic not to have to think, 'I can't do this or that because I've got to watch my throat.'

Henrik was still fairly reserved. He tended to express his feelings by surprising me with gifts and kind gestures, like offering to help pay my bills back home in Yorkshire while I wasn't working. When he took me on a trip to Las Vegas, I popped my birth certificate in my handbag and kept it close for the entire three days, just in case he whisked me off to the chapel to get married – he didn't, though.

I have two abiding memories of that trip. The first is of throwing a coin into the fountain outside Caesar's Palace and making a wish that Henrik and I would stay together. The second is of Henrik asking me how much I weighed and, when I told him, of him saying, 'Jane, you'd be perfect if you lost half a stone.'

He was very clever, was Henrik. He could see so much potential in me, but if somebody tells me to do something, I will do the exact opposite. I was extremely hurt that he wanted me to lose weight – and who wouldn't be? The problem in any new relationship is that you get content and go out for dinner a lot and drink wine, which puts weight on. Still, when we got back to Fort Lauderdale, I went to the gym every day and soon shed the extra pounds, whereas if Henrik had said, 'You need to lose half a stone,' I would probably have put another half on, just to show him.

Henrik's next surprise was to show me a piece of land he had bought in the grounds of a former estate called Lakes of Newport, about 20 minutes' drive from Fort Lauderdale.

'This is where our house will be built,' he said, pulling up near some trees beside a lake.

It's funny, I was less interested in the house than I was in his use of the word 'our'. 'That must mean he's thinking of a long-term future for us,' I thought. And yet I still wasn't entirely sure of his feelings for me, not even after he bought me a brand-new silver Mercedes as his next surprise gift.

We were due to move into the new house in Lakes of Newport four days before Christmas and, while Henrik was away on business, I started packing up the flat in preparation. I was excited about moving, but wished that he had given me a say in how the house was to be decorated. He claimed to have chosen all the colours and finishes because he wanted to surprise me, although

I couldn't help but suspect he had doubts about my good taste. I didn't feel I could complain, though.

As I carefully packed up the tea set Henrik's mother had given him, the phone rang. It was another surprise: just over six months after I had left the *Century*, Celebrity wanted me back as the headline act, on a new ship, with a pay hike and a passenger cabin – in fact, with all passenger facilities and rights.

'Are you joking?' I said, stunned.

'People miss you,' they said. 'Whenever we have a press event, they ask, "Where's Jane?" '

'When would you want me to start?' I asked, looking at the boxes piled up all around me.

'Immediately,' they said.

I sat down on a box. 'Not before Christmas, surely?'

'Yes, it's for seven weeks, over Christmas and New Year.'

I said that I would think it over and get back to them. Putting the phone down in a daze, I shook my head in wonder at this latest development. I hadn't regretted leaving the *Century* for a single second, but now it struck me that if I hadn't resigned and walked away, vowing never to return, I would never have been offered the job as a headliner on this new ship, the *Galaxy*. What a year 1996 had turned out to be! I was starting to realise that you have to make space for good things to happen.

I talked it over with Henrik and decided to take the job after he promised to join the ship for a few days over Christmas. I was sorry to be leaving him to move into the new house alone, but it was too good an offer to turn down and, anyway, with Christmas coming up, I wanted to earn some money of my own.

A few days later, I was still asleep when the phone rang early one morning. 'What's going on?' I thought, rolling over and glancing at the clock. 'Nobody ever rings me at this time.'

I picked up the phone. 'Hello, is that Jane McDonald?' said the voice at the other end. 'This is Chris Terrill from the BBC—'

I giggled.

'Course you are,' I said, and put the phone down.

A few seconds later, it started ringing again. I picked it up and said, 'You're having a laugh, aren't you?'

'Can you just hear me out?' he said. 'This really is Chris Terrill from the BBC and I'm going to be making a documentary about life on the *Galaxy*. Your name has been put forward as someone I could potentially follow in my film, if you agree to appear.'

'Okay, but you've got to understand I don't do mornings,' I said.

I wasn't entirely sure what sort of film he was imagining. Remember, those were the days before reality TV took over our screens, before docusoaps like *Driving School* and *Airline* had gone out, let alone *Big Brother*. I remembered seeing one or two fly-on-the-wall documentaries capturing people going about their everyday life, but Chris said this was a different concept.

'You and the other people I'm filming won't be able to forget about the camera, because I'll be right there, focusing it on you every hour of the day. Part of what we'll be showing on the programme is the interaction between the two of us. We'll be spending a lot of time together, Jane, so we need to get on.'

'I see, Chris, and are you handsome, love?' I asked.

He laughed uproariously. 'Could we meet up and see whether we both think it would work?'

My dressing room on the Galaxy,
the ship that changed my destiny.

A headline act on
the ships at last
and my very own
photo shoot.

Yorkshire Woman of the
Year 1998, what an honour:
Mum, Tony, Me, Henrik, Wendy.

Las Vegas, at one of the
lowest points of my life.

Drama and
sequins after
The Cruise aired
on the BBC.

Mum and me,
always laughing.

However bad you feel,
Dr Showbiz always
kicks in.

Ed and me,
13th May 2008:
our first meeting
after 27 years.

Back together again and already
wearing his 'n' hers jeans.

The Cats crew: playing Grizabella gave me the confidence to call myself a singer.

Quinny, me and Gabby: lifelong friends after Cats.

The cast of Cats in Blackpool: I've never been so nervous.

Back to Blackpool for the Making Memories tour in 2016.

Writing songs with Steve Cooper, my main man on stage.

With Kay Heeley, my dressmaker, who loves sequins as much as I do.

My touring family: the laughter never stops among this special group of people.

Outside the BAFTAs with my handsome beau,
Ed, the love of my life.

11

Be Yourself

You've got to be yourself in life, haven't you? As I later learned to my cost, there is absolutely no point in trying to be anybody else.

I didn't feel I had anything to hide while Chris Terrill was filming me over those seven weeks of the *Galaxy*'s maiden voyage, so when *The Cruise* aired the following January, viewers saw the real me: a hardworking Northern club singer with three chins, wearing her heart on her sleeve. Having said that, for some reason I was talking *very much like that* and sounded like Lady Di half the time.

My mother said, 'You're a bit posh, aren't you?' when she watched the first episode.

'I had to, Mum. It's the BBC!' I told her.

You've got to make yourself understood. It was a lesson I'd learned after seeing my grandmother tone down her Scottish accent at the Spiritualist church. Either that or face constant bewilderment, like my friends from Barnsley, where the accent is even thicker than it is in Wakefield. I was mindful of how my ex-boyfriend Ed, and other friends had been baffled by it – 'What did they just say?' they'd ask me, because it sounded totally foreign to them.

So, I took a leaf out of Gran's book while working on the ships and living in America, where people would look mystified my Yorkshire dialect loose. Having a Danish boyfriend was another factor, and even though I tried to speak slowly and clearly, sometimes Henrik saw me making people laugh and said, 'I wish I could understand what you've just been saying because I bet it was really funny.'

To people watching *The Cruise* who weren't from Yorkshire, I probably sounded like I had a thick accent, but to my friends and family, it was as if I'd turned into HM The Queen. In every other way, though, I was myself, from my terrible hair and awful stage frocks to my sheer terror in the run-up to my first show as a headliner.

And my goodness, that first show was terrifying! That was the night I realised how much your audience picks up on how you're feeling. You must learn to leave your life and problems and whatever else is going on at the stage door. People want to be entertained and it's your job to make sure they are, so make them smile. I tried to be too clever with my choice of songs when I should have known to stick to what people want to hear.

Chris Terrill was of the opinion that the documentary needed to show every aspect of what life was like on a cruise ship, but when he filmed the audience getting up and walking out of the show, people said he shouldn't include it because it was too exposing. It really hurts when an audience doesn't like you and there was a lot of pressure on, because getting bad ratings could easily have led to me being fired in front of the cameras – my career would have been over in a second.

I had to pull something out of the bag quickly and with the help of our dance captain, Jack Failla, I worked hard at making my act more appealing to the *Galaxy*'s audience. Jack was an inspiration and I have so much to thank him for, because he could see the artist I was destined to be one day. We changed the choreography and setlist and, fortunately, my next show knocked them dead. My ratings soared and so I kept my job.

There was only one other time when it all went wrong for me onstage and that was when there was a mass stampede out of the theatre in the middle of my set. I had no idea what it was about, but this time I knew not to take it personally.

'It is what it is,' I thought as I watched everybody leave. 'I've done the best I can, I can't make it any different.'

When it turned out they were all off to investigate a new, late-night 'chocolate buffet', I understood.

'Sometimes it doesn't matter who you are, how good or how bad – if there's a flipping chocolate buffet going on halfway through the show, people will want to go and have a look,' I told Chris. 'That's the reality of being an artist, so you absolutely should show it on the programme.'

I think one or two people were worried about how up close and personal Chris was getting with his camera. He was practically in bed with Henrik and me when he filmed us opening our Christmas presents. What a devastating moment it was when Henrik's Christmas gift to me turned out to be a pair of earrings instead of the big, sparkling engagement ring I was hoping for!

'Is that it?' I thought, as I opened the little box wrapped in gold paper. My face was a picture, because I've never been any good at hiding my feelings.

Chris seemed to appreciate my trust in him and, as the weeks went on, I opened up to him more and more. At first, he was my confidant, then he became a friend. I talked to him about my feelings for Henrik, we went knicker shopping together, he even got me paragliding . . . The growing bond between us was there for all to see.

After a while I started to get the impression that he might be holding a candle for me, but I was soon put right about that.

'Don't think you're special, because he falls in love with

whoever he's filming,' one of his team warned. 'You could be an orangutan in a zoo and he'd fall in love with you if he was making a film about you.'

In February 1997, when my contract ended and I left the *Galaxy*, Chris asked Henrik and me if we would be willing to fly to the UK and finish my strand of the documentary up in Wakefield. I had talked endlessly about my mother on camera and he felt the viewers would want to see her – 'They will feel they know her,' he said.

But I didn't need an excuse to go home and see my mum – I had really missed her over Christmas, so I was at the airport like a shot. It meant that Mum and Henrik met for the first time in front of the cameras, which was a bit strange, but they got on very well and that was all that mattered. Mum was used to men being abrupt and Henrik's manner was just like my dad's, so she thought he was perfect for me. He in turn loved her bacon sandwiches and of course her vivacious charm won him over completely, as I knew it would.

It was wonderful to be at home in Silcoates Street, although I don't think Henrik was enthralled. In fact, I'm surprised he didn't make a run for the airport, because his family were very posh. They lived in a big, beautiful, detached house back in Denmark and when I visited them there, a week later, I thought, 'Blimey, I'm glad we went to mine first!'

Even without seeing his family home, our three-up, two-down looked small and cramped when I saw it through his eyes. But for me it was home and I loved it. All things told, it really didn't make a difference what Henrik thought of it, as he was never going to be doing more than visiting.

I would have liked to spend more time with Mum, but Henrik had to get back to work after we had visited his family in Denmark, so it was only a few days. Soon we were in Florida again and it was great to be back in the sunshine and I was excited about moving into the new house at Lakes of Newport, especially as I still hadn't seen how Henrik had decorated it. As he drove me there from the airport, I wondered what it would be like.

'I really hope you like it,' he said.

I gasped when he led me through the front door. The house was decorated in a beautiful palette of rich colours: the walls were burnt orange, oxblood and mustard, the floors were Mexican tiled, and the worktops and shelves were hewn from different shades of sleek, waxed wood. Everything was clean-cut and straight lines, with few curves to be seen and not a trace of chintz. It was a style I now call 'hospital corners' and it summed up Henrik, really.

'Wow,' I said. 'It's amazing.'

Henrik was happy to let me do the flower arranging and I found you could transform a room with a vase of gorgeous blooms and foliage. I was madly in love and threw myself into being a corporate wife (well, girlfriend!) again. I loved every bit of it, even ironing his shirts. I'm a chameleon, so, if I'm not singing, I'm doing something else and I enjoy whatever it is. I love life! My cooking went from strength to strength and we started having Henrik's associates over for dinner. Those dinners were always a huge success, because while I made sure the food was delicious, Henrik served our guests the best wines and brandies.

Henrik's business partner, Ken, was very complimentary about my cooking. The first time he came over, he said something like, 'You should stick around, Jane, especially if you always cook like this.'

'Believe me, I intend to stick around, Ken,' I said.

'Hasn't Henrik told him I'm here to stay?' I wondered. I understood that Henrik didn't like to discuss his personal life at work, but it seemed strange that he hadn't told his closest colleague that we were living together.

While Henrik was on a trip, I decided to soften up the bathroom, which I felt was just that bit too stark and Scandinavian. I had seen a wisteria mural painted in somebody's house and thought something similar would look nice around the bathroom door frame, so I went out and bought all the materials to create a pretty ivy leaf design. I took my time over it and was very happy with the result when it was finished.

'Oh my God, I hate it!' Henrik cried when he saw it.

'I've spent days doing this,' I said, unable to believe what I was hearing.

'I know you have, but it's awful,' he replied and, the following day, he painted over it.

He was probably right and it was awful, but after that, I got it lodged into my head that Henrik thought I didn't have taste. I was even more convinced of it when it came to buying a piano. Henrik knew that all my life I had wanted a white grand piano, but he absolutely refused to have one, so our seven-foot concert grand piano was made out of a beautiful chestnut cherry wood, which matched the floor, because coordinating the décor came first. Never mind. The piano was the centrepiece of a fantastic domed room that had great acoustics because of the slanting ceiling and tiled floor, and while Henrik was away, I wrote some of my best songs on it. I have that cherry wood piano to thank for 'The Hand That Leads Me', 'Winner' and 'I See It In Your Eyes', which have all gone on to become huge favourites with my fans.

Who knows where life might have taken me if *The Cruise* had been edited down to a one-off documentary, as had originally been commissioned? Or if the expanded 12-part series had gone out in the 11pm slot on a Monday night? I could easily have carried on living a life of leisure with Henrik in Fort Lauderdale. It was a great life: I was deeply in love and enjoyed not having to work. But, in early January 1998, a full year since I had been on the *Galaxy*, I had a call from Chris.

'I think you'd better come back to the United Kingdom,' he said.

'What for?' I asked.

'Well, this is going a little bit bigger than we thought. The programme's going out at eight o'clock on BBC1, straight after *EastEnders*. The press want to talk to you.'

'Okay, I'll come back for a little break,' I said. 'I'll book some gigs in to keep me busy while I'm over.'

Before I left, Henrik sprang the ultimate surprise and asked me to marry him. Perhaps it shouldn't have felt so unexpected: it was typical of him to take his time and give an idea careful consideration before he took action. It won't come as a shock to anyone to hear that I said yes in a flash.

'What's brought this on?' I asked him later, scarcely able to believe that my dream had finally come true.

'It's hardly sudden, Jane. We've been together for nearly two years,' he laughed.

I flew to the UK with a song in my heart, ready to brave absolutely anything, but back home in Silcoates Street, it was a shock seeing myself on the telly. I sat through the first episode of *The Cruise* with my mother, thinking, 'Oh my God, I didn't know I was that big!'

'Oh dear, look at my chins,' I said. 'Who's done my hair?'

Boom, that was it! I flew in and never left, because things went berserk after that. The viewing figures started at 11 million and grew to 13 million. Chris Terrill told me the bosses came to him with the numbers and said, 'You're not going to believe this.' It was the biggest shock of his life, nobody could have predicted it.

There were a lot of characters on the show, but as the weeks went on and the media glare focused on me, Chris started to edit the episodes differently. The strange thing is that I don't think he originally filmed me as much as some of the others – people like Mary and Dale Nathan and Jack Failla – but he went back and added more footage of me, and then more. Very clever was Chris. By the end it was the Jane McDonald show, really.

I took it as it came. I knew nothing about viewing figures, so when the bosses told me, 'You're very, very popular,' I thought, 'They've liked it, that's nice.' Now, I look back and think, 'Flipping heck!'

My mother didn't get worked up about it, either. When I came off the phone saying, 'Mum, you won't believe this. A record company's got in touch and they want me to record an album,' she said, 'Lovely. Do you want a cup of tea?'

People think, when you're on television, you're worth a fortune, but *The Cruise* was a documentary and I was paid nothing to appear in it. I needed my club bookings to tide me over while I was staying at Mum's, but when it all kicked off with the programme, my gigs were suddenly packed with people who wanted to see 'Jane McDonald off the television'. The regulars couldn't get in and neither could I. There were skirmishes at the door and, when I turned up at one club, the bouncer put out an arm to block me and said, 'Sorry, love, you can't come in. We've been full since half past six.'

'Don't be daft,' I told him, 'I'm the turn!'

It was no joke, really. The crowds and the fights made me feel unsafe. Eventually, I had to ring the agent and say, 'I can't do this anymore.' I felt bad about letting him down – but not too bad, because he was the agent who hadn't wanted to pay me the same as his male acts, a few years earlier.

Meanwhile, the phone at Silcoates Street was ringing off

the hook with offers from record companies, publishers and TV production companies. I was relieved when Chris rang one afternoon and said, 'How is everything? Do you need any help or advice?'

'Should I sing on the midweek lottery and press the button for the draw?'

'Go for it!' he said. 'It's primetime TV, it'll be great for your career.'

Chris had known for a while that Henrik and I were getting married. When I'd first told him, he immediately asked if he could film it for a *The Cruise* special.

'But we want to do it on a beach somewhere sunny,' I said.

'That's fine,' he said placidly, perhaps already planning the scenes in his head. 'People will love it even more because of the romantic setting.'

After talking it over, Henrik and I agreed to Chris's plan, even though it was daunting to think of sharing our wedding day with half the world. Henrik wasn't especially comfortable in front of a camera, but it was lovely that the public wanted to see a fairytale ending to our romance and definitely added to the sense of occasion.

I couldn't believe it when OK! *Magazine* asked for exclusive rights to cover the wedding. They were offering us a fee, which meant that we could fly our family and friends over for a party. But with all these offers flying around, people started saying, 'You'd better get an agent to help you sort through it all.'

I can see why people thought I needed an agent – I was a club singer, I wasn't media trained and I had no idea how the business worked. If I had, I would have known that all I really needed was my sister-in-law, Wendy McDonald, to answer the phone for me, because when you're a success, everybody contacts you. It's simply a question of deciding, 'Yes, I could do that,' or 'No, that's not for me.'

Being naive, I got a London agent: 'You're already a star, but you have so much untapped potential,' he said. 'Our vision for you is to make you into an even bigger star and take your career into the stratosphere.'

'Okay,' I said, 'that sounds good.'

I signed a record deal with Focus Music International and the next minute I seemed to be surrounded by a load of people saying, 'You can't do this anymore,' and 'You can't do that,' and 'You need *us* to do *this* for *you*.' That was the way it was 20 years ago: people created stars, and so all these people came in and tried to fashion me, stage me and style me.

'I'm 35, I don't need all this,' I thought.

They set about trying to erase my working-class background, because in their eyes, it seemed to me, I was common: 'Stop talking onstage,' I was told. 'Divas don't tell jokes.'

I rebelled against everything – I was a nightmare. 'No, please don't try to change that about me,' I protested.

For once, I found it difficult to make myself heard. I was a huge success and people were zooming in, thinking, 'I want a piece of that.' They wanted to make money in all the different categories, from TV and concerts to records and books. Before I knew it, I'd signed a record contract, which was amazing, something I'd always dreamed of doing. Yet it didn't feel real, because it felt like something that happened to me, rather than something that I made happen. Since I didn't know the industry, I had to leave everything to the people who did, which made me feel uneasy. They didn't know me and, right from the start, they seemed to have the wrong idea about me: they didn't understand that I was proud of being a club singer, proud of where I came from, proud that I had schlepped up and down the motorway with my speakers in the back of the van, entertaining people all over the North. I thought being a club singer was a great job – and then I progressed onto the ships – but up at the top of the music industry, clubs and cruises were frowned upon and 'cabaret' was a dirty word, it seemed.

I couldn't understand it. 'Tom Jones started as a club singer, so did Shirley Bassey, but nobody is saying they're not good enough. That's how you came up in those days, you had no choice,' I remember saying.

'Yes, but they're big stars now,' I was told.

'Why is it different for me?' I wondered.

People didn't seem to understand that I've always been funny – I do more than introduce the songs I sing. What the public loved on *The Cruise* was that I was just being me. There were no airs and graces, I wasn't a star that had been created – I was more Marti Caine than Shirley Bassey.

'You're not a club singer anymore, you're something else now,' they said.

'Well, I'm not actually,' I thought. 'I'm still that person who's come up the ranks.'

It was a confusing time and I was glad to get away from it all and join Henrik in Florida for a break.

'Congratulations, you've got a record deal!' he said, putting his arms around me when he met me at the airport. He looked into my eyes. 'Is something wrong?' he asked.

'How could it be when I'm marrying you?' I said. 'It's just that everything's happening so fast with my career that I can't seem to catch my breath.'

'Just forget about it while you're here and have a rest,' he told me.

That was wishful thinking because my mind was full of the challenges that would be waiting for me when I returned to England. First, I was set to start work on recording my own album, which was huge. I would be singing songs made famous by Dionne Warwick, Whitney Houston and Dusty Springfield, so my voice needed to be in the best possible shape. I was also lucky enough to have been invited to do a show at the Blackpool Opera House, which in some ways was an even more nerve-racking prospect, because Chris Terrill would be filming it for the documentary. Yet my worries seemed to lift in the Florida sunshine and I spent happy days at the piano, working out arrangements for the songs I was planning to record and sing at the concert.

It was comforting to think that, if all else failed, I would always have Henrik. One night, while we were having dinner, the subject of spiritualism came up.

'I believe I've met you before and that we were destined to meet again,' I told him. 'I really do.'

Henrik laughed. 'My approach to life is pragmatic and science based, so your beliefs are very different to mine,' he said, 'but I feel I should know more about the psychic world now that we're getting married.'

Touched by his willingness to explore spiritualism, I made an appointment for him with a Florida psychic, who had been recommended to me. Henrik was sceptical about anything that couldn't be scientifically proven so I was curious to know how the session would go.

He returned from the appointment wearing a puzzled smile.

'What happened?' I asked.

'It was interesting,' he said. 'But the psychic predicted that I will change profession within 90 days. I of course said that would be impossible.'

'What did he say you were going to do instead of engineering?' I asked, intrigued.

'He didn't say. But apparently there will be problems with you and, if I can sort them out, everything will be all right.'

'Really? Did you believe him?'

'I'll try to keep an open mind, but he must be wrong about my business. The company is thriving and expanding every day. I'm not planning to change direction in three months' time.'

'Mmm,' I thought, knowing full well that life has a way of trampling over plans.

Soon I was back in England again, rehearsing for the Blackpool concert and the album sessions. I had to pinch myself when I saw the full orchestra waiting for me at Abbey Road Studios. I just couldn't get over the idea that all these talented people – the orchestra, the session singers, the arrangers and producers – were there to record my album. You could have put pins in me and still I wouldn't have been able to take it on board.

Henrik flew over to be with me for my big debut in April 1998 at the Opera House in Blackpool, which was another dream come true. I picked out a beautiful silver lamé dress and silver shoes for the most important performance of my life so far and felt like Cinderella going to the ball when I looked in the mirror and saw my reflection. It was such a big deal: my family would be in the audience, along with people who had seen me come up through the clubs and others who had shared my highs and lows on the *Galaxy* – and all the while Chris Terrill would be filming me for a TV audience of millions.

My nerves kicked in with a vengeance before the show. So, what do you do when you're about to go onstage in front of nearly 3,000 people and you feel sick, your throat is dry and every nerve and sinew in your body is quivering with fear?

I had a brandy, took a deep breath and walked on.

It's hard to describe how it felt to be on that stage in front of all those people. 'Scary' and 'fantastic' are the first adjectives that spring to mind. It wasn't so much the size of the audience, because I had performed to big crowds before, at places like the Maid Marian near Skegness: it was the sheer fact of appearing at the Opera House in Blackpool that made the difference – and this time everybody had come to see me.

I wasn't bad. Thankfully, nothing went wrong and the audience seemed to like me well enough, but I came off feeling I hadn't given it my best without quite knowing why. It's not surprising: with hindsight, I just wasn't ready to perform in a theatre of that size. There's a big difference between a club act and a theatre act and you can't transform from one to the other overnight, it's just not possible. Being a performer is not something you can play at. You have to learn it and hone it and be constantly evolving into who you want to be. I got there too fast and I wasn't prepared.

Years later, the pianist and songwriter Bobby Crush gave me one of the best compliments I have ever had when he came to see me in concert.

'As soon as you walked onstage, I knew we were in safe hands,' he told me – and this, of course, is exactly the effect you want to have on your audience. You want them to feel, 'This is going to be great.' But it's not something you can learn overnight, it comes with experience.

There were some beautiful moments that evening and best of all was seeing my grandmother at the concert with my mum. Gran was 92 and hadn't been out of her house in ages, so it meant a lot to me that she could make it.

'I've waited all my life for this day,' she told me. 'I just wanted to see you be a star.'

My grandmother had been in the room with my mother when I was born. Scenes from Monifieth, Eastmoor Road and the Wakefield Spiritualist Church replayed in my head. As I thought of all the predictions Gran had made about my life that had come true, I started welling up.

'Thanks, Gran, I do love you,' I told her, giving her a hug.

'That was great,' Mum said.

I took this as a compliment, since she usually said, 'It was all right, but . . .'

'Well, you have to keep your feet on the floor,' she said in her defence when I teased her about it.

Later, an agent who was watching from the dress circle gave me a constructive piece of criticism: 'All I ever saw was the top of your head,' she said. 'You never once looked up.'

It was a great tip: I was so used to playing to a club crowd that I found it hard to reach out and connect with a bigger, wider theatre space and didn't pay enough attention to the people in the dress and upper circles. It's quite possible to include everybody when you're performing, but I didn't have the stagecraft. Still, it was a mistake I never made again. I learned from it, as I always do, and when I was booked for a series of Sunday night shows at the Opera House during the summer season, I made sure to look up at the dress circle and above throughout the show.

The whirlwind continued. I finished off the album in London and, the next thing I knew, I was flying to St Thomas in the American Virgin Islands for my dream wedding to Henrik on 26 May 1998. Only, by the end of it, I didn't actually feel like I'd had the lovely wedding that was later shown on TV, because it turned out to be just another hardworking day spent with Chris, making the documentary. We had the *Radio Times* and OK! *Magazine* out there. We had the film crew. Every morning we were up at five o'clock to film and do photoshoots. So, although it looked beautiful – and I had a gorgeous designer dress and celebrity stylist Trevor Sorbie flew out to do my hair, so it really was very beautiful – we never stopped and were exhausted by the time we got to bed. It looked like our happy-ever-after when Chris had edited it down, but actually, the best part was getting into bed and going to sleep when it was all over. When we woke up, Henrik kissed me and said, 'Are we really married or was it all a dream?'

Afterwards it was pretty much straight back to the UK for more meetings and appearances for me, while Henrik flew back to Florida. Once again, there was pressure from the London lot to shed the real me and put on a slick, styled diva persona. I kept having to fight my corner to stay true to who I really was, but it wasn't easy. I had always been strong and independent, the stakes seemed so high now that I needed an ally to help me stand up for myself.

I rang Henrik and said, 'This is not going well, I'm not enjoying it at all.'

He must have been able to tell from my voice that I was close to breaking point. 'Hang on, I'm on my way,' he said. 'I'll get a flight tomorrow, but I can only come for two weeks.'

Two weeks sounded long enough to sort out my career. 'Thank you,' I said, feeling extremely relieved.

'I've bought a book that tells you everything about the music industry,' he added. 'I'll read it on the flight.'

Being a trained engineer, Henrik was well versed in reading thick, technical manuals. He read *Everything You'd Better Know About the Music Industry* in its entirety on the flight to England and seemed to know whole passages off by heart by the time he got off the plane. By then, he was ready to take on the entire record business, I think.

We went straight to a meeting with my agent. I can still see them now, the agent leaning forward in his chair, talking nineteen to the dozen at Henrik, and my husband sitting back in his chair, listening intently.

As we left the agency offices, Henrik said, 'I'm taking over as your manager.'

'Thank God for that,' I thought.

Unfortunately, it would have been better if he hadn't. But we weren't to know that at the time.

12

Higher And Higher

The week I released my debut album, *Jane McDonald*, in late July 1998, I arrived at the Blackpool Opera House to find a pack of photographers waiting at the stage door. The minute they saw me, they started running towards me, snapping photos.

'What's up?' I asked.

'Don't you know?' one of them said.

'Why? What is it?'

'Your album's gone to No. 1!'

'Oh, that's nice,' I said.

It was incredible news, but I honestly don't think there was enough room left in my brain to take it in. So many things had been happening, so quickly, one after the other, that I couldn't keep up. It was like walking round the fair and winning all the prizes, which never happens in real life.

It was only a few months since I'd been doing club gigs at my old haunts in Manchester. Now, I was waking up every morning wondering what the heck was going to happen next. When the No. 1 was announced, I was still getting to grips with the idea that, two weeks earlier, 13.5 million people had watched my wedding to Henrik on *The Cruise Special: Jane Ties the Knot*.

'No one can believe the viewing figures,' Chris Terrill told me. 'They're over the moon at the BBC.'

Now, I was going in the *Guinness Book of Hit Records* as the first artist to enter the charts at No. 1 with a debut release. My shows at the Opera House were all sold out. Henrik had booked a 30-date nationwide tour to start in October. It made me dizzy just looking at the schedule.

I was always working. I travelled hundreds and hundreds of miles by car, train and plane to promote the album, visiting every local radio station and TV company that would have me in for a chat. Although I felt very grateful for the opportunity, it was exhausting. Whenever an interviewer said something like, 'I bet you can't believe how lucky you are to be sitting here talking to me about your incredible success,' I'd think, 'Yes, but I'd like to be at home, having a cup of tea with my mum.'

I lived in hope of Henrik saying, 'You've got the day off today.' It wouldn't have made a difference, would it? Just one day? Yet I couldn't help worrying that, if I took my eye off the ball for one single second, all the success would disappear.

'Where do you go from the top?' I thought.

The only way was down.

'You must be minted now, Jane!' one of the photographers said.

'No, can you tell my bank manager I've gone to No. 1?' I laughed.

I can see why people thought I'd be in the money, because everything I touched was golden. But somebody else was taking care of the financial side of things and I had no idea where the money was going. I got a monthly allowance paid into my bank account and that was all I knew.

Stupid me.

Although the music journalists weren't bowled over by it – and one reviewer said I had a voice like a 'faulty clutch' – my album stayed in the top spot for three weeks. People kept saying, 'Wow, you've got a No. 1 album!'

'Enjoy it now, because it's not going to happen again,' I'd say.

That was the realist in me talking, keeping my feet on the ground. In my mind, people had watched *The Cruise*, got into it and thought, 'Oh, we like her,' and even if they weren't fans of my singing, they were buying my album because they'd bought into the idea of me, or because it was a great gift for their mother or somebody else who'd enjoyed the TV show. There was a huge momentum behind it that I knew could never be repeated.

It wasn't a bad album – I don't think I've made a bad album yet – but when someone told me that their daughter or husband had given it to them, I used to say, 'Don't worry, you don't have to listen to it. Use it as a beer mat or put your cup on it instead!'

Henrik would tick me off for remarks like that. He didn't like to hear me doing myself down – I think he felt that I should behave more in keeping with the star I was becoming, although I never thought of myself as a star, and still don't. I wanted to please Henrik. He was my husband now, and he had given up a lot to be my manager, taking on a partner on the engineering side of his business in Florida so that he could be with me in the UK as much as possible. But I couldn't change my humour – not for him, not for anyone. It was so deep-rooted that it was like a physical reflex.

Henrik would probably have preferred us to be based in London, but I stood up to him.

'I like Wakefield, my family are here,' I explained.

'In that case, we need to move,' he said.

I was aghast. 'We can't move from Silcoates Street! I feel safe in that house, it's in such a great area.'

There was quite a bit of discussion about it, but Henrik prevailed and found us a house in Howcroft Gardens, which was lovely and just round the corner. He did it up in his style and picked everything, just as he had at the Lakes of Newport house – I wasn't allowed to do any of the decorating. The results were very minimalist. Now, we had two lovely houses, both very, very Scandinavian.

I took it as read that my mother would live with us: 'We need someone to be in the house to keep it homely while we're away on the tour,' I said. 'I don't like to come into the cold and switch everything on. I like to come into a home where there's a full fridge, a pie in the oven and a warm welcome.'

Since none of my mother's things matched Henrik's décor, she had to throw everything out before we moved, from her 'Best Mum in the World' mugs to our enormous oak dining table. It was difficult for her to let it all go.

'Throw out the dining table?' she said, perturbed.

We'd had that table since the 1960s when Mum and Dad had kitted out our big house in Eastmoor Road with heavy Edwardian furniture. The table top was beautiful, because Mum kept it polished, but otherwise it was a bit of a wreck after all the years – the legs were scuffed and the chairs had definitely seen better days.

'What is it you think you're hanging on to?' I asked her.

I could see both sides of the argument. Henrik was right, but I felt for Mum too – it was everything she was used to.

'Oh my God, my whole life's just gone into a skip!' she wailed the day we left Silcoates Street.

But Mum quickly grew to like the house in Howcroft Gardens, as I knew she would, because everything was new and she had her own en suite.

At first, we operated an office out of a room in Wendy and Tony's house, with my sister-in-law doing all the administration single-handedly. She was such a support to me, was Wendy, then and always. There was an awful lot to do. The phone never stopped ringing and we had calls coming in from America as well as

England, so we never switched off. Soon Henrik moved the office to a smart Georgian building near Wakefield train station and Wendy became his PA, while Caroline Eccles came on board to do the admin and run the fan club. She had been at school with Wendy and me and the three of us got on like a house on fire.

One of the nicest offers came in September when Prince Charles asked me to appear at a Prince's Trust concert. It was a brilliant experience and I couldn't believe it when the Prince himself told me afterwards that he had seen *The Cruise*. It's just not the sort of thing you imagine the heir to the throne to be watching, is it? I told him about how Princess Anne had been partial to my music on the Royal Yacht *Britannia* – and that's been it for me and the royals to date, although I believe one of their butlers follows me on Twitter.

My tour started in October 1998. At last, I had a proper band, although it was a bit like the house in Howcroft Gardens in that the musicians were chosen for me.

'Okay, you can set the band as long as I can bring my own backing singer,' I told Henrik, thinking of Sue Ravey. Sue was a great singer in her own right and a good mate, so I was lucky that she agreed to join us. She's so dry-humoured, is Sue, and everybody loves her. She brought along Sue Drake, another lovely singer, and they were soon known among the crew as 'The Two Sues'.

The concerts were fabulous, they really were. After my years performing in the clubs and on the ships, I was used to going out and working an audience. My time at the Opera House in Blackpool had been great practice for reaching out and engaging with big theatre crowds. I'd had time to rehearse. I knew the songs well. I had my mate backing me. I was better than I'd ever been. But I was still throwing up before I went on and I was a complete wreck before I went on the first night: sick, shaky, everything.

When I came off, feeling fantastic, I thought, 'Why can't I feel like this all along?'

Midway through the tour, I performed at the London Palladium for the first time. Chris Terrill was filming it for a *The Cruise* special that would be going out on New Year's Eve, so I had nerves off the Richter Scale that night. While we were backstage waiting, someone said, 'Don't get disheartened if the crowd doesn't go wild. London audiences are famously tricky. It's not like a gig in the North, it's the Palladium – they're used to seeing everything here.'

Needless to say this piece of advice didn't help to calm me down one bit.

All of a sudden, the intro started onstage and the audience began whooping and cheering. 'I think we're going to be all right, you know,' I said.

The waves of energy and warmth that crashed over me as I walked onstage nearly knocked me for six. It was a fantastic night and I felt completely at home on that Palladium stage. About halfway through the show, I sat down to play the piano. It was part of the act: since it would be a surprise to most people that I could play, I was going to mess around like a beginner before going into a complicated classical piece.

So, I sat down and plonked about a bit. 'Where's Bobby Crush when you need him?' I joked.

A voice from the stalls called out, 'I'm here!'

I couldn't believe it: Bobby Crush was actually in the audience! It was an amazing coincidence that I'd mentioned him.

What I liked most about the tour, apart from the performing, was meeting fans and making friends along the way. I've been incredibly lucky with my fans and I'm so thankful for each and every one of them. Back then, we were only just getting to know each other properly and I couldn't believe how lovely everybody was. I began to recognise faces in the front few rows and always took an hour or so after a show to meet people and sign autographs, which was a special time for me.

Still, I was tired out after the final show, which took me back to the London Palladium. It had been nose to the grindstone every day, travelling from one place to the next, doing phone interviews in the car and planning my schedule with the team in every spare moment. It's the same for anyone who is on their way up: hard work, long days and no time to yourself. There were decisions to be made every day: what would I wear on this TV show? What would I sing? Could I make it to Birmingham if I had an interview in Manchester?

I missed my life of leisure in Fort Lauderdale, where I never seemed to get irritable or upset. Henrik and I had started to have quite a few arguments and they were often about money. I'd had a No. 1 album for three weeks which had stayed in the charts for 26 weeks and gone platinum; I'd just finished a sold-out tour. I couldn't understand why we were short of money. The record industry system of advance payments and recouped balances meant that I was always waiting to be paid. It felt like there were problems every day. Nothing was as I expected. Then again, how was I to know? I was a club singer and my manager was new to the business.

Henrik was very, very bright, but I was beginning to worry that he might be out of his depth. 'As a manager, you have to know every side of the business,' he once told me and it has always stayed with me, because it's true. 'You have to learn how to be a lawyer, a promoter, an accountant and a whole lot of other jobs.'

If I could go back, knowing what I know now, I would take a closer look at some of the contracts I signed, because at the end of the day it was my responsibility and I suffered the consequences. There was a scene in one of *The Cruise* specials when a limo turned up for me and you could see that I was absolutely delighted that the record company were treating me so well: 'Is that for me? Oh my God!' I squealed happily.

I didn't realise that the limo hire came off my artist's royalty, and that every lovely restaurant meal I had with record company executives came off the artist's royalty, as did the hotels I stayed in and countless other expenses. If I had known, I wouldn't have sat down to the expensive meals, stayed in the posh hotels or had drivers taking me everywhere. I'd have said, 'No, I'll make my own way,' as I was used to doing.

I should have made it my business to know about the financial implications of what I was doing, but I was gullible and clueless. Clearly, I wasn't ready for all that fame. It was just too much of a change for me to cope with. I like to learn things as I go along, bit by bit, but this was everything at once. I had always been in control of my life – of my own destiny – and I had liked it that way. Now, I had to give all the control away: I had a manager, PR people, record company execs and television producers who were all saying, 'Right, you're doing this, you're going to look like this and you're going to say this.'

I should have asked more questions, because why would I take advice from someone who can't write music, can't sing and can't perform? It's amazing how many record industry people are not musical. They're business people who don't understand the human side of the business. They don't seem to realise or care that the more you control an artist – and say hurtful things to keep them in check – the lower the artist will sink.

I should have been allowed to flourish, but everybody was saying to me, 'You can't do this or that anymore because there's too much money riding on it.' Only, it was their money they were worried about, not mine. And they were being paid such a huge amount that I assumed they knew what they were doing.

'I've worked with this big star and that big star,' they'd say.

So, I thought, 'Goodness, they must be really good at what they do.'

They weren't the only people controlling me: it felt like

Henrik was at it as well. In the music industry, your manager is your boss and tells you what to do, what to wear and who to be, so our relationship naturally changed almost from the moment he took on the role. Henrik seemed to be always looking for ways to improve me: 'You've got so much potential, but you're not there yet,' he kept saying.

I loved Henrik with all my heart, but I couldn't help but feel that he had stopped looking at me as a wife and I became a product in his eyes. I don't think he heard me when I questioned him, because he had his own vision of what I should be – a superstar, an international diva, not Jane, the singer off *The Cruise*. I found I couldn't flourish in a relationship like this. It worked for Cilla brilliantly, but it didn't work for me, because I often thought, 'He's making the wrong choices here. I wouldn't have done that.'

Again, why would I follow his advice? He was another one who wasn't musical or a singer, and he was new to the business as well. Yet if he said, 'Look, believe me, this is the right decision,' and I said, 'No, it's not,' then it was argument time – not only between manager and artist, but also between husband and wife. The lines were too blurred and I didn't want us falling out. Perhaps, for this reason, Henrik always got his own way: 'Come on, let's go and have a walk,' he'd say and we'd go for a stroll round Newmillerdam, a beautiful spot just outside Wakefield.

I'd be thinking, 'I know what I want and I know it's right. I'm going to win this argument.' But by the time we'd walked round the dam, he would have talked me into whatever it was he wanted. It happened every single time.

Our biggest problem was that he wouldn't let me in.

It was such a mistake. After a while I didn't really feel as if we had a marriage – it was far more as if we were working together. From the moment we woke to the moment we went to sleep, we talked about the industry. We never shut the door on it and we argued a lot. It was the opposite of romantic. Meanwhile, everything I did flew and, with all the success I was having, I was like honey to the bees. In came the stylists, who were on huge amounts of money, saying, 'You need to change your appearance.'

I was a slightly overweight Northern woman in her thirties – just like many of the women in my audience, no doubt – and suddenly I was paying for all these experts to come in and dress me and style me. They wanted me to be classier, more polished – 'Cut your hair, lose weight, stop talking, put your arms away,' they said.

Some of them had good advice and I think they were genuinely trying to help me, but I didn't realise that they wanted a completely new image for me.

'You need a different hairstyle,' they said. 'Something fresh and modern and light!'

I had an appointment booked for me, a smart hairdresser in London. On the train down from Wakefield, I was looking forward to a bit of pampering and a glam new hairstyle. Just as long as nobody cut it too short, mind – I loved my big hair.

Little did I know that the stylists had already been in and said, 'We want the impish look.'

I sat down and the hairdresser cut all my hair off. My intake of breath was as sharp as his scissors.

'Did you not know about this?' he asked.

'No,' I said in a very small voice.

I nearly cried in my seat – I knew nothing about the impish look and hated having short hair. Since I didn't want to upset the hairdresser, I said, 'God, it's fabulous!'

This was the moment I really started to lose myself. People were taking me and stripping me down. I lost confidence and went through a stage of being very introverted. I couldn't do an interview without having two people from my team in the room with me. I didn't know how to speak anymore – I was afraid and looked to them for guidance.

'I'll have to turn to Henrik for the answer to that question,' I'd say. 'Henrik?'

I had really short hair all through my next tour and recording my second album, *Inspiration*, because that was the image everybody wanted for me, though heaven knows why. Henrik said it made me look sleek and polished, but I thought it was too severe.

My second tour, in 1999, was 27 dates nationwide and finished with a concert at the Royal Albert Hall, which was out of this world. I'd never been to the Albert Hall before I sang there, I'd only ever seen it on television. The tour was fantastic because of my wonderful fans, but I felt a bit as if I was playing a part rather than being the real me. The record company people had told Henrik, 'You can't have her chatting away between songs – it doesn't look professional, it's not polished enough.' They tried to stop me ad-libbing by giving me scripts to learn. It was ridiculous. I did my best to stick to what we'd rehearsed, but I kept slipping up. One of the shows was filmed for my DVD, *Jane McDonald In Concert*, and there's a moment when I'm talking about the great gigs I've been doing and, suddenly, I correct myself: 'I'm not supposed to say gigs anymore. They're concerts now, aren't they?'

Thousands of people had paid to come and see the Jane McDonald they'd seen on the telly, but they got a polished version instead and I'm not sure they liked her quite as much. It was hard for me, because I wanted to go on and say, 'What a day! Are you all right?' and start chatting about the soaps – I didn't want to be some great superstar that nobody could touch.

Henrik wasn't keen on me socialising after a show (he was worried it would affect my voice and health), and it was a very lonely existence. I just wanted a drink and a chat with Sue Ravey and some of the crew as I came down from performing, but I'd think, 'If I stay up and have a good time, I won't be able to do the job tomorrow.' I was ever so grateful that Sue was my backing singer, because at least I could have a joke with her onstage, if nowhere else.

At the end of the tour, the two Sues had my star chart done by a friend of Sue Ravey's cousin, Elizabeth, who was an astrologer called Pauline. When it was finished, the astrologer told Sue, 'I don't actually want to give her this.'

The chart predicted utter devastation: the stars were saying I would fall from the top to the very bottom and go from having everything to absolutely nothing. Sue came and spoke to me about it.

'We've had your chart done, but I don't think you'll want to read it,' she said.

'No, I'll take it, because if it's in the stars, then it's in the stars, isn't it?' I replied.

'Oh blimey, look at this!' we said, laughing, as we read it and tracked my downfall. 'We'd better make the best of things while we can.'

We took it with a pinch of salt. After all, unless I murdered somebody, it was hard to imagine how things could go wrong for me. After a successful pilot, the BBC had commissioned an 11-part series of a new primetime Saturday night television talent show, *Star for a Night*, and I was presenting. It was a triumph for Henrik, who had been very focused on finding me the right TV show for a long while. A lot of offers had come in for daytime programmes, but he had turned down every single one because he wanted me to have a Saturday night show. I admired him for sticking to his guns, even if he rubbed a lot of people up the wrong way in the process.

Back in the noughties, *Star for a Night* was the biggest

entertainment show on the BBC. It was great but it was also really hard work, because for me it was a huge step from being a cruise-ship singer to presenting my own Saturday night show. I was reading from an autocue, singing on the show and all the while thinking, 'Somebody's going to knock on my door in a minute and say, "Hang on, you can't do this, can you?"'

I felt I wasn't good enough: I wasn't trained, I was a fraud. I literally made everything up as I went along, so it was stressful, because I wasn't as practised at thinking on my feet as I am now. There was always so much going on in the studio: we had contestants, judges and special guests, and when I was out of the studio, I was travelling the length and breadth of the country, auditioning would-be contestants. *Star for a Night* proved a huge hit and I loved meeting people like 13-year-old Joss Stone, who won the contest the second year; it was great to give airtime to Alexandra Burke and all the many other talented people who took part too. But I wasn't ready: it had all happened too quickly and I didn't enjoy it very much.

I can't look at photos from that time in my life now without feeling sad, because I didn't know who I was then. I was somebody else who was manufactured. It was my own fault for letting it happen, but you're told that's what you have to do to get on. I often used to say, 'I hate my life.' And I started to fight back – I had so little control over my life that I began kicking off about the tiniest things.

I couldn't change my image or my schedule, but I could change my hotel room, so I used to go into a hotel and say, 'I don't want this room.'

'What's wrong with it?' the poor hotelier would ask.

There was nothing wrong with it, but it was the only piece of control I had.

'No, it's just not right. I don't feel right in here,' I'd insist.

One day, as I was leaving the house, my mother asked if I'd be home in time for tea at six o'clock.

'I'm too busy to think about that,' I snapped.

'Who are you? I don't even know who you are anymore,' she told me.

'Well, Mother, this is how you are when your life is like this,' I said.

When I got home, she said, 'What was all that about? I can see you've got some challenges, but don't forget where you've come from.'

I started crying and went up to my room; I felt so alone.

'You don't know what it's like,' I thought. 'No one understands how bad it is.'

Part of the problem, I think, was that, if you spend all your time in a highly controlled environment, it rubs off on you. It was a big lesson for me and that's why, these days, I'm careful to surround myself with light, like-minded people who get me and know me.

While I was busy being bad-tempered, Henrik was also feeling the strain. I remember sometimes when he was late leaving for work at our offices in Wakefield and Mum had a full breakfast laid out for him, he'd rush out, leaving it untouched and she'd just scrape it all in the bin.

I felt sorry for her because she'd spent time making that food. But Mum wasn't bothered because she was used to my dad being blunt.

'Aren't you angry?' I'd ask, because I could remember feeling furious in Florida when I'd had a meal ready for Henrik and he'd gone to the pub with some colleagues.

'No,' she'd say, 'he had to get into work early.'

'How can you be so nice about it?' I'd think.

He did some wonderful things, did Henrik. It was just his way of doing them that upset people, because he seemed to step on a lot of toes. I began to realise that, if somebody is representing you, it has to be someone who people want to negotiate with, because they are your ambassador. Just as importantly, I wanted him to be kinder to my mother, who was always doing nice things for him.

It was a really rocky time for Henrik and me. Our saving grace was the house in America, where we'd go whenever I got time off. We had a really nice time out there, away from the cares and worries of work, and sometimes I'd say, 'Let's pack it all in and move back to America. We're happy here. I don't care if I never sing another song in my life.'

'No, your career is too important,' he'd say. 'There's still so much for you to achieve.'

We changed record label to Universal before I recorded my second album, *Inspiration*, in 1999 – and it went to No. 6 when it came out in 2000.

'Why am I never played on the radio?' I asked the execs there, hoping a big label might have some clout to help make it happen.

They looked into it and came back saying, 'They won't put you on the playlist.'

'Why is that?' I asked.

'Because they won't play covers.'

'Right, I'll go and write my own then,' I thought.

Somebody telling me that I couldn't do something always makes me determined to find a way to do it. The next time I was in Florida, I wrote some songs on the cherry wood piano at the Lakes of Newport house, and two of them went on the album: 'The Hand That Leads Me' and 'Winner'. After that, I developed a taste for songwriting and I've written and recorded many songs since. But I still couldn't get on the playlist so I went back to Universal and said, 'Why?'

'Honestly? They just don't like you,' they said.

'Fair enough, I can take that,' I said. 'Just tell me the truth.'

13

Windmills Of Your Mind

One Sunday in early 2001, after we'd had one of my mother's fantastic roast lunches with Tony, Wendy and their daughter, Katie, Henrik and I went for a walk round Newmillerdam.

'Are we going to have a family?' I asked him.

He and I had talked about having children around the time of our wedding, but since then, the goalposts appeared to have changed: all we seemed to focus on was my career.

'You can have everything, but not all at once,' Henrik replied.

There wasn't room for babies in Henrik's plans for me. He had bigger ambitions, it seemed. 'Do you remember when we were in Las Vegas, we threw coins into the fountain outside the MGM Grand theatre?' he asked.

'Yes, and I wished that we would stay together forever,' I said, reaching for his hand. 'Come to think of it, you never told me what you wished for.'

His eyes glinted with excitement. 'I couldn't tell you because it wouldn't have come true. But I can tell you now, because it's all booked: I wished that one day you would play Vegas!'

'What?' I screeched.

He squeezed my hand. 'This is it, Jane. You're doing a concert at the MGM Grand! It's going to be huge. The BBC are going to film it. Chris Terrill is getting a crew together. It's going to be a documentary special called *Jane's Next Step*, about how you're moving on to bigger and better things.'

'I don't believe it,' I said, enjoying the feel of his hand in mine. It had been a while since I'd felt so close to him.

He pulled away. 'We just need the record company to get behind the album now,' he said.

I sensed his mood darkening. 'Is something wrong?' I asked.

'It will be fine,' he said firmly. 'I'm going down to have a meeting with them tomorrow.'

My third album was a collection of songs from films called *Love At The Movies*. The songs I had chosen were special to me for all kinds of reasons, and they were written by some of my very favourite songwriters, ranging from 'Ain't No Mountain High Enough' by Nickolas Ashford and Valerie Simpson to 'Windmills Of Your Mind' by Michel Legrand and Marilyn and Alan Bergman.

Michel Legrand was a particular favourite. The first film I'd ever watched from beginning to end was *Wuthering Heights* (1970) starring Timothy Dalton as Heathcliff, and the only thing that had kept me interested was Michel Legrand's score. Since then, I had come to know and love his music: he had written hit after hit, composed hundreds of film soundtracks and won multiple Oscars and Grammys. So, I was very excited when his agent got in touch with Henrik during the months of frantic preparation leading up to my Vegas show in June 2001.

'Can we set up a meeting? We think Jane and Michel would really work together.'

'He wants to meet me?' I said, when Henrik read out the fax.

A meeting was arranged at Steinway's showroom in London, and it was a meeting of minds. Michel was sitting at a piano in the basement when I arrived and we had a fabulous time, singing and playing to each other. There was so much warmth and joy emanating from him that I thought, 'I'm going to love working with this man!'

Chris Terrill was around and, when I told him about Michel's plans to work with me, he said, 'I've got to film this.'

So, we all met up at the Langham Hotel opposite the BBC in Great Portland Street and Michel and I played piano again.

'I can't wait to work with Jane,' Michel told Henrik. 'She has something in her voice that is quite unique. It's like a cry: it's called emotion. Not many people have it.'

'Flipping heck, he thinks I'm good!' I thought.

Henrik was beaming. He later told me that he was thinking to himself, 'Wow, this is going to be huge.'

Knowing that Michel was a wine buff, I said, 'Shall we have some wine?'

He looked down the wine list and saw something he liked, so we ordered it – and it was absolutely beautiful.

'Ooh, have some of this wine!' I kept saying to everybody around us. 'Let's have another bottle.'

When we got the bill, Henrik went white: 'Oh my God!' he said in a strangulated voice. 'That wine was £750 a bottle.'

No wonder it was the best wine I had ever tasted. It would be, at that price.

After that I had quite a few meetings with Michel. I absolutely loved him. He was fired up with enthusiasm about doing an album – and maybe a musical – together and said he was going to get the Bergmans out of retirement to write the lyrics. The producer Quincy Jones was one of his best friends and he'd rung him and said, 'Would you like to come and work on this album with this new singer I've found?' and Quincy said, 'Yes.'

Henrik and I were over the moon. We went into Universal and said, 'We have this chance to work with Michel Legrand and the Bergmans and Quincy Jones . . .'

The Universal bosses just looked at us and laughed. 'You'll be telling us that Michael Jackson's doing backing vocals next,' said one.

Their reaction puzzled me.

'No, this is for real,' I said.

'It will be massive, it will go worldwide,' Henrik chipped in. 'The BBC have started to film it coming together. We can link it to Jane's show in Vegas and the album. She's already going to be singing "Windmills Of Your Mind". Everything connects!'

A silence ensued. Finally, they shook their heads and said, 'Nobody will buy it. There isn't a market for it.'

I was dumbfounded. Were they mad? Of course, people would buy it – this was one of the world's great composers teamed with two amazing lyricists and a genius producer.

'Don't you see? It's a once-in-a-lifetime chance . . .'

My voice trailed off. Nobody said a word.

'Get your coat, it's over,' Henrik said, and we walked out of Universal. 'Nobody's getting behind you anymore. Nobody cares,' he grumbled as we made our way home, completely disillusioned.

I rang Chris Terrill and told him what had happened. 'I can't believe they've turned it down, especially as I'd already started filming it,' he said.

It was a missed opportunity and a real regret, but I had to let it go. I still went on to sing 'Windmills Of Your Mind' for the album and I did so with a full orchestra, as a nod to Michel.

I threw myself into preparing for my big Vegas show, but then catastrophe struck just as we were about to board the plane to America. Chris Terrill phoned to say that the BBC had pulled out of filming the documentary: 'I'm sorry, Jane. I tried to persuade them not to, I can't understand it.'

It was a huge shock. Henrik had invested a lot in the Vegas concert: we'd got everything set up, the band were already out in

America and a crew were on their way to film the concert for a video release. It knocked Henrik for six; he was beyond disappointed. All his projects were crashing down around us.

'What do we do now?' he said, putting his head in his hands.

'We go ahead and we do it,' I said.

The next couple of weeks were awful. I don't know how I got through the concert. It was a dream come true, the biggest performance of my career – in Vegas! – but I was on autopilot, because it was in Vegas that I realised my marriage was in serious trouble.

We were staying in a beautiful suite in Vegas. It was fantastically luxurious and had a lift up to the bedrooms. The hotel manager told me that it was the suite Barbra Streisand sometimes stayed in when she was in town. We only had one night off during our stay and I was excited about spending it with Henrik: 'Let's have a lovely dinner sent up, just the two of us,' I said.

Just as we were sitting down to eat, the door went – Henrik had invited some of the press up to our suite to join us.

'That's it,' I thought miserably. 'He doesn't want to spend any time with me.'

The Vegas live concert video went into production when we got back to England and it was a big success when it came out, but the release of the *Love At The Movies* album in October 2001 didn't go so well. It was a good album and people loved it, but the record company didn't get behind it. If an album isn't promoted, the public won't know it's in the shops and no one will buy it – it's that simple. Since you're only as good as your last set of sales figures, our relationship with the label was starting to feel the strain.

First, Michel Legrand, then Vegas, now my album and record deal: everything seemed to be going wrong, including my marriage. Meanwhile, Wendy, being Henrik's PA, was concerned.

Wendy worked directly for Henrik because I was off singing and doing TV shows, and of course she was in the office with him every day. She confided in Tony.

'Well, we'll have to tell Jane,' he said.

It was a difficult situation for Wendy. There has been many an occasion when someone has said something about the husband and it's been the family member that's been cast out. My sister-in-law knew she had to tread very carefully and she was wise to do so in the way she did. She told Tony, who passed bits and pieces on to my mother, who drip fed things to me in her own clever way.

'How does it all work? Where does the money go?' Mum asked me one day over a cup of tea, her face a picture of innocence.

'Mother, I have no idea! I just get an allowance paid into my account monthly,' I said.

It got me thinking, just as Mum knew it would: 'Maybe I should pay more attention,' I thought. I started to question Henrik: 'What's going on with this particular thing?' I'd say.

'How do you know about that?' he'd respond. 'Just stick to being an artist and I'll take care of the rest.'

This was something he always said, but the tone in which he said it gradually changed over time. At first, it was Henrik being protective. There was so much going on that he wanted me to be able to focus on my singing and press appearances, and I appreciated the way he tried to shield me from the cut-and-thrust of the business side of my career, but lately, I sensed a change and instead of giving me a paternal pat on the head and saying, 'Don't worry yourself about it,' he would give a curt answer to my questions. I can see now he was under considerable stress, but it was upsetting. I had to be very careful how I handled it, because he couldn't know there was a leak in the office, as it would put Wendy in an even trickier situation.

But Henrik soon worked out what was going on: 'I want to tell you things myself, I don't want it to come from your brother,' he said sternly.

I began to feel lonely in my marriage. There were a lot of things that I wasn't supposed to say (I talked too much, I sounded common) and I found it difficult not to be open about our money troubles.

I couldn't help thinking back to the time on the ships when I had written a list of my ideal attributes in a man. Back then I was feeling insecure and wanted a man to look after me, and I forgot to put down some of the most important qualities, like 'kind, warm heart and loving'. I started to rebel, ever so slightly. One evening, Sue Ravey and I went along to the filming of *An Audience With* . . . I think Ricky Martin was the star of the show that night, though I wouldn't put money on it. What I do know is that I ended up having quite a few drinks. I remember chatting to the comedian Paul O'Grady first, and then he left and we had a drink with some people who worked with the presenter Graham Norton, and then Graham joined us. We had the best night. Sue was on top form, I was cracking jokes, everything seemed funny and we were laughing and laughing . . . until Sue looked at her phone and said, 'Henrik is waiting outside.'

I mulled it over for a moment; I pictured Henrik outside in the car. 'I'm staying in here where I'm having a good time,' I thought.

'Oh, sod it, let's have another drink!' I said.

When we finally made it to the car, I sank down in the back seat, giggling. Sue kicked me to shut me up, but I couldn't stop. 'I've been a bit of a rebel tonight and I've had a drink, and I don't care.'

I rarely stood my ground with him. There's only one other time I can remember, during my tour that autumn. We were in the bar of The Hilton, in Blackpool, where everybody was having a drink after the show. We'd all had a great night and were still feeling high from the concert.

Henrik looked at his watch: 'Right, you, bed,' as he always did.

'No, I think I'll stay here for a bit,' I said.

There was a pause. It was the first time anybody had heard me say no to him. He turned and walked away without a word.

It was around this time that the record company dropped me, which was a big blow. I think it was almost worse for Henrik than for me. He felt he was failing – at managing me and at being married to me. When we'd first started out, he was the shiny new husband, I had a shiny career and everything we touched was gold. Then all of a sudden it was gone. I'm sure he must have been thinking, 'She's come to the end of it now, she's on her way out.' Now, he saw things were declining, that the shine was going off the star a little bit. He couldn't move me on to anything, or get me another deal. A lot of doors were slammed in our faces.

We learned the hard way that you won't get anywhere in this business if people can't make money from you. That's the first rule of thumb – you have to fit into certain boxes and make yourself exploitable, otherwise you won't be a success. And when you are a success, you end up paying an awful lot out to a lot of people. It's not an easy industry to make money in.

Henrik hated seeing me being exploited, because he felt it was unfair to me. At every opportunity he fought my corner, but occasionally upset people in the process. Unfortunately, because he was representing me, his reputation was my reputation, and so I got a name for being a diva. But it wasn't me saying, 'No, Jane won't do this or that.' That's just what managers say, somebody talking on your behalf is not you.

Our marriage was already on the rocks when we went down

to London to spend a weekend with Michael and Janice, my old friends from Casanova's. By now Michael was big in property and assumed we would be looking for good investment opportunities, considering how much money I must have made: 'Maybe you should start investing in property. It's the way to go,' he said.

We went to look at a house together. A breathtakingly gorgeous Georgian house in a quiet square, it had high corniced ceilings and beautiful bay windows.

'We can't afford this,' I said.

Michael laughed. 'If anybody can afford this, you can.'

'No, we haven't got that type of money,' I insisted.

'Well, you should have that type of money,' Janice said softly.

On the Monday morning, Henrik stayed in London to attend a meeting and I took the train back to Wakefield. Mulling over what Mike and Janice had said, I thought, 'Something's not right.' And so I phoned Wendy from the train: 'I'm coming into the office to look at the books.'

'Thank God for that!' she said. 'We can't say anything to you because it would be interfering with a marriage and we work for Henrik, but we've been watching what's been going on and praying something would bring it to light . . .'

I went into the office and scoured the accounts with Wendy and Caroline: there was no money anywhere. I couldn't believe it. After all that work I'd done. For years, I'd never had a minute's peace: I'd had albums out, books out, tours sold out, a top TV show . . . I should have been a multimillionaire, but I didn't have any money in the bank.

Until this point, I had left everything on the business side to Henrik, but now I took over. I looked at everybody on the payroll and thought, 'Hang on a minute, I've got an office in London. I've got this, that and the other, but noughts everywhere.'

I had to let go of quite a few people on the payroll – I couldn't afford to keep them on, so I had no choice. I did a crash course in business, learned everything there was to know about my income, expenses and outgoings, not to mention bought ledger and bookkeeping. I combed the books and had figures running through my head, day and night. Eventually, I came to the devastating conclusion that I really did have nothing left and told Henrik, 'I'm firing you as my manager.'

I was only half-joking and he laughed, 'But I'm your husband.'

He had a point.

'Well, things aren't going right here,' I said. 'I've got to do something.'

It's a shock when you've been so big and then, suddenly, you're fighting lawyers and saying, 'But hang on a minute, where's that gone?'

'Well, you signed that.'

'I did? I signed it?'

Things had been amazing while my career was riding high. Everybody loved my story and where I had come from. They seemed so pleased for me that I never imagined they would want to exploit me. But that's the business, and I had been far too gullible and trusting.

My head was constantly whirring with figures. I bombarded Henrik with questions.

'You don't trust me, do you?' he said eventually.

'No,' I admitted.

We both felt a terrible sense of failure – we could see it in each other's face. My work had dried up, I had no record company, no TV show, the phone seldom rang . . . It felt as if the whole industry had turned their backs on us.

I don't blame Henrik for going – he couldn't get on with the industry and came up against so many people and so many difficulties. It must have been very hard for him: living for me, giving everything up for me and seeing me exploited. He had loved me once but I could see in his eyes that he didn't love me anymore. And you can't make someone love you.

I didn't feel any malice towards him, because he had tried his best and it didn't work – and you have to let people go with a good heart. He wanted to go back to America and live his own life and I loved him enough to let him do that. The day after the tour ended, in the summer of 2002, he left, briefcase in hand.

Boom, everything went from under me, and there was nothing left. I'd lost my manager, my husband, all my money, my self-respect and my work.

'What's gone wrong?' I wondered.

It was a horrible place to be, when everybody shuns you, including your own husband. I had gone from being at the very top and everybody going, 'Isn't she fab?' to nobody wanting me anymore. It was very hard. It felt as if my life was in the gutter.

The welcome that had once been there for me in the industry had gone cold. I used to love going to *An Audience With* . . . but now I wasn't on the list anymore – they had crossed me off. One night, I had to ring up a friend and say, 'Can you get me in?'

I remember seeing someone there that night who was very, very high up in the business. He didn't have a lot of time for me.

'You've got so many bridges to build,' he told me. 'If you ever come back, it'll be a miracle.'

'I've got the cement mixer outside now, as we speak,' I said. 'I'll build as many bridges as you want.'

I felt destroyed, but I had to do something about the mess I was in. My final tour had been amazingly successful, but it hadn't made any money. I don't know why. With no work and no income, I thought, 'Well, it's sink or swim, isn't it?'

'You'll be fine, love,' Mum said. 'There'll be something around the corner, wait and see.'

I imagined I'd probably end up going back on the ships, but later that summer, an offer came in to play the part of the nurse in a new West End production of *Romeo and Juliet: The Musical*.

'It's not for me,' I told Wendy. 'I've had enough, I can't be bothered.'

Wendy looked alarmed. 'No, Jane, you have to,' she said.

'What do you mean?'

'You're in debt, you've got a tax bill coming. You have to take this show.'

I had forgotten about the tax bill and so I took a deep breath and went into the West End to earn money and keep afloat – and I'm very glad I did, because it was a great production. *Romeo and Juliet: The Musical* had come from France and was a really good piece of music. The part of the nanny was perfect for me. I had to cry over Juliet every night, and sometimes I sobbed my heart out.

The director, David Freeman, taught me a powerful lesson. 'As a singer, you sing all these heartbreaking songs and you have to keep it together when you see your audience crying,' he said. 'But I want you to forget everything you've learned. You're acting now, you have to stop holding it in. You have to sing it and howl.'

So, I did. I let everything out, and one of the reviews went on to say something along these lines: 'We knew she could sing, but Jane McDonald is a surprisingly good actress!'

Living in London gave me a chance to regroup. I was working in the West End, earning great money and going out to clubs with the youngsters from the cast. I grew my hair. I lost weight. I got my tiny hips back. The divorce diet worked for me. But I didn't tell anyone that my marriage had ended. I wasn't facing up to everything that had gone on; I couldn't move on and leave the past behind.

Henrik and I met up for one last time on Christmas Day, 2002, after the show had been on for a couple of months.

'Be careful,' my mother warned when she rang the night before, 'because he's going to say to you, "I want to have a family." He's going to want to have a baby with you.' She was very clever, my mum – she knew exactly how Henrik ticked. 'But you can't go down that path again,' she added.

'Don't worry, I've made up my mind to split for good,' I said.

When Henrik arrived, he could see that I was okay again. I was starring in a big West End musical. I had paid off the debts and the tax bill. My hair was flowing. Within two hours of him coming through the door, it felt just like old times again. But in my head I heard my mother saying, 'Don't go down that path.'

'He's left me once, he'll do it again,' I thought.

'No, I want a divorce,' I said. 'Merry Christmas!'

Two weeks later, I went down with the flu – and I mean, proper flu, the type that can kill you. It knocked me out. I had a dangerously high temperature. I couldn't eat. I couldn't get out of bed. At the time I thought it was a reaction to a flu jab, but I think it was also because I hadn't processed properly what had happened to me emotionally.

My brother came to the rescue. Tony drove down to my flat in the van, packed up my things and drove me home, in time-honoured style. I never went back to the show.

Back home in Wakefield, I collapsed. I spent a long time in bed, just getting over my physical symptoms, and when I was better, I didn't want to come out of the house. I was skint, I was beaten down and my spirit was broken for a little while. I cried a lot and went over everything in my head: 'Why has everyone turned their back on me? Why?'

I was the most miserable I have ever been.

I thought back to some of the things people had said, things like, 'Your star has fallen. It was 15 minutes of fame, be thankful you've had it.'

'Maybe they're right,' I thought sadly. 'Maybe my career is over and it's time to stop.'

I dreaded the thought of telling people that Henrik had left. There had been nothing in the press so far and I knew the moment would come when I would be forced to talk about it. Fear haunted me. I was terrified of letting people down. Millions of people had bought into my fairytale life – my wedding to Henrik had been bigger than some royal weddings. But now the dream was shattered, there was no happy-ever-after. After four years of marriage, everything had fallen apart. I imagined a lot of people being disappointed in me.

I was so lucky to have my mother. She was my saviour and she was also a great healer. If you had a headache or a bad back, Mum only had to put a hand on you and you'd start to feel better. Maybe she was only planting the idea of feeling better in your head, but it always worked. My grandmother had been a gifted clairvoyant and my mum had definitely inherited the gift of healing. And Mum managed to coax me out of the house: 'Will you come to the butcher's with me? I can't carry all the bags,' she said one day, after I'd been stuck inside moping for weeks.

'Oh no, Mum, please don't make me.'

'I need your help, Jane,' she insisted. 'Please help me.'

'I've got to go,' I thought.

That was my first day out: going to the butcher's with Mum.

'Hello, Jane,' people said, as we went about the shopping.

All I said was, 'Oh, hi.'

I didn't want to meet anyone. I didn't want to speak to anyone or look them in the eye. I'd gone from being the golden person to nothing. I'd lost everything. I was a failure.

One of my friends – who was a psychologist, funnily enough – came round to see me. 'Oh, God, what's happened to you?' he said, when he saw me huddled up on the sofa, wrapped in a duvet.

'I'm done with the music industry. I want to get a job as a supervisor in Marks & Spencer,' I told him.

'Why's that?' he said.

'Because you get 20 per cent off,' I sniffed.

He laughed. Knowing I'd been left with a huge mortgage, he said, 'Well, if you don't go back to work, you're going to lose this house. Have you thought about that?'

'I can live in a caravan,' I said. 'That'll be fine for me.'

Mum came bustling in with a tray. 'Here we are,' she said. 'There's nothing a cup of tea can't fix.'

My friend looked at me and I looked back at him.

'What about my mother? I can't do that to her,' I thought. 'Right, Jane,' I decided, 'get a grip.'

14
With A Little Help From My Friends

It took me a while to get back on my feet. I watched a lot of TV, cried for hours and tried to work out what had gone so wrong. 'I had everything, and now I've got nothing apart from a disc on my wall,' I kept thinking. 'Why? Why have people treated me so badly? How could they do this to me?' Then one day it dawned on me: 'Hang on, it's not everybody else's fault why you're a failure, you have to take responsibility for yourself. The only common denominator here is you.'

I gave myself a flipping good talking to. 'Why is all this happening to you? It's because you're not taking control. You were a strong woman when you were working in the clubs and then you gave all your power away to somebody who didn't have any experience. What were you thinking? It serves you right!'

My mother was very patient with me. She made sure I ate enough and got out of the house for a walk in the fresh air. Then, one day, while we were watching QVC, I saw an advertisement for a self-help book by Anthony Robbins called *Unlimited Power: The New Science of Personal Achievement*. 'What a load of rubbish,' I thought, but ordered it anyway.

It turned out to be a very helpful guide and reminded me of a book I'd read on the ships about positive visualisation and vibration: *Excuse Me, Your Life Is Waiting: The Astonishing Power of Feelings* by Lynn Grabhorn.

'Have you still got that book I lent you?' I asked Mum.

She found it on the bookshelf in her bedroom and I re-read it eagerly.

Both of these books had a positive message and lots of practical advice. 'Stop being a victim and start being who you should be,' I told myself. I began to look after myself properly, went swimming or to the gym every day and worked on thinking more positively. Within a couple of months, I was feeling better.

I began to see more of my old mates. 'I don't want to make the same mistakes again,' I told one particular friend, a very wealthy businessman.

He gave me four tips I've never forgotten: 'Be careful who you choose as your partner,' he said. 'You are a very strong woman but you've got a vulnerable side.

'Always, always sign your own cheques! Never let anyone sign them on your behalf.

'Keep a separate account for your tax and your VAT and subtract them from your earnings before anything goes into your business account.

'And don't take advice from anyone who doesn't earn as much as, or more than, you do.'

It all made sense, and I realised then that the only way I could take control of my career was by knowing the entertainment business inside out so I found Henrik's copy of *Everything You'd Better Know About the Music Industry* and read it from cover to cover. I learned about advances, percentages and promoters' fees and vowed to read everything before I signed it in future, after seeking advice from an independent lawyer.

My fight came back. 'You've had all that success and it's been brilliant,' I thought. 'You've lost almost everything, but look what you've got. You've still got the golden goose – you *are* the golden goose! That's what you have to remember.'

When Henrik rang in early 2003 and asked when I would be coming back to America to pick up my belongings, I said, 'No, I'm not coming back. Just give it all to charity. I don't want anything from the house.'

'You want nothing? What about your piano? What about all your clothes here and . . . ?'

'Give it all away. It's not important to me, Henrik.'

I knew that, if I went over to America to collect my things, he would talk me into staying. He was a master in the art of talking me round and getting what he wanted. Anyway, I believe it's not worth fighting over a sofa. Let it go, start afresh and change. When, eventually, I did have to go over to Florida to get some keys to some safe deposit boxes a few months later, I took my mother with me to keep me grounded. Otherwise I could easily have waltzed off into the sunset with Henrik again, against my better judgement.

Henrik and I met in the foyer of my hotel. I was feeling fantastic: slim and fit and healthy. He took one look at me and said, 'Why on earth have we split up?'

'You know why,' I said, laughing.

'Shall we get back—' he started saying.

Part of me was tempted. I still respected and admired Henrik for everything he'd done for me, and we'd had some very happy times together. Yet I couldn't forget how unhappy I had been when our marriage ended.

'It was amazing while it was good between us, but I couldn't cope with it going wrong again,' I cut in.

He cocked his head and looked puzzled. 'Don't tell me: your mother's upstairs, isn't she?'

'Yes, she is!' I said.

His face fell for he knew there was no chance of talking me round if my mother was with me – Mum was my guardian.

A couple of weeks after I got home, I had a phone call from a friend in the media, saying, 'The press have found out that Henrik's gone. You need to put a statement out.'

So I put a statement out the next day and wondered what would happen next. A daytime panel show called *Loose Women* was among the first to contact me.

'Will you come on as a guest to talk about your marriage breaking up?' they wanted to know.

I liked *Loose Women*. My mum and I sometimes switched it on at lunchtime, because it was easy to watch and had a light touch, even when covering serious subjects. Kaye Adams was the anchor in those days and she's a really intelligent, funny woman. We enjoyed watching Kaye lead a panel of three female media figures in discussing the issues of the day.

Any interview about my divorce was going to be uncomfortable, but I felt I would probably be safer in Kaye's hands than anyone else's. And at least I had long hair again – I felt fit and had glowing skin – so nobody watching would be saying, 'Oh dear, look at the state of her! What's happened here?'

So I travelled up to Anglia Studios in Norwich, where they filmed *Loose Women* in those days. To start with, I felt very nervous but the panel were so welcoming that I soon relaxed. I had planned more or less what I was going to say and, as the interview progressed, I felt I was coming across quite well. Then they took me by surprise and showed a clip of my wedding to Henrik, without any warning at all.

Suddenly I was transported back to being happy and madly in love, with a gorgeous man by my side and a soaring career ahead of me. My expression was full of hope and laughter, the setting was breathtaking and my dress exquisite – everything about the scenes I was watching unfold on the screen seemed beautiful and untarnished.

I put my head in my hands and tried to absorb the shock of seeing into the past after such a long time.

'Oh no, I don't know what to say!' I burst out. 'I haven't seen this since it was broadcast, six years ago.'

Later, I was told that you could see emotions flitting across my face like shadows as the memories flooded back. I remember longing for the lost love and tenderness of my early days with Henrik and feeling heartbroken all over again that my marriage was over. After that, I went to pieces and poured out my heart live on air. People seemed surprised at how open I was, but I always have worn my heart on my sleeve.

Watching the TV monitor behind the scenes, the *Loose Women* producers said, 'She's so real! We need her on the show.'

When the interview was over, I left the studios feeling as if a huge burden had been lifted from my shoulders. I'd been so worried about what people would think when I told them my fairytale bubble had burst, but there had been only warmth and sympathy coming from everybody in the *Loose Women* studios. Something told me that things were going to be all right, after all.

I'd be the first to admit that I couldn't have got through it all without my mother. She helped me through the worst of times; she got me up on my two feet again like nobody else could have done. So, as soon as I had a bit of money after paying off my tax and debts, I thought, 'Right, I'm going to spend it on my mother and me.

'Enjoy your money,' I decided, 'because otherwise someone's going to take it off you!'

I had a friend who had been a commanding officer for Celebrity Cruises and was now working for Silversea. 'Why don't you go on a cruise?' he suggested. 'Just treat yourself and have a break.'

'Do you fancy going?' I asked Mum.

She did.

So, I took my mother on a cruise to the Seychelles. We went first class as well, so it was a dream holiday for both of us, and the sunshine and fine dining did us the world of good. I was proud to be with Mum – she was so funny and vivacious and always looked amazing. She loved her clothes, did my mother, she dressed immaculately, and of course never skimped on shoes. She was also quite canny about underwear.

'Jane, you're getting older,' she told me. 'Now you're 40, you need a foundation garment.'

It was a slightly depressing thought.

'Mum, I'm a size 12. I don't need a foundation garment,' I protested.

Actually, she was right, because modern shapewear can work wonders. It smooths out the lumps and bumps and gives you a great contour, especially if you're wearing a gown.

I did a lot of thinking on that cruise to the Seychelles. As I looked at all the happy couples around me, I tried to work out why both my marriages had failed. I thought about my brother and his wife and their lovely relationship, and my sister and her husband's fabulous marriage. Was my problem that I compromised too little or too much? I couldn't seem to find a balance, I couldn't work out how to get it right.

Mum and I got talking to a well-known psychologist at dinner one evening.

'There's nothing behind your eyes, what's gone on with you?' he asked me, looking concerned.

I laughed it off by saying I was tired and hadn't had a holiday for a while, but Mum took me aside later and said, 'Please talk to him.'

'I don't need to talk to anyone,' I insisted, but somehow, I ended up telling him everything, coaxed along by my mother.

The psychologist was quite direct. 'You're picking all the wrong men, you need to go for somebody completely different,' he said. 'You're following the same pattern again and again and you have to stop. You are attracted to powerful men. In turn, they are drawn to your vulnerable side, but when they inevitably try to control you, you fight it.'

It was true that I always went for a certain type: I went for what I knew. Now I had to break the pattern and go for someone with a big heart. I reviewed my checklist.

'What do you want?' I asked myself. 'You've got the ability to earn your own money. Why do you feel you need someone who matches you financially? I'm going for the wrong things in life,' I realised.

I didn't need a great deal of wealth or success to make me happy; my ideal man didn't have to be rich or powerful, he just needed to be kind and loving.

There was a sax player from Poland playing in the band on the ship. His name was Jarek Pyc and I noticed him immediately because he was really talented. He was also handsome, kind and gentle. I wouldn't normally have gone for him, but I thought, 'Well, he's different.'

When your husband has left you, you need verification that you're all right, and that's what Jarek gave me. He was there for me at the right moment and we had a lovely holiday romance that spilled over into real life and continued for a couple of years, on and off. Jarek brought joy back into my life and made me feel attractive again. He was a ray of sunshine and I'm very grateful for the way he helped me heal after my divorce.

One morning on the ship, I looked in the mirror and saw my old self again. There had been times while I was married to

Henrik when I'd seen my reflection and thought, 'Who are you? I don't even know you.' But now I looked at myself and thought, 'Ah, you're back.'

The feeling of being my old self again grew stronger by the day. Back in Wakefield, my good friend Sue Ravey came over for a drink and said, 'After all you've been through, you're still a singer. Why don't you get out on the road again?'

Sue knew a promoter who was keen to offer me a mini tour and she suggested bringing in some of our mates for the band and backing singers.

'Let's do it,' I said, trying to shake off the vestiges of self-doubt.

At the time I was still seeing Jarek, who was on a break from the ships, so I brought him in to play sax and be my musical director. Sue was the senior vocalist: she was also good at keeping people in line and making sure that everybody knew what they were doing. It felt great to be surrounded and supported by friends; it was a time of rebirth. During our rehearsals I thought, 'Yes, I can do this as long as I've got people I feel safe with.'

As the first night of the tour approached I started to feel anxious, however. I had played the Royal Albert Hall and Vegas, but this concert at the Wolverhampton Grand Theatre in autumn 2003 began to feel like the most important gig of my life. It was also the most petrifying. I had worked alone for 15 years before I got married, but now I was worried that I couldn't do it without Henrik by my side. Suddenly, I was Miss Insecurity without him.

Every critical comment I had ever heard came swarming back into my head. I had to bat them away, one by one.

'Stop talking! You're so common.'

'No, I'm not. It's just that I'm not the superstar you wanted me to be, I'm a Yorkshire lass.'

'Don't show your arms! You're too old.'

'Stop carping! I like this dress and I'm having my arms out.'
Your career is finished.

'Get out of my head! I've got a packed house tonight and I'm going to give it all I've got.'

But I was scared. My confidence had been knocked. I had gone from being the golden girl to being told, 'Nobody wants you anymore. Nobody cares.' And I had believed it.

Chris Terrill came along to film me: 'I feel I should be here,' he said. It was good to see him. He followed me on tour and edited the footage into a documentary called *Being Jane*.

'I hope they still like me now that Henrik's gone,' I thought. People had loved me for my dream-come-true story. I was worried that divorce and heartbreak had taken away my shine.

Thankfully, walking onstage felt like coming home. It was so emotional to see the familiar faces of my fans out in the audience.

'You're here,' I thought, relief washing over me. 'Thank you.'

The fans were so glad to see me. They sang along with me and kept me going through difficult songs like 'You're My World', which I had always dedicated to Henrik because it seemed to sum up my feelings for him when we were first in love. It was bittersweet to be performing it without him looking on from the wings, but my friends in the crowd gave it new meaning by helping me to sing it again, and that felt very special

'We're on your side, Jane. We'll help you make it through,' they seemed to be saying. They held me up and carried me through a very difficult evening.

I owe my fans a great deal. They have been there for me, no matter what, and they've kept me going and given me joy during some of the most tragic times of my life. Their reaction when I go onstage and the energy they give me always lifts me up. It may sound a bit strange when I talk about loving them, but why wouldn't I love them when they've helped me so much? You've got to love your fans and I love mine with a passion; I need them and they need me. I will always be grateful to them.

It wasn't an easy tour, because I kept reliving the heartache with Henrik at every stop. In one way, it was like therapy, and it was affirming to have to keep on explaining to people, 'Henrik's gone, but I'm all right.' But it took its toll, because every night I had to open up about how my life had fallen apart. By the end I wanted to leave the past behind and move on – which was probably why I was finally able to do just that.

Everything started to fit into place, and in 2004, when *Loose Women* moved from Norwich to be based in London, I was invited to join the panel. Getting a job on the lunchtime panel show was a lifesaver: it gave me the chance to build bridges and start afresh in the industry. And it was the ideal job for me, in many ways, as I like working with women and find talking a lot easier than singing. When you're singing, you have to think about so many things, like pitch, projection and emotion, but anyone can talk, can't they? The great thing about *Loose Women* was that you could be yourself. You didn't have to pretend to be anything you weren't and that made it very enjoyable.

Whoever picked the pool of women did a good job, because we were all very, very different, but complemented each other really well. There were eight of us in the beginning: women in their forties and fifties with massive personalities, who loved having a laugh. After a while, I couldn't help thinking, 'I love this group of girls.' You cannot insult each other as much as we did without being good mates and that came across very strongly on the programme. It was a huge part of our appeal, I think – we could insult each other and then laugh about it in the next breath. We were the 'Loose Women'.

I was lucky to work with a group of women who were my bezzie mates. Good, strong women like Lynda Bellingham, Jackie

Brambles, Andrea McLean, Denise Welch, Carol Vorderman, Coleen Nolan, Kate Thornton, Lisa Maxwell, Sherrie Hewson and Carol McGiffin, among others. I felt that I could have rung any of them if I was in trouble, and they'd have all been there. We went through a lot together.

I used to love being on with Carol McGiffin. We were a brilliant double act because we never agreed on anything. I remember once she said to me, 'I'm not calling you a liar, but I just don't believe you.'

Carol could say things like that to me, and I would laugh and say, 'You misery! What's up with you? Just cheer up!'

Lynda Bellingham was very forthright. God, I loved Lynda. She was so full of life and very wise with it, so you always had a good time with her. You had to be punctual if you went out with Lynda, though – she was very particular and couldn't stand anybody being late.

Denise Welch was cheeky, she was a terror. She used to just say something provocative and I'd think, 'How are we going to get out of this one?' She was really good at making us go, 'Hmm, okay . . .'

Then there were the anchors, who have the hardest job in the world, because they can't really take sides. They have opinions, but they've got to sit on the fence and stay neutral. All the anchors I worked with – Kaye Adams, Kate Thornton, Jackie Brambles and Andrea McLean – were all fabulous. Andrea McLean is such a sweet girl. There isn't a bad bone in her body, but she's also strong and holds her own. It's inspiring to work alongside people who are really good at what they do, and all the 'Loose Women' were exceptionally good at what they did. They were well read and knew what they were talking about. I upped my game straight away, and started reading the papers every day.

Sometimes our debates reminded me of being at home as

a kid, watching my brother and sister kick off. 'Here they go,' I'd think every time we discussed something controversial. 'They haven't even realised what this is actually about.' Often I couldn't get a word in edgeways, so I'd leave them to roll on. Then, all of a sudden, the producer would say, 'Will somebody let Jane speak?'

I'd come in at the end with a completely different point of view: 'Why would you think that? What about this angle?' I'd say.

Now that calmed them down.

'She's done it again,' they'd say. 'Oh, flip!'

You couldn't help opening up about your life on the show, but I never bad-mouthed Henrik, because I didn't feel any resentment towards him. He made a lot of things happen, from *Star For A Night* to the show in Vegas; he fought my corner, had my professional interests at heart and valued my abilities and talent. I learned a lot from him and I've always been grateful to him for all that he taught me, even if our divorce was expensive. People were shocked that I still had a mortgage after all the success I'd had, but I look back and think it was probably good for me, because it meant I had to go out and work. If I'd had all the money that I should have had, I might have become a recluse after Henrik left. Instead, I had to look after my mother and make sure she was okay, because she'd got very used to the lifestyle – she'd become accustomed, as they say.

My mother was the best part of me, the good side, and I valued her advice. I used to ring her and say, 'We're discussing this on *Loose Women* today and I'm going to approach it this way.'

'You can't say that,' she'd say. 'Why don't you say it like this?'

Her mantra was always: 'It's nice to be nice' – she was the fifth Loose Woman, really.

Eventually, I thought, 'I'm going to have to live my own life sooner or later. I can't just keep ringing my mother to ask, "What shall I say?"' So, I started ringing her after the show instead of before it: 'I agreed with every word you said,' she'd tell me. I was happy when she thought I'd got the balance right.

Mum was never critical of me unless I needed it. There was a point when I started to put on quite a lot of weight and she said, 'You're getting a little bit . . . I'm your mother, I can tell you this. Cut down a little bit.'

'Okay, thanks, Mum.'

Then, just like mothers do, she'd feel bad and say, 'Right, do you want a scone?' or, 'Can I do you a bacon sandwich?' It was all good material for the show and I used to make people laugh with my stories about living with my mother. There was an endless source of anecdotes, because Mum was very funny in herself, and so kind and loving.

I loved being on *Loose Women*, but felt a constant pull towards performing and recording. People kept telling me, 'You can't do both. You're either a TV star or you're a singer.'

'Why?' I'd ask.

'Because that's just how it is,' came the answer.

'Says who?'

I couldn't help myself, though – after all those years of singing and live performing, it was as if a powerful magnet kept drawing me back to the stage. And if there was anything I had learned by now, it was not to listen to other people when they told me I couldn't do anything. Now that I was back in the public eye, I knew I was a viable proposition as a singer again and, on the back of my comeback tour, I brought an album out on the DMG label, *You Belong To Me*, in early 2005. It did fairly well, but when I did the sums, I thought, 'There must be another way to do this.'

I went back to Henrik's book about the music industry, which said that the only reason you need a record company is if you haven't got the money to produce your music yourself. Since I now had my own resources, what was stopping me? When you're with one of the majors, you will get an awful lot more sales, because a major company can get radio play and promote you worldwide. But if you have a fanbase who will buy your albums, you don't need that kind of promotion.

It was a light-bulb moment. 'I don't need a record company!' I realised. 'All I need to do is fund my music and have a distributor.'

I started to invest my money in my shows, my records and my songwriting. It took a lot of bottle because I was often risking everything I had, but it made total sense, because every expense was tax deductible. I went on to do further tours and, as the company began to build, I brought out my first album on my own label in 2008. Entitled *Jane*, it went to No. 7 in the UK charts, and I probably earned as much from that album as I had from my first album, which had gone platinum, because this time around I wasn't paying all the record company cuts and percentages. It was a revelation to me. The only downside was that I was never going to get on any of the major playlists, but I felt I could live with that.

It's funny: you're told, 'You can't do this. You can't do that,' and you think you need a man in charge, even though sometimes they're nowhere near as bright as you are. By then I had signed up with one of the biggest agencies in the world, because I thought I needed a manager, but I had such a success with the *Jane* album and tour that I decided to manage myself. I went to see the agency boss and said, 'I don't think this is right.'

'You're a better manager than I am,' he replied, and I thanked him for saying so, because his words helped firm my resolve.

But I'm skipping ahead . . . Back in 2006, it probably came as no surprise to people that, ultimately, things didn't work out with

Jarek, lovely as he was. I had to learn all over again that it's very hard, if not impossible, to mix business with pleasure. I can't be the boss and the girlfriend or wife at the same time – the pillow talk ruins everything! – and some guys don't enjoy being given orders by their romantic partner. Also, Jarek, being a musician, needed to go wherever the work was, and so when we weren't touring, he went back to Poland or on tour elsewhere. It wasn't a good basis for a stable relationship: things were always on and off, and eventually we were apart so much that it just fizzled out. Still, I was fine with it and so was he, and he's gone on to have a family and I hope he's very happy. Jarek came into my life at a time when I really needed him, and it was great while it lasted.

Meanwhile, *Loose Women* was going from strength to strength and I wore my Loose Women badge with pride. To this day, it's a great show. Everything felt new and fresh to me when I first joined. I remember walking down Bond Street and thinking, 'I'm going to shop on this street one day.' I was determined to rise up and be strong and financially independent again; 40 was the new 30 and I had been given a second chance to follow my dreams, only this time I would rely on myself to make the most of my luck.

In the early days, we filmed two shows on a Tuesday and two on a Thursday, so I used to stay down and get my London fix for three days. At the end of filming, we'd head off to have a meal somewhere like Studio 6, a restaurant on the Southbank.

The number of letters I used to get saying, 'I'd love to go out with you lot for a drink', 'I'd love to go and have dinner with you all.' I could understand why: it was always such a laugh, we had the best time! All of a sudden, we started winning all the awards and, honest to God, we were like the girls in *Sex and the City*. When we went out, everybody knew we were out. The press were all over us and you'd hear people say, 'Oh my God, the "Loose

Women" have just walked in!' My weeks were exciting, glamorous and fun, and then I'd take the train back to Wakefield for the weekend.

'This is it for me now. I'm going to spend the rest of my days living with my mother,' I'd think happily.

Of course, Destiny had something else in store for me.

15

I Second That Emotion

I wasn't looking to fall in love, but some things are just meant to be.

Living with my mother worked for me. She ran the household like clockwork and I could talk everything out with her. When I came in, we'd sit down, have us tea, and I'd say, 'Oh gosh, you'll never guess what's happened today.'

'What?' she'd say, and we'd be off.

I had been on my own since things had fizzled out with Jarek: I'd dated, but nothing serious, because I didn't want anybody serious. I was happy being single and running my company. My work came first; my career was back on track. I could have lived like that for the rest of my life.

My mother wanted a bungalow, so we decided to move in early 2008. Mum found a sweet little house on a plot of land in the nicest part of Wakefield, where Henrik and I had once hoped to live. She chose it and I bought it, so I still haven't ever picked my own house. This time at least I got to do the decorating and went for warm creamy colours with Italian furniture and vibrant landscapes on the walls. I realised then that I did have taste after all – it was just that my taste was not the same as Henrik's.

Steve Holbrook, my psychic friend, came to see me just after

Mum and I had moved in. 'There's a very tall, blond guy going to walk through this door,' he said.

'Will he be sorting out the extension?' I asked.

Steve laughed. 'It's the guy you're going to end up with,' he said.

'When's all this going to happen, then?'

'I'd say six weeks – within six weeks,' he said.

'We'll see,' I said doubtfully.

Another psychic had told me that I was going to end up with someone I'd known years before.

'I don't think so,' I told him. 'My mother always says, "Never go back." '

The following week, we did a show on *Loose Women* about famous ex-boyfriends. Jackie Brambles was the anchor, Sinitta, Carol McGiffin and I were on the panel. Jackie said she'd known one of Bros. Sinitta said, 'Brad Pitt,' and Carol said she'd been married to Chris Evans.

'I can top all of you,' I said. 'I went out with the drummer of Liquid Gold.'

Two weeks later, I was in The Ivy having dinner with Lynda Bellingham when Frank Allen from The Searchers came up to me.

'You used to go out with our drummer,' he said.

'Oh, yes? What's his name?' I said.

'Ed.'

I shook my head. 'I've never been out with an Ed, he's lying to you,' I said.

'Oh, you probably know him as Wally Rothe.'

It was a shock to hear this name after so many years.

'Oh my God, Wal! How is he? He's in The Searchers now, is he? I haven't seen him since I was 19 or 20, when he was in Liquid Gold. How's he doing?' I said.

'He's great. You should give him a call.'

'Yes,' I said. 'It has only been 26 years, after all!'

*

A couple of weeks later, I was at the *Loose Women* studios having my make-up done when I looked up at the TV monitor and saw The Searchers talking about their new album on *This Morning*. And there was Wal, their drummer, looking every bit as hand-some as he had all those years ago.

'I used to go out with him!' I told Donna, the make-up girl.

'Well, you've got to go and say hello,' she said.

'I can't,' I said. 'He's probably married with kids.'

'It doesn't stop you saying hello, does it?'

Donna literally dragged me up to the *This Morning* studio.

'Hello, do you remember me?' I asked Wal, my heart fluttering.

His face lit up. 'Jane!' he cried. He picked me up and swung me around and it was such a lovely, spontaneous reaction that it felt as if the years had just melted away.

'He's exactly the same!' I thought.

Everybody went, 'Ah!'

I started to giggle, Donna started to well up and I think the band were really chuffed. 'So he *was* telling the truth!' they thought.

'I just can't believe I've met you again,' Wal said, beaming at me. 'Look, here's my number. Give me a call.'

'Thanks, I will,' I said, beaming back.

Donna and I raced back to the *Loose Women* studios. 'What a lovely moment that was,' she said.

I couldn't wait to get off air. The moment the show was over, I went straight back to the hotel and phoned Wal.

'Wow, I didn't expect you to ring,' he said.

We talked for ages and ages. He was just as lovely as ever and we couldn't stop laughing as we raked over our memories of the Pussycat days and the time Wal had come for Sunday lunch with Mum and Dad at Silcoates Street.

'Do I call you Ed now?' I asked.

'Ed, Wal – you can call me whatever you like!'

'He's as nice as he ever was,' I thought, 'and just as funny.'

Two days later, I went on holiday to Majorca with a friend. While I was away, I found myself thinking about Ed loads. I was surprised by how much I was looking forward to seeing him again.

'I really do like him!' I thought.

Back in the UK, I went up to see him in Alnwick, where he was playing with The Searchers. I don't often fancy people – I'm just not like that – but I thought Ed was gorgeous. He was tall and dashing, warm and friendly, and I felt proud to be by his side. I was falling in love with him all over again.

'I've met someone, and he's just lovely,' I told my old friend Sue Ravey.

'Hang on, I've never heard you say that before,' Sue said. She told me later that she knew straight away that it was serious. 'Hmm, this is different,' she thought, and it was.

It's funny how Denise Welch, Carol McGiffin and I all met our partners at the same time. It was a life-changing couple of years for us, with Denise meeting the artist Lincoln Townley, Carol meeting Mark Cassidy and me meeting Ed. It was an exciting new chapter in our lives and we were sharing it with the nation.

It was clear for everybody to see how crazy I was about Ed. The only downside was that The Searchers did 250 gigs a year, so he was often busy, or away. The deeper I fell in love with him, the scarier it felt, especially when I thought back to why we had split up nearly 30 years earlier, because he was always on the road.

'I'm just not good at relationships,' I confided in Lynda Bellingham, 'and I'm terrified that history will repeat itself with Ed.'

'Well, I can't give you an opinion if I haven't met him,' she said. 'Will you introduce me?'

So, one evening when Ed was down in London on a day off, we had dinner with Lynda at The Ivy. 'So, what are your intentions?' she asked him. She was interviewing him for the job of my boyfriend!

'I've never been as scared in my life,' he told me afterwards.

'What do you think?' I asked Lynda the next day.

'He's a keeper, Jane,' she said. 'He's lovely.'

I still had doubts. Ed was off all round the world, so how would we ever last the course? And yet we were so good together that we *had* to make it work.

A break in our schedules meant that Ed and I could spend Christmas 2008 together and I was looking forward to having a cosy time at home with him and Mum. But Ed seemed a bit jumpy on Christmas Eve.

'Is everything okay?' I asked him.

'Yes, absolutely fine!' he said brightly, but I could tell something was up.

That night, we went to my local Italian for dinner. Suddenly, Ed cleared his throat and put his hand in his pocket.

'Oh no, what's the matter?' I thought.

'Jane, you are definitely the one for me and I should have done this 26 years ago,' he said. 'Will you marry me?'

I was so surprised and overwhelmed that I started crying. Then Ed started crying! The people on the tables around us were mortified, because they thought we'd split up. I could see them telling each other, 'I can't believe he's just finished with her on Christmas Eve!'

'No, no, he's just asked me to marry him,' I said, laughing through the tears.

A cheer went up: 'Yay!' We had champagne, and it was lovely.

My mother was at home with my Aunt Nancy.

'I've just got engaged!' I said, when we got back.

'That's nice,' Mum said. It wasn't that she didn't feel happy for me, but she'd seen me through so many disasters that she must have been thinking, 'Oh, not this again.'

'Honestly, this one's all right,' I reassured her.

Soon, Ed was back on the road and I was juggling *Loose Women* with singing and performing again. I was touring every year and loving it, but things weren't moving fast enough for me. When I'm doing something, I'm already mentally on to the next thing and the thing after that: I constantly wanted to progress. Yet sometimes it felt as if I was coming up against a brick wall because, although I was working with a great bunch of people, they weren't so driven as I was to keep improving and moving forward.

'Let's do this!' I'd say.

'Why? We're quite happy as we are,' they'd tell me.

I began to realise that I needed to be more of a driving force within the band, so I worked hard at organising my next tour, hoping my enthusiasm for trying new things would be catching. I threw myself into learning as much as I could about every aspect of touring and performing, so that I could always back up my ideas and suggestions with practical know-how. It was a steep learning curve and I found it fascinating, but the progress I was hoping for still seemed out of reach.

The more I focused on my work, the less I saw of Ed, who was away most of the time, anyway. It got to a point where we were apart so much that, by the time we were used to being with each other, one of us would be off again. Things came to a head after we'd tried to have a holiday three times in a row and had to cancel each time because gigs had come in for The Searchers.

'I can't do this anymore,' I thought.

The day before Valentine's Day 2010, I rang Ed in Australia and said, 'I'm really sorry, but this is not going to work. It feels just like it did before, when you were in Liquid Gold. I don't want to be in that situation again.'

'Oh no, Jane! Let me speak to you when I get home,' he said.

'Why didn't you ever try to get me back?' I blurted out, because when you're breaking up with your fiancé, you're obviously going to bring up a 30-year-old grudge.

'What was I going to do?' he protested. 'Say to you, "Stay at home, I'm just going away to Mexico now?" You weren't the type that I could just leave at home – it was all or nothing.'

I heard a phone going in the background. It was late at night in Australia and I thought, 'Who's ringing him at this time? Oh, God, this is ridiculous! I don't want this!'

'I'm sorry,' I said, and put the phone down.

The following day, I went into the *Loose Women* studios with a heavy heart. As I made my way to the meeting room, one of the producers said, 'Hi Jane, Happy Valentine's Day!'

But I said nothing. I didn't want to talk about love – I couldn't bear to share the pain I was feeling inside, or face the agony of another failed relationship.

There was excitement in the air at our morning meeting. Nobody told me that Ed had filmed a special Valentine's message to camera on Sydney Bridge, saying, 'I'm sorry I've been away so much. I love you and I'll be back soon.' It was meant to be a lovely surprise for me, live on air. But when they screened it, I said, 'Oh, God!' and the tears started.

'Jane, what's the matter?' Carol McGiffin asked, shocked by my reaction.

'Oh dear,' Sherrie Hewson said, sensing that something had gone horribly wrong.

It turned out that Ed's ringing phone hadn't been another woman or a groupie: it was the producers at *Loose Women* on the other end, calling to check the filming had gone according to plan.

It was a funny old mix-up, but it didn't take away from the fact that we never saw each other, so when Ed got back, we had a serious talk, which was more like a business meeting than anything.

'If we're going to make a go of this, we're going to have to make some serious decisions,' I said. 'We're either going to be together or we're not, so I can either give my job up, or you can give yours up.'

I knew that I would never meet a better man than Ed, so I was prepared to give up everything for him. At the same time, I sensed that he was feeling weary of life on the road, so perhaps he would actually like the idea of giving it up. I didn't know. All that mattered to me was that we find a way to stay together.

Ed smiled that sunshine smile of his.

'I've also been thinking things over,' he said.

My heart started to pound. 'Yes?' I said.

'I've been on the road a long time,' he went on, 'and I think I'd be happy to stop touring now.'

I gasped. 'Are you sure? Because if you're not, I'm also—'

'I'm sure,' he interrupted.

'Thank you,' I said, my heart bursting at the thought that we were finally going to be together. Not only that, I didn't have to sacrifice my career.

I think the rest of the band were a bit shocked when Ed broke the news as he'd been with them for 12 years. I was thrilled, though. After two years of fitting each other in when we could – which really wasn't very often – we were finally going to settle down. It was Sue Ravey who said, 'If you want to hold on to this one, which I know you do, you've got to make a choice: either move Ed in and your mother out, or it's not going to work.'

'What?' I said, shaken.

I had lived with my mother for so long that I couldn't imagine us living apart. It would be a massive shift for both of us. But I could see Sue's point. My mother had rules: breakfast was on the table at a certain time, dinner at another. She ran the place like a boarding house and didn't know the meaning of a duvet day. If I slept in past a certain time, she'd say, 'What are you doing in bed? Get up!'

Sue continued to insist that I couldn't expect my fiancé to live with my mother, and my sister-in-law Wendy agreed: 'You've been with your mum for all these years. It's time. Your mum needs her own life as much as you do.'

To be honest, I hadn't looked at it that way. 'But if she's moving out, she needs her own house,' I thought. 'Somewhere nice and comfortable.'

After giving us both a few weeks to get used to the idea, I got in contact with the local estate agents and Mum and I went to see quite a few properties. Eventually, we found a beautiful bungalow just around the corner from where we lived.

'This is really nice,' Mum said, as she walked in.

'This is the one. It's perfect,' I said.

It was great having my mother so close; it meant I could pop over every day to make sure she was okay.

The day after she moved, we got home and Ed said, 'I can't smell any dinner.'

'Neither can I. Who's cooking?' I asked cheekily.

'Put your apron on and let's get chopping,' he replied with a laugh.

As we settled in together, I couldn't get over how blessed I was to have Ed – and I still can't quite believe my luck. Every day, he makes me laugh. He cooks a fabulous Sunday roast. He's like my dad in that he can fix anything – but it always turns out well – and he's the nicest, kindest man you'll ever meet. He's been the drummer in Liquid Gold, Mud and The Searchers, but he revels in the role of house husband and is a brilliant businessman, too. He helps steer and guide me in everything I do: everybody calls him 'The Silent Assassin' because he makes a lot of my business decisions with me. I love Ed more than I ever thought possible and I thank my lucky stars that we found each other again so, when he moved in, it was the best thing that could ever have happened.

Once things were settled at home, it was easier to focus on my career. People kept asking me when I was going to film another live DVD and so I decided to put on a concert at the London Palladium in 2010 and executive produce it myself. It was a huge amount of work, but we got there, and it was a big success, an amazing, sell-out show with a 15-piece orchestra and a fantastic mix of fans, friends and celebrities in the audience.

But life can turn on a pin, or in this case, a zip, and we nearly had a complete disaster with one of my costumes. We'd got this young designer in and her designs were lovely but very static, with no stretch, which isn't ideal when you're performing. Among them was a gorgeous silver dress that I chose to wear regardless, because I loved it so much. But while I was putting it on during a costume change, the zip went up and came off the top, the silver dress came apart and I was left standing there in just my G-string backstage.

'What the flipping heck do we do now?' I thought, frozen in panic.

Luckily, I had a spare red outfit, because you just never know – and thank God I did! Someone had to run around and get it from the dressing room while the band played filler music. That wait felt like an eternity. The audience must have been thinking, 'Where is she?' The band would have been wondering, 'What's going on?' It was the longest seven minutes of my life. Eventually, I got the red dress on, and it was probably the best outfit of the night, even though it was never supposed to be worn at the Palladium. And thank goodness for an edit to cut that long, slightly anxious, musical interlude out of the DVD footage!

The Palladium show reminded me of how things could be when we had proper rehearsals and a committed band. I felt it could be a great springboard for bigger and better things, but the team I was working with didn't appear to share my passion. A feeling of stagnation began to set in. No one seemed motivated to try anything new, so the show stayed the same and everyone got bored.

The problem with employing session musicians, however good they were, was that they weren't emotionally involved. They weren't necessarily big fans – they came in, did a good job and left to go on to the next. Sometimes I felt as if they didn't want to be there, that they were turning up, thinking, 'Not this again.' But I couldn't have that – I wanted everybody to be happy.

'This is show business. We should be going out there and having a brilliant time,' I thought.

Our sound engineer, Martin Hudson, was the one person on the team who I felt really shared my enthusiasm. At first, he and I just chatted about the music we liked and we never seemed to run out of things to say. Then, as time went on, I started confiding my hopes and dreams in him.

'I know this sounds a bit daft, but I feel like there's much more ahead for us,' I said one evening after a show. 'I can see me in arenas. I don't know if you feel the same.'

'Yes, I do,' he said. 'When you're ready, let's work on it.'

First, things had to change. I had reached a point where I couldn't move any further with what I was doing – it was getting harder to sell tickets, the shows weren't filling up enough. I needed to regroup in my head so that I could change and grow; I needed time to sit down at the piano and write songs, to rest and think about what I really wanted to do next, so I decided to stop touring.

Now I turned my focus back to *Loose Women*, which was a good laugh, paid the mortgage and gave me time to be at home with Ed and my mum – I needed time at home. I still loved going down to London. One night, shortly after Carol Vorderman had joined the *Loose Women* panel in 2011, she and I went out to dinner. You could hear the lull when we walked into the restaurant – that's what happens when you're with Carol. We had so many bottles of champagne sent over to our table, we didn't know where to put them.

I really enjoyed my dinners with Lynda Bellingham, too. She and I were alike in many ways and had even looked physically similar when we were younger. In fact, Ed and I were coming back from a party at Lynda's one night and he said, 'It's a bit weird that she's got photographs of you everywhere.'

'They're not me, they're Lynda!' I laughed.

Over Christmas 2012, Lynda starred in panto in Bradford, playing the Fairy Godmother in *Cinderella*. I used to go and have dinner with her quite a lot, just the two of us, and sometimes Ed and Lynda's husband 'Mr Spain' joined us to make up a foursome. Lynda absolutely loved doing panto – 'You should do it sometime, Jane,' she said. 'You'd enjoy it.'

But I wasn't sure – it looked like a lot of hard work to me. Anyway, I was enjoying my break from live performing. I wrote some cracking songs on my white concert grand piano at home, including a tribute to my fans called 'The Singer Of Your Song'. I still wasn't sure how to get my career back on track, but I had some lovely peaceful days with Mum and some much-needed holidays with Ed.

One evening, Sue Ravey came over for a glass of wine.

'Don't waste these years, will you?' she said. 'Don't wait too long to use your voice again.'

'What do you mean?'

'I'm just saying, be careful. Your voice loses power as you get older and, one day, you won't be able to do what you do.'

Her words hit me like a ton of bricks. 'She's right,' I thought. 'I might not have another shot at this.'

Around the same time, Martin Hudson, our sound engineer on the tours, got in touch. 'You're too good to stop,' he said. 'I can't believe I'm saying this, but if you let me be your tour manager, I'll make it crack. I'll do everything and keep you in the loop every step of the way.'

I wasn't sure I needed a tour manager, as I already had Mark Worrall, who booked the tours, looked after my admin and website and drove me to the concerts. But Martin persuaded me that I needed someone to oversee the band, crew, logistics and staging.

'Okay, you're on,' I said.

That's how Martin left the sound company where he was working and became my tour manager. In turn, we gave his sound people the next tour to work on. This gave them the financial backing they needed to get all the best equipment, which improved the quality of our sound. With Martin, everything started to make sense.

We wanted the show to be bigger and better, and so we invested heavily. I put my house up as collateral and Martin helped me pick the band. Our 2013 tour was called 'The Singer Of Your Song' and, although I wasn't making any money and sometimes it was a struggle to fill the venues, I felt that we had taken a step in the right direction. I could see small improvements everywhere, because Martin worked as hard as I did and paid a lot of attention to detail. The shows went up a notch, my musicians seemed happier, and so was I.

Midway through the tour, Lynda Bellingham rang me and

said, 'Look, there's going to be something out in the papers tomorrow, and you're not going to like it.'

'Oh no, what have you done now?' I joked.

'I've got cancer,' she said.

For a moment, the world seemed to stop turning. I couldn't believe it.

'Oh no, love! Are you all right? Is there anything I can do?' I said.

'Don't worry, I'm going to beat it,' she told me firmly.

I believed her, because if anyone was going to beat cancer, it was Lynda. She was such a strong, loving, positive person. Still, I was sad for her that she had to go through it. And it gave me pause for thought, as news like hers always does.

By the time the tour closed towards the end of the year, ticket sales had picked up and we'd decided to take the same show on the road again the following year. Martin was full of ideas about how to improve production – 'We need your brand on the stage to be the same every night,' he said. 'When people come into the theatre, they should look at the stage and think, "Jane McDonald's on tonight."'

'How, though?' I asked.

I couldn't see how we could achieve any kind of uniformity when each theatre, auditorium, stage and rig was different from the next.

'By having a lighting designer on the tour with us,' he said.

'Okay, let's do it,' I said, instantly seeing why this would work.

Martin commissioned Dave Catley, a lighting maestro, to build our first touring stage set and create a distinctive look for our concerts. After that, stage production became a big part of our tours and you could always tell a Jane McDonald set from any other by the set-up, floor arrangement and lighting colours. However, it was still a struggle to sell out some of the venues on my 2014 tour. Usually, ticket sales picked up in the days before a show, but there was one gig where the sales were so poor I had to scrap it. The manager rang up and asked, 'Why have you cancelled?'

'I can't sell enough tickets!' I said. 'I'm not going to lie to you and say I've got a bad cold or an upset tummy, like most people do. I just can't sell tickets in your town.'

'Blimey! Thanks for being so honest,' he said.

Other venues sold out as soon as the tickets went on sale, especially in the North, where my fans have always been very loyal. Martin and I took note and discussed this and every other aspect of the tour as it went on. And the more we talked, the more I thought about how things could be improved.

Before we went out on the road for the 2014 tour, I had recorded an album called *The Singer Of Your Song*, which I also executive produced. There were three of my own compositions on the album, including my tribute to my fans, 'The Singer Of Your Song' and 'I'll Be There', a song I'd written with my guitarist, Steve Cooper. Our audiences were always very receptive when I sang these songs, and Steve and I decided to focus on our collaborations whenever we could.

People often asked whether it was hard to juggle the different sides of my career. 'At times it is,' I'd say, 'but I'm enjoying life too much to think of giving any of them up.'

This was true until things started changing at *Loose Women* in 2014. New producers came in and there was a shift towards a more newsy agenda.

'Perhaps I should leave,' I thought. 'I'm not very good at news. I'm not a journalist or a newsreader, I don't know enough about what's going on in the world. I'm better talking about things that affect my friends, family and my local community.'

Part of me didn't want to leave the show. It was safe, easy and fun, and I enjoyed spending time with the other girls. But I think the producers thought it was getting a bit samey. We'd had years of the same cast and they wanted a shake-up, which I absolutely understood. One criticism was that the viewers knew me so well that they could guess what I was going to say – but then some people like that, don't they? It's like going out with an old mate: the familiarity is comforting.

Staying at *Loose Women* was the safe option, but sometimes you've got to jump off a cliff to see if you can fly. Although a lot of people asked me, 'What on earth are you thinking?', I decided to leave the show to focus on singing and touring again. Some of my mates, like Carol and Denise, had already gone and it didn't feel right to stay.

I left *Loose Women* on the best of terms and they gave me an open door to come back, for which I was very grateful. The girls and I have remained good friends and that's nice. We're all on one of those WhatsApp things, so we still keep in touch.

It was a turbulent year and we were all affected when Lynda Bellingham dropped a bombshell in September and told us that her cancer was terminal. It was very, very sad news. Lynda took a no-nonsense approach when she spoke to me about it, though: 'I've a favour to ask of you, Jane. I'm supposed to be doing the pantomime in Birmingham at the end of the year. Would you consider taking my part?'

'Oh no, don't do this to me!' I said. 'Yes, of course, I'll go and audition. Thank you.'

I was on tour at the time and had to go onstage that night as if nothing had happened. Usually, I'm good at keeping my emotions back, but I just couldn't manage it after hearing Lynda's dreadful news. When it came to singing 'I'll Be There', the song I had written with my guitarist, Steve Cooper, I couldn't help thinking of Lynda and crying when I got to the line

'Picture me beside you and I'll be there, feel my arms around you and I'll be there.'

Steve looked at me as if to say, 'Are you okay?' because I never cry onstage. I walked behind him and rested my head on his shoulder to shield my face from the crowd.

Oh, God, it was so hard to sing that song.

16

Memories

Lynda Bellingham's funeral was held in November 2014 at the beautiful, fifteenth-century church of St Bartholomew's in Crewkerne, Somerset. There was so much love in that church for Lynda. Looking around at the packed pews as I took my seat, I thought, 'How wonderful to have been so special to so many people.'

Many of the mourners had known and loved Lynda for most of their lives and several of them gave eulogies. I didn't write down what I was going to say because I wanted to speak from the heart and so I can't remember exactly what I said. I know I started off with something like, 'I was a latecomer to the Lynda Bellingham party, but I was there at the end.'

Lynda was one of life's good people, and I'm very honoured to have known her. I lost a very, very good friend the day she died and her death had a profound effect on me. The day of her funeral was very emotional and I was ready for bed by the time I got back to my hotel. But when I looked at my phone, I saw that I'd had ten missed calls, all from my brother, Tony.

'Jane, I need to talk to you. Can you ring me straight away?'

'Mum,' I thought, my heart pounding as I phoned him back. But it wasn't my mother, it was my brother-in law.

'It's Gary, he's passed away,' Tony said.

I felt dazed with grief and shock. 'No, that can't be right. I'm at Lynda's funeral,' I said. 'It's Lynda who has died.'

This is what happens when you get to your fifties: you start losing people very, very close to you. Gary's passing was a real shock and sadness for us all. It was an awful time and we did our best to rally round my sister, Janet. That's one thing about our family: we're not in each other's pockets, even though we're only five minutes away, but if there's anything wrong, boom, we're all there in an instant.

Losing Lynda and Gary changed me. It made me think about my own mortality and ask myself, 'What do you want? Where do you want to be?' Unfortunately, I didn't have enough time to think about it properly before I dived straight into rehearsals for the pantomime I had promised to do for Lynda. You don't have a spare minute when you're doing 12 performances a week of *Jack & The Beanstalk* for six weeks. I played the good fairy, working with the director Michael Harrison, who was amazing, but I was exhausted by the end of it – pantomime is great, but it's tough.

We had Lynda's picture up backstage during the whole run. By the end, I had nothing left inside me except sadness. Tired and depleted, I didn't help myself by eating all the wrong things, like Chinese takeaways and pizza. I needed proper food to fuel me and give me energy, but I was going for quick-hit sugar and carb-heavy meals that left me feeling drained.

I have a body that will fight everything and then, all of a sudden, I'll go down like a sack of spuds, which is what happened now. I had worked so hard, for so long, that I was totally knocked out and had to spend three days straight flat out in bed.

'I need to stop and think about where I am,' I realised, as I battled a high fever. 'I need to take my foot off the accelerator and live a bit more.'

I thought about Lynda, who had written her final book right up until she died, getting up at five every morning so that she could finish it. Lynda wouldn't slow down, and yet she knew how important it was to live well and nourish close relationships. She kept on about Ed – 'He's a good one,' she told me, several times. 'We need them, you know – we need them.' Now her words came back to me and I thought, 'Yes, I need to spend time at home with Ed and with my mum too.'

I invited my agent, Craig Latto, to see one of the shows at the Birmingham Hippodrome. Craig is fabulous. He's a like-minded person who never tries to talk me into doing a job just because it's prestigious or well paid: 'If you don't think it's right, it's not right,' he says.

'I'm exhausted. I can't do this anymore, I need a year off,' I told Craig when I saw him after the show.

'A year,' Craig echoed, going slightly pale.

'I'm that tired that I need a complete break from everything,' I said.

The great thing about Craig is that he trusts me. He understood that I wanted to step back and sit on the rim of the soup bowl for a bit; he knew that I was a great believer in the saying 'When in doubt, do nowt'.

'Right, I'm going to garden. I'm going to learn to cook like my mother,' I decided. I wanted to know how Mum did her soups, sauces, gravies, Yorkshire puddings and oven-cooked braising steak.

It was so nice to be at home! It's no wonder my favourite sign in the world is 'M1 North', because Wakefield is my safe place, and every time I've needed to regroup, to rest and to heal, it has done that for me. I'm a home girl, and yet I've been away for huge chunks of my life, which doesn't make sense, does it? So, it was fantastic having quality time with Ed, my mum and the rest of my family.

Mum taught me her recipe secrets and, once I had mastered them, I added bits and pieces to make them my own.

'Oh, this is nice! What have you added there?' she'd ask, when I made something for her.

'A splash of red wine and some Worcester sauce,' I'd say. 'Do you think it works?'

Six weeks into my year off – and I was loving it, believe me – I got a call from Craig.

'Are you sitting down?' he said.

'Why? What have you got?'

'Do you fancy a musical?'

'Well, it depends what it is.'

'The Really Useful Group have asked if you want to take the starring role in *Cats*.'

I nearly dropped the phone.

'You what?'

'Yes, but you've got to go and audition for it in London.'

My heart sank. 'Well, I'm not going to get it, then, am I? So, what's the point? Think of who I'll be up against.'

'Actually, I think they would really like you to do it, because the show is in Blackpool, where you've got a big fan base,' Craig said.

Blackpool! Ask anyone and they'll tell you that there's something magical for me about Blackpool, always has been. The Opera House is one of the biggest theatres in the country and the audience are always up for it, because they've come away for the weekend.

'Well, if it's Blackpool, then I'll do the audition,' I said.

I arrived at The Really Useful Group offices with half an hour to spare, so I popped into Reiss in Covent Garden for a browse. There was a gorgeous jacket on the rail and it looked fantastic on.

'I'm just off to an audition round the corner,' I told the shop assistant. 'If I get the part, I'll come back and get that jacket.'

'See you in about three hours then,' she said, although she didn't know me from Adam.

It was like *The X Factor* at The Really Useful Group offices. I had to sing in front of Andrew Lloyd Webber, who composed *Cats*, Trevor Nunn, who wrote the lyrics and directed, David Ian, the show producer, and Gillian Lynne, the associate producer and choreographer. *Cats* is based on a TS Eliot poem, *Old Possum's Book of Practical Cats*, and I was trying out for the part of Grizabella, an ageing Glamour Cat who has seen better days.

Grizabella sings 'Memory', the best-known song of the show. 'Memory' is her plea for acceptance among her old tribe of cats, who have shunned her. It has three key changes and the climax is in D flat, so it's a very difficult, very emotional, song to sing.

When I arrived, Andrew Lloyd Webber said, 'Ah, you're the girl who does it all on her own, aren't you?'

'Yes, but it didn't happen through choice, Andrew!' I said.

It was just me and a piano at the audition. I sang 'Memory' as well as I could and reached the top Db with ease. As the last note died away, Graham Hurman, the music supervisor, grabbed my hand, as if to say, 'That was great.'

I thought I could have done it better, but you don't get a second chance. However, while I think Andrew Lloyd Webber needed convincing that I was right for the part, the voice coach, Fiona Grace McDougal, had no such doubts.

'Definitely take her on. I can work wonders with her,' she told him.

On my way to the station, I thought back to something that had happened earlier in the week, when I'd looked out of the kitchen window while singing 'Memory' to see four cats sitting on the wall outside. It had to be a good sign, didn't it?

So, I bought the jacket in Reiss and, on the train home, Craig rang to say I'd got the part.

'Oh my God, I've got the lead in *Cats*!' I screamed. I couldn't help myself – I hadn't been so excited for a long time. I had been touring, doing *Loose Women*, appearing in panto – happy, but not really going anywhere. This was different, it was the next step! I wasn't just 'Jane McDonald, the cruise-ship singer' anymore, now I was 'Jane McDonald, starring in *Cats*'. It was a seal of approval and I felt accepted. I really started to believe in myself, at last.

Fiona Grace McDougal was right in thinking she could work wonders with my voice. 'You've got no idea how big you can sing!' she said at our first rehearsal.

Up until then, I'd been lazy. I used to think, 'Make it easy: just lower the key, I'll be fine. I won't go for a top Db, I'll just go for C,' because I knew I could get the C. Now I learned to do a proper, disciplined warm-up before a performance instead of knocking back a Drambuie and walking onstage, and I found I was singing better than I had ever sung in my whole life, and singing bigger, too: my range expanded and I was able to hit notes even higher than the top Db, right up to F or G. My confidence soared.

We had a good few weeks of rehearsal time and I worked closely with the musical director, Adrian Kirk. All the while, I watched and learned how to put on a really slick, stylish production. The cast were a group of incredible, talented West End performers and I was amazed to find that they had heard of me – they even seemed impressed that I was in the show. I loved getting to know them and made some friends for life among them.

After intensive rehearsals in London, we arrived in Blackpool in early July 2015, excited about opening night. My nerves were terrible, as usual – and especially so, because everybody in the audience is waiting to hear 'Memory' at the end of the show. To stop myself shaking and feeling sick, every night before I went on I'd go to the bottom of a deep stairwell backstage and ask one of the musicians to give me the top Db. Then I'd sing, 'Touch me . . .' to be sure that I could reach the note.

'I can do this,' I'd think, and then we'd go on and bring the house down.

As the season progressed, I could feel myself growing and changing. I loved playing Grizabella; I didn't miss a single performance during the entire run and wanted it to last forever. I had a strong sense that I was coming into my own and fulfilling my potential as a singer and a performer.

Adrian Kirk and the band often came up for drinks and a chat about the show. They were a talented bunch of musicians and it was great to swap stories and experiences with them. I was always in my element when they came to see me. Ed was with me in Blackpool throughout the season, which was lovely. Instead of staying in a hotel, we rented a fabulous house that had a jacuzzi, a steam room and loads of bedrooms.

One day, after a matinée, Matt Krzan, who was playing Munkustrap, complained of muscle ache.

'I've got a Jacuzzi at mine . . .' I started to say.

'You haven't!'

'I have! Do you want to come back after the show?'

I had already become mates with Jane Quinn, the talented actress and singer who played Jennyanydots, and she came along that first time with Matt. Soon, I was regularly inviting members of the cast over to my house on a Friday for pizza and a hot tub. We called it the Friday Club and it became quite a popular event, so we had to stagger the invitations as we only had room for 12. People came over for something to eat and drink, or for a jacuzzi and a steam, and then the young ones went off clubbing and the rest slept over in the spare bedrooms. They were great nights, and I tried not to let Henrik's words ring in my head: 'If you spend the night drinking and talking and having a good time, you won't be able to do a show the next day.' We were all mindful of this, and careful, and very disciplined – but it did us the world of good to relax and have a break from worrying about the show, just for one night. We had two performances on a Saturday and they were always the best shows, because we'd had so much fun the night before.

We were such a close-knit group that I was distraught to learn that I hadn't been picked to go to London for the West End run later in the year. During the last performance in Blackpool, I was shaking with emotion because I didn't want it to come to an end. I remember I cried onstage and the rest of the cast gathered round me, still in character, to say, 'We'll miss you' – it was very emotional. Still, it didn't stop me going down to see them do it in London and Beverley Knight, who took over the role of Grizabella, was brilliant.

Things happen for a reason. At first, I kept thinking, 'I haven't gone to London with *Cats*, I haven't gone with the rest of the cast.' It made me want to go on working and achieving, so when Craig rang up with news of two offers that had come in, I didn't immediately turn them down flat.

'The first would involve going into the jungle,' he said.

'Eating bugs, you mean?'

I asked a few friends for their advice.

'No, you're not doing it,' Jane Quinn told me adamantly.

'But, you know, I suppose it's a good—'

'No, you're not,' she interrupted.

'Maybe you're right,' I said. 'I couldn't be seen without my make-up, darling – I frighten children without my face on, and my hair, in the humidity . . .'

I went back to my agent. 'It's not for me. I love watching it, but I couldn't go on it,' I said. 'What's the other offer?'

'It's a reality programme for ITV called *Sugar Free Farm*,' Craig said. 'Six celebrities live and work on a farm in Hampshire, eat natural food and go sugar-free for three weeks.'

'I'm not sure that sounds right, either,' I said. 'I don't need to lose weight. I'm only a size 14. I eat well and I haven't got a sweet tooth.'

If I sounded defensive, it might have been because I'd had enough of people telling me I was fat. From my ex-husband to people in the music industry and on the ships, I was always being told, 'You've got to be a certain size and weight.' When I had started managing myself, I'd decided, 'I don't have to slim down anymore, I'll be whatever weight I want to be.' But actually, I wasn't doing myself any favours. Although I felt healthy, there's only so long you can go on eating pies.

I wasn't big, but I was curvaceous, because of course with age you get bigger – and if you're not careful, you can get a bit of middle-age spread. I assumed that I generally ate a good diet, but when I really thought about it, I realised that I was always grabbing snacks and ready meals on the road, before and after gigs, interviews and meetings. Perhaps I did need a lesson or two in nutrition, I realised – and I liked the idea of giving my body a rest and a detox in the countryside. So I went back to Craig and said I wanted to do the programme.

On my first morning at Laverstoke Farm, where *Sugar Free Farm* was filmed, I woke at six, just as the sun was rising over the fields. As I looked out of my bedroom window, I was filled with wonder at the peace and beauty that surrounded me. That amazing first sunrise set the tone for a life-changing few weeks. Every morning, we were up at the crack of dawn. We milked the cows and the buffalo, worked in the fields, picked vegetables, looked after the animals and learned to cook sugar-free, making and eating delicious organic food. At one point, I actually thought, 'I love this so much that I could easily be a farmer's wife' – it was the chameleon in me talking!

It was bliss because I didn't have to think about anything except what was happening that day. Those few weeks taught me to stop worrying about things, to switch off and focus on whatever I'm doing at the time. I was there with comedian Rory McGrath, quiz mastermind Mark Labbett, actress Tupele Dorgu, TOWIE's James 'Arg' Argent and dancer Jennifer Ellison and we all got on well. There was no television in the farmhouse and, in the evenings, we'd simply have dinner and go to bed. I used to relish coming into my bedroom after a really tiring day: I'd run a bath and add a few drops of the Molton Brown bath scent I'd brought along with me as my one and only treat; I'd find a radio station on my iPad, lie back in the bath and relax. Once in bed, I was always asleep the moment my head touched the pillow. I've never slept so well in my life – it felt like a cleansing of the mind as much as the digestive system.

I took the diet seriously and followed it to the letter. That's me – if I'm going to do something, I do it thoroughly. The first week was difficult, because we weren't even allowed to eat fruit due to its high sugar content, but things became easier as the days went on. I became great friends with Angelique Panagos, the show's nutritionist, who taught me some valuable lessons about eating well and eating healthily. Angelique suggested preparing a big bowl of salad every morning and putting it in the fridge, so that, if I ever fancied a snack, I would always have something healthy and delicious there waiting for me.

'I don't think I can be bothered with that,' I told her, 'I don't like tomatoes very much and I think lettuce is a waste of time.'

'Well, what do you like?' she asked.

'Cucumber, peppers, radish and onions . . .' I said.

'Fill the bowl with all the things that you do like, then.'

It was a lesson well learned: look in my fridge today or any other day and you'll see a bowl of delicious, fresh vegetables.

What I found incredible about those weeks at Laverstoke was that, even though I was eating twice as much as before, I was losing weight. I lost two stone, boom, like that, and went straight down to a size 10. By the end of my stay, I felt so much better: not only was I slimmer, but I also had a lot more energy and a feeling of being in control.

'This is it, clean eating is the future,' I decided.

My diet wasn't the only thing *Sugar Free Farm* revolutionised. Being surrounded by nature, away from the noise of the outside world, gave me precious time to think and re-evaluate. Now it occurred to me that maybe doing the London run of *Cats* wasn't the be-all and end-all – and maybe it was a good thing that I hadn't been picked to do it. Perhaps it was enough to have done the Blackpool run, in fact. There was no doubt in my mind that it had completely changed my life. It had given me a massive confidence boost and brought me back to the joy of singing. To star in an Andrew Lloyd Webber musical and bring people to their feet every night made me feel like I'd arrived. Now I could think of myself more as a singer than an entertainer – I was finally ready to write 'Singer' on my passport under 'Occupation'!

An idea started to form in my mind. What if I toured again, only this time taking the live shows up to a completely different level professionally? A crash course in discipline and world-class voice tuition had helped improve my singing range beyond belief. Surely my show should reflect the quality of my new performance abilities – and hadn't I just seen close up how to stage a dazzling production? I needed a brilliant band, proper staging and lights, fabulous costumes, great promotion . . . Having seen what the production team had done with *Cats*, I could visualise it all in my head. All of a sudden, I was thinking, 'I'm really *glad* I haven't gone to do *Cats* in London.'

As soon as I left the farm, I got in touch with Martin Hudson, my tour manager, and we started working on new show content together, formulating a plan for my 2016 tour, which went on to be the most successful tour I'd ever done. His attention to detail was phenomenal and I couldn't fault him when it came to production values; he was all about stage production and he was brilliant at it.

The band was by far and away my top priority. I wanted a tight group of musicians who would help me to shine, as I had on the stage at Blackpool during *Cats*. Also, I wanted to do more than just break even on this tour and so I said to Martin, 'Let's do it all ourselves this time: booking venues, promotion, everything.'

'Ready when you are,' he said, without breaking a sweat.

To help us get it right, I consulted Ian Sime, the manager of the Leeds Grand Theatre and a good friend of mine. 'I'm planning to tour again next year,' I told him. 'But this time I'm planning to spend so much money on the production that I'm going to have to increase the ticket price. What do you think to that?'

'It sounds great,' he said. 'It'll be worth it if the show is brilliant.'

Ian told me how everything works financially when you book and play a venue. I believe it's something that every artist should know. If you don't know how the costs break down, you will be spending far more than you expect to and won't be able to understand why you're earning relatively little for filling huge venues. What you always have to remember is that there's VAT charged straight from gross: that's 20 per cent before you even start. The theatre cost is another 30 per cent. Then add on the show cost and your tax. What's left is yours, and it's generally not a lot, so it's better to know the figures in advance.

Talking to Ian taught me everything I needed to know about the business side of touring. Pleased that he thought it was a good idea to invest in production values, I stretched myself to the limit to make the new shows the best they could possibly be.

'This is going to take us up to a whole new level,' I told Steve Cooper, our guitarist, excitedly.

Steve has stood by me and supported me ever since we started working together in 2008. But back then when I didn't know him as well as I do now, I wasn't quite so sure of him as I am today. Then I had a dream about Steve that was so vivid and reassuring that it changed my relationship with him forever. In the dream, I was in a massive hall, sitting down with about 15 people. Steve got up, walked towards me and kissed the top of my head – 'I will always have your back,' he said.

It doesn't sound like anything much – other people's dreams never do – but the feeling it gave me has never left me and I always look to Steve for encouragement when I'm feeling nervous before a performance. He's my main man onstage and our writing collaboration has produced two songs that will always be in my repertoire: 'I'll Be There' and 'One More Day'. He's the one I turn to when I'm trying to narrow down my selection of songs, or if I've got a problem with something I'm planning to sing. 'Do you think we should do this?' I'll ask, and he'll always give me his honest opinion.

Steve is brilliant at what he does, onstage and off. He's a great guitarist and a nice person. I've never seen a side of Steve that I don't like: he's good fun, he's very pleasant, he loves his wife and he loves his family. As we started to plan the new shows, I felt lucky to have him and Martin on my side.

Steve was instrumental in helping me put my band together for the tour, which I decided to call the 'Making Memories' tour because I wanted to sing 'Memory' from *Cats* as part of the show's finale. I was hoping Sue Ravey would be my main backing singer and couldn't wait to tell her about my plans, but she came to me and said that she was having a few issues with her voice and had decided to stand down. This really upset me because she had been a source of strength and support for even longer than Steve had – she knew exactly how I ticked, she was fantastically organised and dynamic, and it was clear to me that things would be far more difficult without her.

'Okay, but do you still fancy a job?' I asked.

Her face lit up and, much to my relief, she said, 'That would be brilliant!'

'Why don't you take over as PA? It's a big job, but you already do a lot of it, so it's a natural progression.'

'I'd love to,' she said.

When it came to the new tour, everything seemed to be clicking into place – but you can never speak too soon, can you? While we were deep in the planning stages, I had a devastating call from Tony: 'Mum's had a fall,' he said. 'She's at the hospital now. She's broken her spine in three places.'

I dropped everything and was by Mum's side in a flash. It was terrible, poor thing – this amazing woman, who was up and out of the house every morning, taking the bus into town, going shopping and meeting friends for tea and coffee, was suddenly laid out flat and needed 24/7 care. She was absolutely helpless.

'Jane, we need you to help out,' Tony said.

'Don't worry, I'll take time off and nurse her back,' I said.

The next few months were a very special part of my life because I was able to give Mum back some of the loving care she had given to me over the decades. I was literally with her night and day at the hospital, making sure she was comfortable, had enough pain relief and food, soothing words and a hand to hold. I was determined to help her make it through the worst of it. Some months later, when I happened to visit Pinderfields Hospital while I was helping out with fundraising, I bumped into one of the surgeons who had treated Mum.

'She wouldn't have made it if you hadn't been here,' he said.

Once we got Mum home – bent double, bless her – I went on caring for her 24/7. It was like having a baby: I was on alert all the time, always listening out and getting up in the night, thinking, 'Is she okay?'

It may sound strange, but I'm really glad I had this time with Mum. It was a good time, a time of deep love and care between us, and I was very grateful that I was able to be there for her when she needed me, as she had been for me from the day I was born. It helped that I had a rainy day account set aside for an emergency, an account that I had paid a tiny amount into every month ever since I had been on the ships. I had gleaned the idea from a self-help book and after all this time had almost forgotten the account existed – I was surprised to see how much it had gradually accumulated. It was a godsend, because it meant that I was able to devote myself to Mum without having to worry too much about where the next pay cheque was coming from: to pay the bills and mortgage and buy everything Mum needed while I looked after her and nursed her back to health, cooked for her, tended to her cuts and bruises and washed her feet every day.

I lived at my mum's for months. Ed hardly saw me and yet he never complained: he was such a support. He came to visit us a lot and had his tea with us on a night; he was my rock through it all, giving me the strength to be with Mum and do everything for her until she was back on her feet again.

Timing is everything and being unable to work while I was looking after Mum gave me space to visualise how I wanted my next tour to be and to make sure I produced it properly. In the meantime, I had a phone call from Craig, my agent.

'Ben Frow, the Director of Programmes for Channel 5, would like a meeting with you. Would you be able to go down to London next week?'

'Yes, I could arrange it,' I said.

I had heard only good things about Ben Frow and was intrigued to meet him. He definitely lived up to the hype and we clicked instantly at that first meeting. I went down to London and he explained that he'd had an idea for me to present a travel programme exploring a range of different cruise ship holidays. 'How brilliant!' I thought. Ben was so enthusiastic about it that I instantly loved him: he's a visionary, a leader, not a follower, so he'll take chances and think, 'Let's go for it.' I felt sure we could have a great working relationship.

Ben and I had a lot in common and were on the same page regarding the show, apart from one thing: he insisted I sing at the end of each programme, but I was reluctant. Still, I have to salute him: he was right, it was a great idea. Everybody waits for the song at the end of each episode of *Cruising With Jane McDonald* and tries to guess what it will be.

Clearly, I wasn't going anywhere until Mum was a bit better and Channel 5, bless them, were happy to wait. I nursed Mum from October 2015 to May 2016, and when I felt she was well enough to cope without me, I set off on my first cruise – to the Bahamas.

17

On Top Of The World

One of the things people like about *Cruising With Jane McDonald* is that it's very spontaneous. It's just me on my holidays on a cruise ship, saying, 'Oh, look at this! Look at that!' I've got no script, I don't know where I'm going from one minute to the next and I make a lot of it up as I go. It was a stroke of genius to give me a GoPro camera stick so that I could go off alone and explore without a camera crew – that's when you see the real Jane and when people open up to me. My little GoPro camera stick is so unobtrusive that people don't feel self-conscious when they see it, they're just themselves.

Viewers liked the programme from the start and the audience figures grew until *Cruising With Jane McDonald* became the biggest show on Channel 5, which is something I can't get over. (The first series was broadcast from February 2017 and we're now on our seventh series, believe it or not, averaging more than two million views for each episode and reaching an overall audience share of as high as 10.8 per cent.) Of course, I had no idea whether it would be successful or not while I was making the first episode, which was surprisingly hard work, as it turned out. Most days, we got up at dawn, filmed all day and didn't finish until around 10pm – that's a long time to be thinking on your feet. From the start, it was one thing after another and I barely looked up when they said, 'Tomorrow, you'll be swimming with sharks.'

'That's fine, I'll be in a cage,' I thought to myself.

But no, I wasn't in a cage – I was totally exposed – and not only that, I was carrying shark bait! It was a day of very rough weather and everybody was feeling sick, me included. When the sharks suddenly appeared and surrounded me underwater, I felt that nauseous I had no fear: I was looking at all these sharks circling me, thinking, 'And you can eat me as well if you want.' When I finally made it back to the surface and onto the boat, the entire film crew were hanging over the side, throwing up!

My next trip, a Scottish cruise aboard the *Glenn Tarsan*, was an altogether gentler experience. Firstly, the sun was shining for the whole time we were there. Secondly, the ship was too small for the crew to stay overnight, so they got off at 6pm every day, which was wonderful because we had a bit of time off for a change, instead of working every minute.

Sue Ravey and I had a very special moment after dinner on our first night aboard the *Glenn Tarsan*. We were among a lovely bunch of new cruise friends and had just eaten the most delicious meal, followed by a very fine whisky. Usually, when people ask us singers to sing, we make every excuse under the sun not to, but this time when we were asked, 'Would you sing a song for us?' we decided to go ahead and sing 'The Rose' together. It was such a lovely setting and we were among such warm, friendly people that I felt privileged to sing a duet with my best friend.

It was fabulous to be back on the ships again. Every trip was a voyage of discovery and I felt incredibly lucky to be along for the ride, doing a job I love. What I've discovered over seven series of *Cruising with JMD* is that there's a cruise for everybody. You can have a really expensive, luxurious cruise, eating rich food and drinking champagne, content to stay on the ship and watch the world go by. Or you can have a cheap and cheerful cruise, where you get your cabin and board and leave the ship at every stop.

Being curious, I like going off to explore, and one of the most beautiful places I've ever visited is Dunedin in New Zealand. I'll never forget the extraordinary view of hills and sea that met my producer and me as we stepped out onto a balcony at Larnach Castle near Dunedin. Our mouths dropped open. 'Oh!' we said, in unison, because it was so stunning that it looked unreal, like a scene from the movie *Avatar*. It was a moment to treasure – I wouldn't have missed it for the world.

It has been eye-opening having a nosy around all the different cruise ships. There are some amazing cabins and state rooms: onboard, accommodation ranges from penthouse suites on two floors, with pianos, luxury carpets and silk drapes, to plain, functional family rooms for four. A lot of people cruise now and so it's much more affordable than it used to be, if you choose the right cruise – but it can also be a fabulously expensive and opulent holiday.

I've been on some amazing trips and seen some sights I never thought I'd see, from Fingal's Cave in Scotland to the Marjory Glacier in Alaska. I've also had a good share of hair-raising adventures, because these days, if I'm faced with a challenge and I think, 'I really can't do that,' then I'll do it. That's why I agreed to get into a perspex tube inside a pool of crocodiles in Australia, mad as it seems when I think back on it.

Before I got in with the crocs, I had to sign a document to cover their owners in case anything went wrong.

'Sorry, you want me to sign what?' I asked.

'A death waiver,' they replied.

'Always read the small print, because you could die,' I said in the voiceover. It was actually terrifying to find myself with a centimetre of perspex between me and a crocodile eating its dinner – it's not something I'd rush to do again.

Jumping 192 metres off the 53rd floor of the Auckland Sky Tower wasn't anywhere near as bad, but it had its moments. At first, when I leaned over the side and looked at the ground, I thought, 'I'm going to lose my breakfast here.' About two seconds later, I was thinking, 'What the heck am I doing? I'm going to die!' Instinct is telling you that you're about to go splat on the ground and you're trying to override it and tell yourself that everything will be fine. You've got all this going on in your head and adrenaline pumping through your body and then it's: 'Oh, flipping heck, they've let me go!' Down you drop, trying not to let the terror show on your face. Thankfully, I'd had a lot of practice in hiding my nerves onstage.

Sue Ravey comes with me on the cruises and, frankly, I can't imagine going without her. Along with everything else she does, she works wonders with my hair and make-up in all conditions. Being a force of nature herself, she refuses to be outdone by the weather: 'It's going to be windy out there, I'll plait it today,' she'll say. She makes me look so much more glamorous than I normally would.

Getting your look right when you're at sea isn't as easy as you might think, but having cruised more than most, I know my way around the ideal cruising wardrobe. The key element is fabrics that work with travel. You need clothes that will wash through on a cold wash and don't need ironing – I'm always thinking of that side of things! If you can't wash and iron it, don't buy it, that's my rule. I'm not one for dry cleaning.

I have a full wardrobe of cruising gear, which is mainly made up of clothes by the Canadian brand Joseph Ribkoff, because their fabrics are so fantastic. Joseph Ribkoff garments are cut in such a flattering way that you look a million dollars, no matter what you've got on, and the fabric is just right. They're quite expensive, but they're an investment, especially if you're a cruiser. A good pair of their trousers is a must: I've got a white pair, a black pair and a culottes pair and I can team them with just about everything.

After the first series of *Cruising With JMD* wrapped in late summer, 2016, it was time to rehearse for the tour. I couldn't wait to start, because we had lots of new people on the team, including a couple of younger backing singers, Sarah Rhodes and Gina McKendrick, who brought a whole new element to the shows. Sarah and Gina are members of a trio called The Bluebirds when they're not singing with me, and they are amazing. They're a joy to watch because they're always smiling; they gave the show a completely different vibe.

Jim Pitchforth on percussion was a real find. A great guy, Jim is very funny and uplifting to have around, and very protective, but also a real talent. I found him through Richard Hammond, our bass player – and what a bass player! – who happens to live across the road from me. I was surprised when Richard suggested Jim for percussion and in the next breath said that he lived in our village. I had always heard that London musicians were the best, but without a doubt the best band I've ever had is made up of musicians from the Midlands and Yorkshire – and half of them live within a mile of my house.

The new show took a long time to rehearse, but it was worth it for the difference it made. We wanted to make it spectacular, so the lighting was dramatic and, instead of standing in front of the audience singing, I made an entrance: we wanted to knock them dead. Ticket sales were slow until we did our two preview shows in Woking and Blackpool, which went down a storm. Every single part of the production was a step up from the previous tours – the staging was spectacular and I was bang on, hitting all the notes. The coaching and tuition I'd had for *Cats* had really paid off.

I always introduced 'Memory' by explaining that I had starred in an Andrew Lloyd Webber production of *Cats*. It changed people's perception of me, I think. When the song came to an end, the reaction from the audience was overwhelming: I got a standing ovation that went on and on and on. And once I'd sung 'Memory' at the previews, ticket sales for the rest of the tour went through the roof, thanks to this wonderful thing we have known as the internet, so I've got a lot to thank Andrew Lloyd Webber and his producer David Ian for.

I was more disciplined about preparing for shows now: I didn't drink alcohol, I looked after my voice and always warmed up. I became meticulous about everything on my outfits being correct. All my costumes had just one zip so that I could change in and out of them quickly. I worked with my own couturier, Kay Heeley, who made big, wonderful dresses and put lace in the sleeves so that I could move around easily and lift my arms up, which you can't do if you've not got any stretch in the material. Some of Kay's dresses had trains on them, so I had to practise swishing them and I learned how to manoeuvre myself in a sparkly jacket during a performance. My old critics would be glad to know that these days I do cover my arms up – not completely, but just enough. But I get what they were trying to do with me now: they had the right ideas and vision, but I couldn't be turned into a diva overnight. It took me 20 years to get there.

I used to spend an hour or more at the stage door every night after a show, meeting fans, signing autographs and taking photos. This was always a very important part of my concerts, because my fans mean the world to me and I want to give back to them as much as I can. However, as the tour went on, gathering pace and popularity, the crowds waiting for me at the stage door kept growing in size. It put my tour manager Martin Hudson on edge – 'There are autograph hunters out there who haven't even been to the show,' he'd complain. 'They're here because they've heard you never turn anyone away.'

One Saturday in October 2016, after the show had finished at the Watford Colosseum, Martin was called to the stage door: the staff had received a menacing phone call from a man who said he was waiting outside for me. I think it was just someone who was desperate to see me: maybe he didn't have a ticket and was trying to get in, perhaps he had come a long way. That's my mother in me, seeing things from the other person's point of view! I honestly don't know what it was all about, because my team tried to protect me from the details.

The first I heard of it was Martin saying, 'We've got a problem with somebody outside. You can't sign tonight. Go in the dressing room, open a bottle of wine, and have a sit down for a bit. Don't for goodness' sake leave until I come and get you.'

'What the heck's going on?' I said.

He explained the situation, glossing it over (he told me later) so it didn't sound so scary.

'What about all the fans?' I asked.

'No, they're going to have to go,' he said.

Outside the dressing room, I could see people looking worried and running about.

'What's happening?' I asked.

'The police have been called,' somebody said.

'Whoa! I'm sure it's only someone playing games,' I said, suddenly taken aback. I didn't feel threatened, but everybody else must have been thinking, 'This could go two ways.'

Sue and Martin went outside to announce to the waiting crowd that I wouldn't be signing autographs.

'For your own safety, you should start to make your way home,' Martin said.

At first, nobody moved – they were so used to seeing me after a show that they didn't quite believe it. A police car arrived and two officers began to check the surrounding area. People started to leave and the officers came into the building to speak to us.

Alone in my dressing room, I had no idea what was going on so it was a shock when one of the officers said, 'You should think twice in future about meeting your fans after the show.'

'Why's that?' I asked.

'You're putting yourself in a very vulnerable position, because there's no security around you,' he told me. 'You are a target and, if somebody really wants to get to you, they can, because they know you're going to be outside the stage door after a show. Even if they haven't been to the show, they can come round and see you.'

'But it would be terrible if I couldn't meet my fans,' I said.

'I would advise you to stop doing stage door meets,' he replied firmly. 'Now, if someone could bring your car round to the stage door, we will give you a police escort to the motorway and make sure no one is following you. As soon as we're sure there isn't, we will leave you to go on your way.'

'A police escort? You're joking, aren't you?' I said.

At this the officer looked pained that he didn't seem to be getting through to me: 'As you can see, we are treating this as a very serious incident,' he said.

As Sue and I left Watford in our car, with our police escort alongside us, I thought about what the officer had said. I could see the sense in it, but I had never felt a threat from any of my fans before. What bothered me about the crowds outside the stage door getting bigger was that it was pouring with rain half the time and I didn't like people to be standing out there in the wet, waiting for me to appear. Sometimes they had to wait for ages, because I'd have press, family or special guests coming in to have a glass of something after the show. I often felt guilty as I thought about the people outside.

The bigger crowds also meant that it was taking an awfully long time to get round everybody. It's quite gruelling, after two and a half hours of performing, to be talking and talking to people, especially on a rainy night in February. Your throat is sore and people are coming up and hugging you, so you're catching colds and all sorts.

It used to upset Sue when she saw the sea of people outside. 'Jane's tired, how are we going to get through all these?' she told me she was thinking. She would growl like a Rottweiler whenever people put their arms round me – 'Please don't hug her!' But poor Sue didn't stand a chance.

'Aw, she's all right with me,' I'd say, returning the hug, and it was as much my fault as anybody's that all this hugging took place, because I realise how important a hug can be for people and I was only too happy to oblige.

On the journey home from Watford, Sue admitted that she had been worrying about security for quite some time. Before the 'Making Memories' tour, we'd travelled to and from gigs with Mark Worrall, the tour booker, and his partner, Andy, who used to drive us and sell the merchandise for us, providing a bit of security into the bargain. But now Sue was driving us to each gig and it was usually just the two of us in the car. After I'd done an hour of signing and taking photos, she'd look around us and think, 'Hang on a minute, the crew have gone. Everyone has gone. We're the only ones left here.'

It wasn't until the next day that it dawned on me that the threatening phone caller in Watford might actually have wanted to hurt me.

'I must have had a delayed reaction,' I told Martin. 'I couldn't see what the fuss was all about last night, but I can see now why everybody was upset. Thank you for dealing with the situation so calmly.'

What happened forced us to think seriously about security – and not just for me, but for my fans and for my band, too. Reluctantly, I had to decide, no stage doors from now on. Maybe it's for the best. It's upsetting that I don't get a chance to see my fans, but it's too difficult with so many people, especially as I'm not one who can just say, 'Thank you, bye.' I just can't – I've always got to say, 'Oh, hello, how are you?' I can't just walk away.

We tried doing meet-and-greets instead, but they don't work for me. At one time we had 30 people in at Blackpool and I chatted to them for three hours, which was longer than the actual show! The staff were saying, 'You need to hurry, because we're going into overtime in a minute.'

'This isn't going to work, because you can't just do a thank you, hello, photograph, thank you, next,' said Martin.

To make up for it, we made the tour the best it could possibly be. Meanwhile, *Cruising With JMD* was a smash hit and my filming schedule became packed out with trips around the world, from Europe to South America and Australia. I was hardly ever at home – I lived on planes, trains, cars and ships, just as my gran had predicted all those years before. Although I loved the work and felt incredibly lucky, sometimes it was a real wrench to pack and leave the house again. It wasn't unheard of for me to go into a plane toilet and cry, which sounds ridiculous, but I missed Ed and I missed Mum and the rest of the family. I missed Wakefield and just being at home, pottering around in the garden and playing the piano.

'Oh, get over yourself,' I'd think, and then I'd throw myself into the trip and love it. It was like being a child again: getting on the stage was a nightmare, but once I was up there I absolutely adored it.

I worried a lot about my mother while I was away. Mum was over eighty now and you could see she was poorly. She had never fully recovered from breaking her back in three places and the fall had knocked her confidence, so she wasn't getting out much. It was awful to see her growing weaker. She was well looked after by family and friends, but every time I got back, I could see a decline in her, because I wasn't there to nurture and care for her.

I felt that nobody could do it like I did it. I cooked for her and got the washing in, I was there at teatime; I helped her get ready for bed, put fresh water by her bedside, rubbed her feet and did a hundred other things to make sure she was okay. Still, it was a comfort to know that, while I was away, my brother was there every day and my sister was popping in when she wasn't working. Tony took Mum out shopping right up to the end. He used to send me little videos of her drinking her coffee and saying, 'Hiya, Jane, can't wait for you to get back.'

I used to send her clips, going, 'It's a hard life, this, Mother,' trying to be cheerful and make it look like I was having a fabulous time, even though my heart was breaking because I was yearning to get back to her.

When I got home, I'd drop my bags and be straight round to my mother's. Ed was so understanding and patient.

Mum would say, 'You'll have to go back home, darling. You've got Ed waiting.'

'He's fine. He's got all night with me,' I'd reassure her. 'I want to be with you.'

Meanwhile, Ed would have a hot bath ready for me when I got back from Mum's, teary-eyed and exhausted from looking after her. He supported me through every single day of her illness.

Cruising With JMD was proving such a success that in the summer of 2017 the wonderful Ben Frow at Channel 5 called me in for another meeting and asked, 'How about doing another programme for us? What else would you like to do?'

'Come and see what we do on tour,' I suggested. 'People live in a bubble in London. You need to come out and see what's happening in the provinces.'

Greg Barnett, one of the top commissioning editors at Channel 5 and who is responsible for the *Cruising With JMD* series came along to my Wimbledon concert in September 2017, when we had all the Londoners in. It was a fantastic show and I had a lot of my friends there. Wimbledon was one of those nights when I sensed something special happening.

Greg loved the show: 'I totally get it! This is exactly what we need to capture and recreate on television,' he said. 'We need a primetime entertainment show with you fronting it.' He and Ben Frow commissioned that very show and *Jane & Friends* was born.

Sometimes it's hard to know what you want, but once you do, life gets a lot easier. A couple of years earlier, I had thought to myself, 'I want to go back on primetime, I want to be playing arenas.' Now I was halfway there, all of a sudden. In my mind, it was just a matter of time before I booked out an arena.

The great thing about *Jane & Friends* was that there wasn't anything else like it, because television schedules were full of talent shows or repeats at the time. 'I'd like to do something that's a nod to what I used to watch every Saturday night,' I told Ben and Greg at Channel 5 when we met up. I was thinking of the great entertainment shows that kept the nation going through the 1970s recession, power cuts and strikes. I wanted *Jane & Friends* to be a feelgood variety show, a mix of songs, chat, jokes and audience participation. I'm so grateful that Ben and Greg shared my vision, because I absolutely love working for both of them and Channel 5, as well as everyone at Viacom International Studios, who make both the shows for the channel – it's a marriage made in heaven and long may it continue.

We had some fantastic guests on *Jane & Friends*. It's an astounding array when I list them: boyband Collabro, Elkie Brooks, Alexander O'Neal, Bonnie Tyler, Michelle Gayle, Gilbert O'Sullivan, Odyssey, Shane Ward, Russell Watson and Duncan James from Blue . . . and so many more. All these incredibly talented artists wanted to come on the show because they knew they were safe with my musicians and sound people – I'm so lucky to have such a great band and production team.

I wanted my arrangements to be full of excitement, so I worked with Jon Dixon, my producer, to give audiences that tingle up the back of the neck. You don't want your audience thinking, 'Oh, this is nice,' you want them thinking, 'This is amazing!' You want them leaning forward in their seats.

After Jon and I worked on an arrangement, Seán Barry, the musical director, sprinkled magic dust over everything. Then the band started putting in their own ingredients and it was just like *Bake Off*, when the cake is rising in the oven. As the singer, I was the cherry on the top!

It was my guitarist Steve Cooper who said, 'We need Seán Barry,' for *Jane & Friends* and our first meeting with Seán was in Jon Dixon's kitchen after a day of recording the *Cruising With JMD* songs. Jon's two young boys had just come in from school, full of excitement, and they were running around the kitchen, telling us about their day. The meeting took just half an hour: we all knew he was our man, the missing piece of the jigsaw – and he's been with me ever since, on tour and on television.

We brought in Ami Evans, the third singer in The Bluebirds, to join Gina McKendrick and Sarah Rhodes on *Jane & Friends*. She sounded great at the first rehearsal. Martin said to Sue, 'I know what's going to happen here: Jane's going to say, "We want three backing singers on the tour."'

'How long before she says it? Two, maybe three hours?' said Sue, smiling.

By three o'clock, I was saying, 'We need another singer on the tour . . .'

'Here we go!' said Martin and Sue, chuckling.

My instinct was right, though: when Ami joined us, we were complete.

I was petrified, literally shaking, when we came to film the first episode of *Jane & Friends*, because we were recording it with a live audience. It's a good thing that I work well under pressure and the best in me comes out when I'm stressed, otherwise it could have been a complete disaster.

'Right, let's do it!' I thought, as the minutes ticked away.

Having a live audience was a bonus, in fact, and as soon as filming stopped, I would go into entertaining mode: 'Oh, ay, you'll never guess what's happened today . . .' and 'Flipping heck, have you seen this over here?'

Backstage, the fabulous Mark Powell, who is my executive producer for both *Cruising With JMD* and *Jane & Friends*, heard the audience roaring with laughter.

'What's going on out there?' he said. 'What's she doing to make them laugh so much?'

They kept the cameras rolling and half of the off-air stuff ended up in the show, because that's when I was at my most relaxed and just being daft.

We've had so many great moments on *Jane & Friends* and sharing the stage with Tony Hadley was definitely among the best. The former Spandau Ballet singer and I had been friends for some years, ever since I'd interviewed him on *Loose Women*. I had his number in my phone, which I was always very proud of, and when it came to recording my album of original material, *Hold The Covers Back*, my producer asked if I knew any celebrities who might be up for singing a duet on 'I See It In Your Eyes'.

'I don't really know anybody,' I said. 'Wait, I've got Tony Hadley's number in my phone. Do you think I should ring him?'

'If you've got his number in your phone, just try!'

So I did: 'Tony, it's Jane McDonald,' I said, 'I've written this song. If you don't like it, I'm not precious at all. Please just say, "No, Jane." '

I was expecting him to say no, to be honest, but after I'd sent him the track, he rang back and said, 'It's fantastic!'

'Really?'

'It's like a Disney track. I'd love to sing it.'

So we did the duet on the album and I was lucky enough that he came and sang it with me on the show as well. That was a lovely thing to happen – to have somebody like Tony Hadley singing your song.

Duets can be difficult because the arrangements are so complicated, but people love them. I've also done 'Enough Is Enough' with Hayley Tamaddon and 'Tell Him' with Claire Sweeney, and there are more in the pipeline.

One of my favourite sections of the show is 'Jane's Heroes', which celebrates the special people in life who do an awful lot for others but don't see themselves as special. It was humbling to meet every single one of the heroes we featured, because they were all utterly awe-inspiring. There was one particular lady called Brenda Jones, who's in her eighties and has been volunteering for hospital radio for 20 years. Brenda loves what she does and she's vital to the patients, because if you don't feel very well, it can be nice sometimes to have earphones on and to drift away to some music and chat, so that you don't get bored or think too much about the pain you're in. Although Brenda had been a fan for many years, she didn't recognise my voice when I rang her up, pretending to be somebody in the hospital.

'Have you got any Jane McDonald?' I asked her.

'Ooh, I don't think I have!' she said.

'What do you mean, you haven't got any Jane McDonald tracks?' I said, sounding a little disgruntled.

'Oh dear, I'll just put you on to somebody else,' she said.

'Don't you put me on to anybody else, Brenda!' I said, and as I was saying it, I walked into the room and surprised her. Her face was a picture! The tears came and it was just lovely to see how happy she was. We took over the radio show for the rest of the hour and had a real hoot, although I dread to think what the poor patients thought about it.

The year 2018 was a really busy one: I was here, there and everywhere. We stepped up another level for our 2018 'Celebrate 20 Years' tour, because I never like to stand still. We really went to town with the staging and presentation – after all, 20 years in the business is a real milestone – and we were flying high, selling out every theatre and concert hall.

'Wouldn't it be great if we tried to do Leeds Arena?' I said to Martin.

'I think you could sell it out easily,' he said. He emailed the Arena asking for possible dates, but heard nothing back.

Jane & Friends did really well with viewers (well over a million of them) and it seemed a logical step to make a Christmas show. At Christmas, there are so many repeats of the old-style entertainment shows that it's clear to just about everybody that it's what people still hanker after. On our Christmas special, in December 2018, we had carols, children singing and lots and lots of tinsel. The only thing that wasn't Christmassy was when we filmed it – in May, in a break from the 'Celebrate 20 Years' tour.

During the break, Martin Hudson went off to work on another show at the Leeds Arena. He later told me that suddenly he had a brainwave and thought, 'They still haven't answered my emails. Why don't I try to speak to someone in person about Jane doing a concert here?'

'Is the manager about?' he asked.

When the manager came down to see him, Martin explained the situation. Luckily, she was a fan: 'Oh, my word, we've got to have Jane here!' she said. 'You don't fancy doing a show in the next six months, do you?'

'Well, we've always spoken about doing a Christmas show,' Martin said tentatively, 'but the theatres all have pantomimes on at Christmas.'

'Arenas don't put on pantomimes,' she said, smiling.

That's when Martin called me – 'I'm with the manager of

Leeds Arena and she's suggesting we come and do a Christmas show here in December. What do you think?'

I didn't have to think twice.

'It's a brilliant idea,' I said. 'Let's do it!'

Of course, it meant that suddenly we had to get a live Christmas show together before we went back on tour again, which was a lot of pressure, but it was a huge adrenaline rush picking the songs and outfits and working out the staging and setting. Then, when the Arena show went on sale, it sold 1,000 tickets on the first day.

I instantly phoned Martin: 'If all these people are coming, we should film it,' I said. 'We might never get another chance.'

'Blimey!' he said. 'Who's going to pay for that?'

'I am,' I told him. 'I'll put my money where my mouth is and then I'll own the rights.'

At this Martin raised an eyebrow: it was a huge undertaking to underwrite the concert and, if anything went wrong, I would lose my house.

'Trust me on this one,' I said.

Martin did some research and found a camera crew and a director. The Leeds Arena Christmas Concert was to be the finale to a fantastic year. We'd had the success of *Jane & Friends*, I'd won a BAFTA for *Cruising With JMD*, we'd had a sell-out tour, and now we were set for a sell-out Arena concert and a DVD.

I was on the crest of a wave!

18

My Heart Will Go On

No matter where I was in the world – up a mountain, in a desert or on a ship in the middle of the ocean – I would always ring my mother. The time difference sometimes made it difficult, but I'd stay up into the early hours if I had to, because I needed to know she was okay. Then one day in the autumn of 2018, while I was filming a four-part series of *Cruising* in Australia, I couldn't get hold of her. I rang Tony, I rang Wendy . . . they didn't get back to me.

'Something's wrong,' I thought.

Later that day, Wendy got in touch to say, 'Don't panic, it's just that your mum's gone into hospital. She's not very well.'

Mum's blood counts were down; she was going downhill. I began to fear the worst. Thank goodness my friend Sue Ravey was there with me to comfort me and talk it through.

I was constantly ringing my sister-in-law: 'Is Mum going to come home from hospital?' I kept asking.

'They're saying she'll come home soon,' she said.

As the days went by and Mum stayed in the hospital, Wendy's messages became more cryptic. She'd say things like, 'She's okay, but she's not very well,' and 'She was feeling awful earlier, but she's chatting away now.' Wendy tried to sound positive, but one day she said, 'It's not a good diagnosis.'

'I need to get home,' I thought.

So I cut short the trip: my four-parter in Australia became a three-parter.

'She's got pancreatic cancer,' Wendy said.

I was expecting bad news, but her words hit me like a ton of bricks. On the long plane journey back, I cried a lot – I was in bits.

'This is it, this is the end,' I thought miserably.

I rushed straight to the hospital from the airport.

'I'm back and I'm not going away again,' I told Mum.

'Thank God you're here,' Wendy said. She looked exhausted.

We were in the hospital for a week. Ed was amazing – he always had a meal cooked or a bath run for me when I went home for a sleep or a change of clothes. Things would have been so much harder without the love and support he gave me during that time. I desperately wanted Mum to come out of hospital, but it was a shock when the doctors said, 'We can't do any more for her, now. She can come home.'

I had always thought I'd take care of Mum, but now that it came to it, I started having doubts. She was in such agony by then.

'Can you just keep her one more night while I get my head around this?' I asked.

'We can't discharge her until the morning, anyway,' I was told.

I came home and sat on the sofa, not knowing what to do next. My first thought was, 'I can't look after her. I don't know what to do, I'm not a trained nurse – I'll kill her!' I gave myself a talking to, went to Marks & Spencer and got all Mum's favourite foods in. She could hardly eat, but I got everything in for her, just in case. Then I went to her house, put all the lamps on, sorted the bedding out, put the heating on for her and thought, 'Right, I've got my head around it now.'

Wendy rang: 'Are you going to be all right?' she asked. 'Don't worry, when you're not there, Tony and I will come and sit with her.'

Looking after my mother suddenly felt like an impossible task; I started crying.

'I don't think I can do this, Wendy,' I said.

Wendy started to cry too. 'I couldn't do it with my mother, either,' she said. 'And there I was, thinking, "God, she's Superwoman, is Jane. She's only just come in from Australia and now she's going to nurse her mother at home."'

It was a comfort to know that Wendy had been in a similar predicament.

'What about the hospice?' I asked her.

She sighed. 'Funnily enough, the surgeons said, "What about the hospice?" but nobody has mentioned it since. I suppose they thought that you would naturally want to take her home.'

'I'll give them a ring,' I said.

I've been a supporter of the Wakefield Hospice for a long time, so when I rang and said, 'It's Jane McDonald here,' they said, 'Is it our Jane McDonald?'

I burst into tears.

'My mother is very ill and I just can't look after her,' I said.

'That's what we're here for,' they replied. 'It's our turn now.'

They found Mum a room and within three hours we got her out of Pinderfields Hospital straight into the hospice. It was a huge relief for me, but also a tremendous guilt, because if it had been the other way around, I know my mother would have taken care of me. And yet the hospice was warm and welcoming: Mum's bed was comfy, the nurses were amazing and there were nice people on hand to get everything she needed. What's more, they didn't just look after my mother, they looked after us. There was tea coming every two minutes and pies being made every day, I could get a cup of coffee anytime.

'It's lovely in here,' said Mum.

'Thank God for that,' I thought. 'We're in the right place.'

Tony, Janet and I did split shifts. I stayed with Mum all night – I went in at six and stayed until nine the next morning. Tony took over from nine to two and then Janet would do two until six when she wasn't working.

Over the next week, Mum and I said everything that we needed to say. I thanked her for being the best mum ever.

'Have I made you proud?' I asked.

'Are you joking? I don't know what I've done to deserve a daughter like you,' she said.

That was it, I was off.

'Oh, Mum!' I said, tears running down my face.

'Don't be upset, it's just my time,' she told me gently. 'And I'll be at every concert from now on, I can come to every one of them.'

'Absolutely, you will,' I said. 'I'm going to miss you so much, though. Thank you for sticking by me and coaxing me and helping me with everything. I was such a maungy [peevish] kid and you helped me overcome it.'

She laughed. 'You were a nightmare! But look at you now . . .'

Then she asked me about Ed: 'Do you think this is the right one?'

'Definitely,' I said. 'He's a kind man. He looks after me, he lets me do my job and helps me with the business side. He's a great cook and he makes me laugh.'

'As long as you're happy,' she said.

'Yes, I am,' I said, which made her smile.

Unfortunately, right in the middle of all of this, I had to go to Oakham in Rutland to lay down my vocals for the *Cruising* album. It was bad timing, but I was told there was nothing I could do about it. When I got back, Mum had taken a turn for the worse. She was quite poorly, then – she couldn't really speak, she wasn't even drinking fluids.

I took up my vigil again, and during the long hours by my mother's side, I sometimes struck up conversations with the doctors and nurses. At one point, I must have mentioned that I had the Christmas concert at Leeds Arena coming up, because everybody seemed to know about it.

One of the nurses said, 'I'm afraid you won't be able to do that concert.'

Even the doctor said, 'No, sadly, you won't be able to do it.'

Ed was sitting with us. 'With respect, you don't know Jean and you don't know her daughter,' he said.

'And I'm going to lose my house if I don't do it!' I thought.

'Don't you dare cancel that arena concert,' my mother whispered to me later, to my amazement. I didn't expect her to be thinking about it. Then again, of course she was.

The following day, I had a phone call to say the computer had crashed in Oakham and I would have to go back and lay down my vocals all over again. I couldn't believe it – the timing just could not have been worse.

'I'm so sorry, Mum. I'm going to have to go,' I said, 'but I'm going to do it one night and then be back in the morning.'

I worked all through the night and bombed back to Wakefield the moment I finished, too anxious to be tired. It was the beginning of the end. One of the nurses said, 'Don't leave her now,' and I never left Mum's side again – I was with her, day and night, for the next four days.

It was an awful time; it was traumatic to watch the one person I've loved all my life die in front of me. She didn't speak and barely made a noise at all.

One night, I sang quietly to her. I sang 'The Hand That

Leads Me', the song I wrote for her, because I knew she loved it. 'Hmm,' she murmured when I'd finished. I think I was partly testing myself out for the arena concert: could I sing it while feeling all that emotion? Then I sang two hymns for Mum: 'Nearer, My God, to Thee' and 'Abide With Me'.

Ed was staying in the hospice with me that night and, when he arrived at ten o'clock, the lights were down and my voice was echoing through the corridors.

'It's the eeriest thing I've ever heard,' he said. 'You could hear it all around the hospice.'

I had a chair at the side of Mum's bed. All through the night I stroked her hair, whispering soothing words. Every now and then I catnapped.

'Why isn't she going?' I wondered – it was as if she was in a coma.

I thought I was letting her go when actually I was keeping her there by having my hand on her head, which was a way of saying, 'Don't you dare leave me.' It was contradictory: I wanted her to know I was there with her, I didn't want her to feel that she was dying on her own.

After four days of this, one of the nurses said, 'Do you think you could step outside the room, just for a minute?'

'Yes, of course,' I said.

Suddenly it dawned on me that it was me who was keeping Mum back. Despite all the pain that she was in, she wouldn't leave me. I wish I had softly said, 'Mum, I've got to go,' but instead I broke down. 'Mum, I'm so sorry for keeping you,' I wailed. 'I'm not leaving the building, and if you need me, I'll be here, but I need to step outside the room. You have to go, I can't keep you here any longer.

'I love you more than anything,' I sobbed hysterically. 'Come back and see me, if you can. Give my love to everyone. I love you.'

I left the room and fell into Ed's arms. 'I can't bear to think

of her on her own,' I kept saying. 'I should be in there with her!'
But when I went back into her room a few minutes later, the
nurse was already there, saying, 'She's gone.'

Mum had passed.

The nurses showed me into a quiet room and poured me a
whisky, the best whisky I'd ever tasted. Tony and Wendy came
immediately with their daughter, Katie, and Tom, her partner.
We drank the whole bottle between us – we needed it.

Something Wendy said got me through the days that followed: 'You have to live the life that she wanted for you,' she
told me.

I thought of my mum's last words to me: 'Don't you dare
cancel that arena.'

My elder sister Janet was down as next of kin and I said, 'Can
you handle everything? I'm done, I'm worn out.' But in the end,
she was too upset and I took over and sorted everything out, as
I had after our father died.

'Please don't put this out. I don't want anyone knowing, I
can't face it yet,' I told the hospice and everybody around me.
Nobody said a word.

I owe the people of Wakefield a great debt for their discretion,
because Mum's funeral was quiet and beautiful and the family
were able to say goodbye in peace. I was grateful that it was just
family as I was not in a good place, and thankfully, it wasn't until
afterwards that the *Sun* found out she'd passed.

'Do you want to put a statement out?' they asked.

So I put a statement out.

'How am I going to face everybody now?' I wondered.

It was very strange because in the week leading up to the
Leeds Arena concert I had a bout of agoraphobia and didn't
want to leave the house. I was fine when I was at home and then
I literally got the shakes as I walked out the door, thinking, 'I've

got to face the world.' I couldn't have people coming up to me in the street and expressing their condolences because I knew I'd break down and yet I couldn't cry either.

'I can't grieve. What's the matter with me?' I thought.

My Christmas concert at Leeds Arena took place two weeks after Mum's funeral. It was the hardest performance I have ever done in my life.

'If I can get through this, I'll be able to conquer the world,' I told my family.

Everybody was worried that I wouldn't be able to do it. They were thinking my voice would dry up, or I'd break down and have to stop. 'What's this going to be like?' people were asking each other. Even the band were saying, 'Is she going to get through the show?', I found out later.

My family were all there and so were many friends. Jane Quinn, my friend from *Cats*, had a show in London that day, but she got on a train up to Leeds and ran from the station in the pouring rain just so that she could be in that auditorium and send me her energy.

Now, that's a friend, isn't it?

Before I went on, I was a bag of nerves. I had lost my voice before when I'd been emotionally upset and was terrified it was going to happen again.

'I'm not sure I can do this,' I told Steve Cooper, my guitarist, before we went on.

'Don't worry, we've got your back,' he said.

I felt safe with my brilliant band, but I couldn't have done that concert without my fans. The love they gave me that night lifted and carried me like never before: it kept me afloat. I was so thankful, especially when the moment I'd been dreading finally arrived.

'This is going to be a bit hard for me now, but I know you'll get me through it,' I said.

That's all I could say – I couldn't bring myself to mention my mother.

There was a collective intake of breath as I moved from singing 'You're My World' into the first bars of 'The Hand That Leads Me'. Five thousand people stood up and started clapping and singing along. 'Oh, my goodness!' I thought.

Five thousand people were singing my mother's song. What a send-off! It was just amazing.

'Now I'm ready to conquer the world,' I told myself.

Epilogue

This year has been a wonderful year in many ways. My tour was my best tour ever and I've loved every minute of being onstage and on our tour bus. But this has also been my first year without my mother and it's been tough. I haven't got used to her absence; I will never stop missing my mum. Still, there is comfort in the thought that I'm living the life she wanted for me. I like to think she's enjoying watching me have the time of my life at my time of life! Because, apart from losing Mum, things have never been better.

It's funny because I often get calls from singers and performers asking how to get on in the music business. My advice is this: sing as much as you can, in front of as many people as you can, and build your fan base. Never forget why you do it: it's a joy to be an entertainer. Start off small and grow. It's the only way. It takes time to learn your craft.

For many of the people I speak to, especially the ones who have come off TV talent shows like *The X Factor*, overnight success is not the blessing it appears to be. I feel for them because it was a big jump for me to go from being the club singer and the cruise-ship singer to being the star. There's a huge difference between a club act and a theatre act: I was the one who used to go on, make it up and sing a few songs. I was an entertainer who sang. Now, I'm a singer who entertains. It took time for me to evolve: it was a slow journey, and it was hard.

I used to have conversations with my fans where they asked, 'Why don't you believe in yourself a bit more? Why do you look so surprised when everybody stands up?'

'Well, I didn't feel that it was worthy of that,' I'd say.

It's taken me all these years to start believing in myself and think, 'Yes, I'm good at this. I can do this.' Now, I'm finally there. I've learned how to face my fears – and I face them head-on. Luck has played a part in my success, but it's what you do with your chances that really matters. I believe there's an instinct within us that tells us what's right and wrong for us, and often we ignore it. That's why we struggle and become unhappy or ill – because we're not free enough to say, 'No, I'm going this way.' You have to go on your instinct: if you believe you're making the right choice, you probably are.

When something ends, I don't think, 'Oh no!' I think, 'Right, next!', and then I get excited about what's ahead, even if I don't know what it is. I love change – 'Make space for great things to happen,' I tell everybody. It's one of the sayings I live by, and it has always worked for me. So many people are closed off and miss out, but you need to be open to let life in. And if you get hurt, that's fine: something better will follow, don't worry!

It's best to shut negativity out, I find. I keep myself in a bubble as much as possible – if I didn't, I wouldn't have the light and the energy to go out and give to others. Fortunately, I've had a lot of guidance along the way. Some wonderful people have come into my life and helped me and taught me. I don't know whether it's luck or fate or destiny, I just seem to be fortunate that way – the right people come along at the right time.

I've had 20 years to grow into the artist I am now – not a star, but an artist – and it's not something you can do overnight.

I'm glad I've done it at my pace because I've had so many lessons to learn along the way: I'm quite methodical and it has taken a lot of hard work. These days, I'm a very straight talker when I go into meetings, because I know the industry so well. I know what it's like to be a manager and a promoter and how much it costs to put a show on; I know what the theatre takes, how much the show costs and how much the VAT and tax are. I know exactly how much everything costs.

A friend gave me some very good advice once: 'Don't go into this business for what you can make. Always think, "What am I prepared to lose?"' There's an old saying in our industry: 'How do you make a million in the music business? Answer: 'Start with two million' and it's very true. It's definitely a mistake to come into the industry thinking, 'I'm going to be a millionaire.' Most people struggle. Even if chance, luck or fate intervenes to help you on your way, as it did with me when Chris Terrell decided to film *The Cruise* on the *Galaxy*, there will always be difficult times. When my career crashed after my marriage break-up, it was really tough, but I was given another chance. After that, I was completely determined and focused, and gave every bit of my life to what I do – everything else was secondary.

What drives me is the feeling I have when I'm onstage, when it's up to me to create an energy that will come back to me from the crowd. As soon as I get on that stage, even if I'm having a terrible day, Dr Showbiz kicks in and I feel fab: 'Every one of these people has come here tonight to feel something,' I tell myself. 'They want to escape from their lives a little bit today.' My job is to bring out their feelings, whether they laugh or cry.

People ask how I was able to do my Christmas show at the Leeds Arena after my mum died – I did it because I needed that energy, I needed to feel joy. I'd gone through such a traumatic time and I needed to see smiling faces again. I needed my fans, I needed to feel good again. And I felt so much better for it.

It reminded me that you can be at the lowest of the low, but when you can't go any further down, the only way is up. It's important to think about what you've got, not what you've lost. If I dwelt on how much I've lost, I don't know how I'd get through another day. Instead, I have peace of mind and a beautiful partner with a kind heart, who absolutely adores me and lets me run the business. Ed is more than my rock, he's my best friend and ally. I don't just love him, I admire and respect him, and I'm grateful he's my partner.

Am I still ready to conquer the world? Absolutely! I have so many amazing plans for next year and the year after that. The second bite of the cherry is so much sweeter than the first and I'm determined to make the most of it.

I hope I will always sing, but trust me, if I get to a point where I'm struggling, I will stop. But until that time, which I'm hoping is a long way off, I'll 'ride the wave'.

Thank you for reading my book.

Acknowledgements

There are many special people I would like to thank:

Ed, first and foremost, my partner, best friend and ally. Words cannot express how grateful I am that we found each other again.

My beautiful mother, what can I say? Wisdom, unconditional love and support throughout my whole life. You were definitely 'The Hand That Leads Me'. I miss you every minute of every day.

My amazing family, including my aunts Nancy and Barbara, who delved deep into their memory banks to help me to get my facts right; my sister Janet, brother Tony, sister-in-law Wendy and niece Katie.

My best mate, Sue, for being an endless source of support, strength and laughter, along with all my lovely friends, old and new, especially Steve Holbrook, Jane Quinn and June Field. Thank you, I cherish your friendship.

Mark Worrall, thank you for all your assistance and for getting me back to singing and Andy Hawkins for all the driving and to you both for being so much fun to be around.

My happy touring family: Martin Hudson, my amazing tour manager; Steve Cooper on guitar and songwriting; Richard

Hammond on bass; Jim Pitchforth on percussion and vocals; Jamie Little on drums; my wonderful singers/dancers Gina McKendrick, Sarah Rhodes & Ami Evans (The Bluebirds); Seán Barry, musical director and keyboards, Dave Catley, lighting designer, Kay Heeley for her incredible stage outfits and the rest of the crew . . .

Greg Barnett and Ben Frow at Channel 5 – thank you for believing in me. From the first encounter it was a meeting of minds from which we have gone from strength to strength. I bless the day I met Ben.

All the girls at *Loose Women*, past and present. You are all incredible women who I have loved working alongside. I wish this programme nothing but success. Thank you for a great ten years.

Thank you to my Elephant House/Viacom Studios family, what a hoot we have. To Mark Powell and Joe McLuskey, on *Cruising* Ray Easmon, David Kirkham, Darren Lilly, Jeff Anderson, Fi Cotter-Craig, Nic McNeilis, Jon Cowen and on *Jane and Friends* John L Spencer, Steve Smith and Jess Davis.

Jon Dixon, you probably make me work more than anyone else but the results are always such a pleasant surprise, thank you for everything.

In Management I couldn't have a better agent than Craig Latto, he is my rock and listens to me and always has my best interests at heart, and to Jamie, and especially Jilliane Hudson, who magnificently manages all the fan's correspondence and the new world of social media.

All the team at Virgin who made this book possible, I would like to thank Lorna Russell, Michelle Warner, Aslan Byrne, Diana Colbert, Claire Scott, Ellie Crisp, Rebecca Hibbert, Nina Winters,

Acknowledgements

Jane Donovan, your teamwork and enthusiasm for a process that I did not always find easy is so appreciated.

A massive thanks to Rebecca Cripps, who spent many hours with me coaxing memories out of me and then crafting what you are reading with finesse and superb storytelling skill.

KT Forster, literary agent, thank you for your efforts in keeping it all going, for your words of encouragement and faith in what we were trying to achieve.

Last but not least, I wouldn't be here without my incredible fans. I feel very lucky to have the best fans in the world and I really do love you all.

Index

Index

Index

Index

Index